Teacher's Edition

Phonics Is Fun

Book 1

by Louis Krane, Ed.D.

MODERN CURRICULUM PRESS, INC.
A Division of Simon & Schuster
Cleveland, Ohio

MODERN CURRICULUM PRESS, INC.
A Division of Simon & Schuster
13900 Prospect Road, Cleveland, Ohio 44136

Design, Production, and Management: The Quarasan Group, Inc.
Editorial Stages: Proof Positive/Farrowlyne Associates, Inc. for The Quarasan Group, Inc.
Cover Design: John K. Crum   Editorial Supervision: Linda Lott

ISBN 0-8136-0217-3

1 2 3 4 5 6 7 8 9 10   92 91 90 89

Teacher's Edition

Phonics Is Fun

Book 1

Phonics Is Fun

Faster-paced instruction for more capable students.
Now, from MCP, a phonics program that maximizes students' ability to learn as it minimizes teacher-preparation time.

Complete, systematic phonics instruction

Phonics Is Fun provides instruction in the minimum number of phonetic skills which will assure word recognition. The sequence of these essential skills is based on the frequency with which phonetic elements occur in the English language. Thus, the scope and sequence of skills is designed to provide students with a viable set of phonetic word-attack skills, enabling them to read an unlimited number of words.

More capable students quickly take responsibility for their own learning

The instruction is accomplished through a multi-sensory approach, using auditory and visual discrimination exercises, sound blending, and word pronunciation, and culminating in reading, spelling, and writing words in sentences. The students are presented with the minimum number of rules and definitions for achieving reading independence. The students quickly develop the ability to relate the printed word to its speech equivalent and comprehend the meaning of words in context.

All new, contemporary artwork

The attractive, clear artwork will hold students' interest as they work through the pages. The picture cues provide for vocabulary development, but since they are easy to identify, they never interfere with the learning of the phonetic skills.

New, expanded Teacher's Edition

This Teacher's Edition maximizes your teaching efforts as it minimizes the amount of preparation time. There is an array of completely described games and activities for multisensory practice of phonetic skills. These games and activities only require common, easily found materials. The pictures are clearly labeled and the answers easily readable. Blackline masters provide for skills assessment, and family involvement activities enable you to keep parents informed of their children's progress.

Student Edition with instruction that moves at a faster, more challenging pace.

More items per page, providing more concentrated practice.

Faster, more challenging pace of instruction.

Variety of formats to hold students' attention.

All-new, interest-capturing artwork.

Students master the minimum number of important phonetic skills, applying them in meaningful contexts.

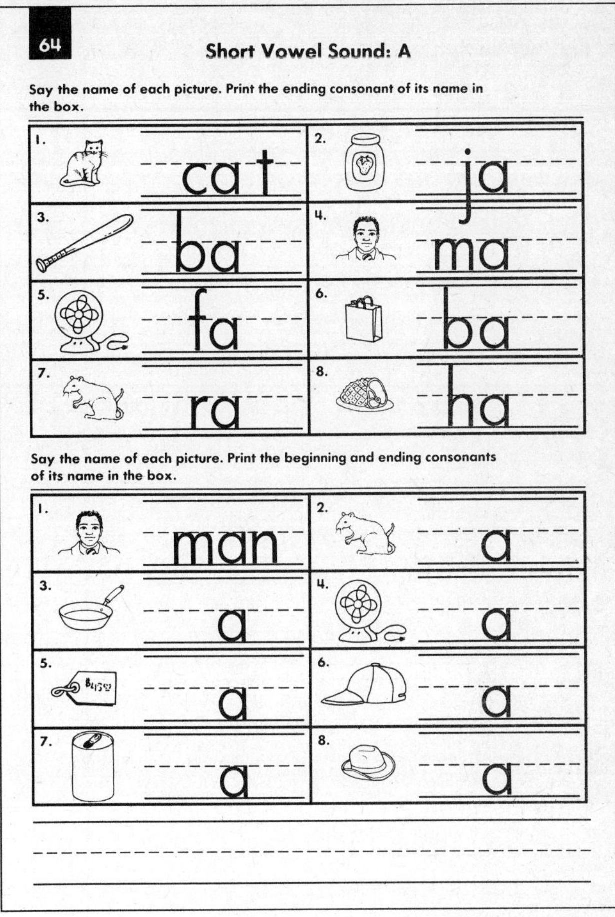
64

Short Vowel Sound: A

Say the name of each picture. Print the ending consonant of its name in the box.

1. cat 2. ja 3. ba 4. ma 5. fa 6. ba 7. ra 8. ha

Say the name of each picture. Print the beginning and ending consonants of its name in the box.

1. man 2. a 3. a 4. a 5. a 6. a 7. a 8. a

Teacher's Edition that maximizes your time.

Review automatically builds in maintenance of previously-learned phonetic skills.

Teaching Ideas describes games and activities that provide multisensory involvement through listening, speaking, reading and writing.

Reteaching suggests activities for helping students who didn't master the skill the first time through.

Extension challenges students who have been successful.

Blackline masters for assessment.

Family Involvement activities that are cross-referenced with reproducible letters to parents.

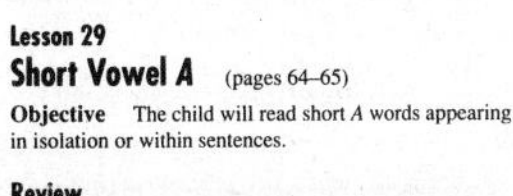
Lesson 29

Short Vowel A (pages 64–65)

Objective The child will read short *A* words appearing in isolation or within sentences.

Review

Listening To reinforce auditory skills, challenge the children to identify beginning and ending sounds in sample words you recite. Help the children fold writing paper in half, draw a line along the fold, and number writing lines. Then direct them to write the letters for the beginning and ending sounds they hear on the correct side of the paper. Choose a variety of short *A* words or picture flashcards naming words with the short *A* sound, such as the following: *bag, cap, cat, lad, hat, fan, can, man.*

Teaching Ideas

Listening Read aloud the words in the following columns. Ask the children to tell which words in each column contain the short *A* sound.

can	*bus*	*fish*	*hen*	*set*	*duck*
yes	*cub*	*cab*	*wag*	*sick*	*doll*
bid	*tap*	*Rick*	*lip*	*sat*	*sack*
Dan	*tip*	*dish*	*ham*	*lick*	*pack*

Speaking Write a list of short *A* words on the chalkboard, or create picture flashcards that name short *A* words. Invite volunteers to choose a word and to read it to the class. Then ask the children to create sentences that use each word. You might wish to use the following words: *jam, and, ran, at, dad, lap, tag, back, had.*

Acting Using the short *A* words or picture flashcards from the previous activity, encourage volunteers to choose a word and to act it out. Challenge the other children to guess the word. Invite the child who guesses the word correctly to write it on the chalkboard.

Extension

Writing Write the following sentences on the chalkboard. Ask the child to identify the short *A* words in each sentence by writing them on a sheet of paper.

1. The lad ran. *3. The man has a fan.*
2. Pass the jam. *4. Jack has a cat.*

Art Encourage the child to create a set of picture flashcards for words that contain the short *A* sound. You may suggest that the child draw the pictures or, alternatively, that the child paste pictures cut from old magazines.

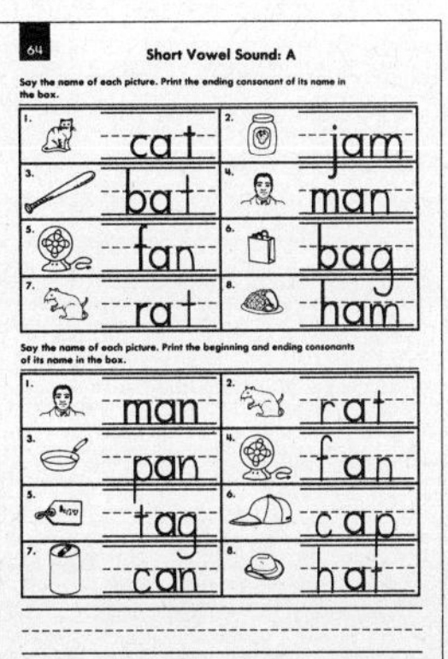
64 Short Vowel Sound: A

1. cat 2. jam 3. bat 4. man 5. fan 6. bag 7. rat 8. ham

1. man 2. rat 3. pan 4. fan 5. tag 6. cap 7. can 8. hat

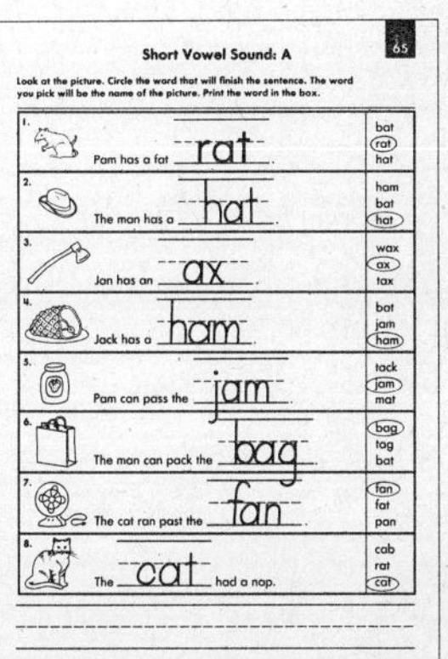
Short Vowel Sound: A 65

Look at the picture. Circle the word that will finish the sentence. The word you pick will be the name of the picture. Print the word in the box.

1. Pam has a fat rat. (bat, rat, hat)
2. The man has a hat. (ham, bat, hat)
3. Jan has an ax. (wax, ax, tax)
4. Jack has a ham. (bat, jam, ham)
5. Pam can pass the jam. (tack, jam, mat)
6. The man can pack the bag. (bag, tag, bat)
7. The cat ran past the fan. (fan, fat, pan)
8. The cat had a nap. (cab, rat, cat)

47

Scope and Sequence for Phonics Is Fun

Lesson Numbers

Skill	Book 1	Book 2	Book 3
Visual Discrimination	1		
Recognition of Letters	2–7	1	1
Consonant Letter-Sound Associations	8–27	2–10	2–4
Short Vowels: *A*	28–30	11	5
I	31–33	12	6
U	34–36	13	7
O	37–39	14	8
E	40–42	15	9
Long Vowels: *A*	43–45	18	11
I	46–48	19	11
U	49–51	20	12
O	52–54	21	12
E	55–57	22	13
Review of Vowels 58			
Suffixes	59–61	36–45	39–44, 57
Consonant Blends: *R* Blends	62	24	15
L Blends	63	25	16
S Blends	64	26	17
Y as a Vowel	65	27	20
Consonant Digraphs	66–68	29, 30, 58, 59	18, 19, 34, 35
Compound Words	16, 23	10,14	
Two-Syllable Words		17, 23	10
W as a Vowel		28	20
Hard and Soft *C* and *G*		31, 32	21–23
Vowels with *R*		33–35	24–26
Contractions		46–49	58
Vowel Digraphs	50–53	27–30	
Kn		58	35
Wr		59	35
Ending *Le*		60	36
Prefixes		61	46–49
Synonyms		62	59
Antonyms		63	60
Homonyms		64	61
Diphthongs		54–57	31–33
Syllabication			37, 38, 45, 50–56

To the Teacher

The *Phonics Is Fun* program consists of a phonetic-semantic approach to word recognition. Characterized by strong auditory training, the program presents a minimum of rules, definitions, and variations of consonant and vowel sounds. In *Phonics Is Fun*, the child quickly develops the ability to associate letters and sounds, relate the printed word to its speech equivalent, and comprehend the meaning of words in context. The program increases the child's reading vocabulary to correspond with the verbal and auditory vocabulary. *Phonics Is Fun* is designed to provide the child with a viable set of phonetic decoding skills, enabling the reading of an unlimited number of words.

Objective of the Program

The specific objective of the *Phonics Is Fun* program is to provide for mastery of the minimum number of phonetic skills that will assure achievement in word recognition. The sequence in which these skills are developed is based on the frequency with which phonetic elements occur in the English language.

Instruction is accomplished through a multisensory approach. Activities include auditory, visual, and tactile discrimination exercises, as well as sound blending, word pronunciation, reading, spelling, and writing words within the context of sentences.

Characteristics of the Program

The focus of *Phonics Is Fun* is not memorization of phonetic axioms. Instead, the emphasis is for the child to identify elements the phonetic principles address, state rules in personal language, and apply each rule, tip, and definition to appropriate words.

Phonics Is Fun, Book 1, presents the recognition of the letters of the alphabet, single consonants, short and long vowels, *Y* as a vowel, consonant blends, consonant digraphs, and endings *-s, -ed,* and *-ing.*

Phonics Is Fun, Book 2, reviews and extends the skills taught in *Book 1.* It also introduces hard and soft *C* and *G, W* as a vowel, vowel digraphs, vowels with *R*, affixes, contractions, synonyms, antonyms, and homonyms.

Phonics Is Fun, Book 3, reviews and broadens the skills taught in *Book 1* and *Book 2* prior to presenting syllabication.

The acquisition of phonetic skills is cumulative in nature, with subsequent levels of instruction building on prior teaching. The following phonetic rules are developed in *Books 1* and *2* of *Phonics Is Fun*, then are expanded upon in *Book 3: Short Vowel Rule, Long Vowel Rule 1, Long Vowel Rule 2, Y as a Consonant, Y as Long I, Y as Long E, Vowel W Rule, Soft C Rule,* and *Soft G Rule.* Rules, tips, and definitions are explicitly defined in appropriate lessons in the Teacher's Manual.

Implementing the Program

This Teacher's Edition presents lesson plans that can be used effectively with an individual child, a small group, or an entire class. Each activity is designated with a boldface title to be easily located. You can choose activities based on time considerations, availability of materials, and academic needs. (For instance, you might conduct the activities in some lessons over the span of two class sessions.) Recommended materials are common to most classrooms. Preparation options are suggested when appropriate, and an effort has been made to include the children in these preparations.

The lesson plans contain the following sections: Assessment, Review, Teaching Ideas, Reteaching, and Extension. The first lesson in each book will begin with an Assessment activity. A Review section appears only when the reteaching of an earlier skill will help the child grasp the new concept presented in the Teaching Ideas section. Skills are developed in Teaching Ideas, redeveloped in Reteaching, and enriched in Extension. While the activities in Teaching Ideas are intended for implementation with the entire class, the Reteaching and Extension exercises are directed to the individual child. Reduced facsimiles of Pupil Edition pages appear on the same page as the corresponding lesson to insure that specific practice follows immediately after instruction.

Involving the Family

Family Involvement Letters are referenced in most teaching units and are provided at the back of each Teacher's Edition for duplication. The activities suggested in these letters are designed to acquaint families with the work their child is doing in *Phonics Is Fun,* and to provide further review and reinforcement of the skills. Families choosing to participate in these activities will find each activity presented in a step-by-step format, with materials that involve little preparation and are common to most homes. While participation in these activities is not mandatory, the teacher may choose to use submitted projects as part of the classroom display or materials.

Contents

Unit 1 The Alphabet

Lesson 1
Visual Discrimination (pages 1–3)

Objective The child will identify differences and similarities among shapes.

Assessment

Listening To review auditory discrimination skills, invite the children to identify rhyming words in books and recordings. You may wish to choose from the following materials and activities.

Encourage the children to share books that display a strong sense of rhyme. Books by Dr. Seuss, Bob Reese, Jack Prelutsky, or Bill Peet—and books of nursery rhymes—are among selections that are successful at this level.

Play a recording of nursery rhymes or jingles.

Suggest words that lend themselves to easy rhyming, such as: *play/day, light/write, rest/nest.* Challenge the children to identify other rhyming word pairs or to create short verses using the rhyming word pairs you suggested.

Teaching Ideas

Tactile Review shape recognition with the children. You may wish to use a tactile approach by selecting one or more of these common classroom materials: flannel-board shape cutouts, paper or cardboard shape cutouts, building blocks, pieces from shape puzzles, modeling clay molded into shapes, and pipe cleaners formed into shapes. Arrange a set of four or five shapes, making sure that at least two of the shapes match. Separate a matching shape from the rest in the row. Challenge the children to find a shape that matches the first one. Acknowledge a correct match. You may continue the activity by using different shapes or by varying the materials. After reinforcing correct responses, you may wish to point out similarities in incorrect matches.

Art Draw simple sketches of three objects (for example: balls, tents, trees, faces) on the chalkboard. Alter the drawing of one of the objects by omitting a part, such as the nose on one of the faces. Invite the children to identify the sketch that is different, name the missing part, and draw the missing part on the chalkboard sketch.

Writing You may wish to extend the previous activity by writing rows of letters on the chalkboard (for example: *BBDB, EEFE, NMNN, ILLL, DDBD,* and *CCGC*). Repeat the visual discrimination activity as described previously.

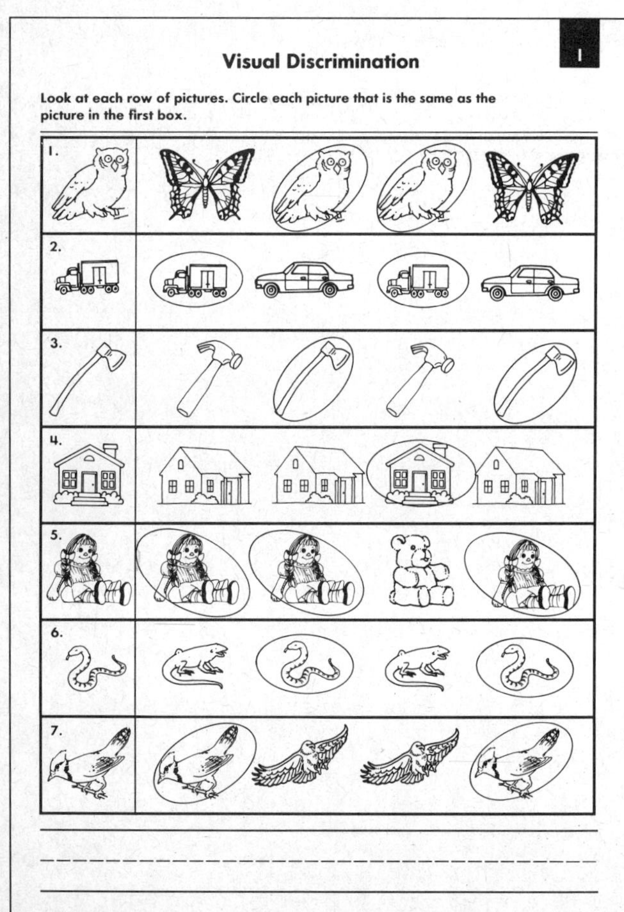

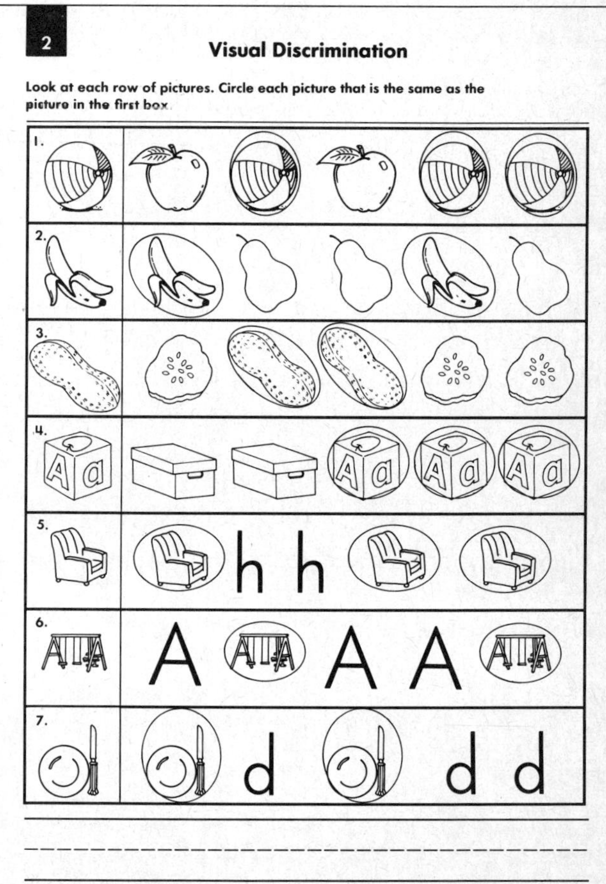

Extension

Shape Game Give the child a manila folder with paper geometric shapes pasted on the right side and an envelope filled with various paper shapes on the left side. (The folder may be prepared either by you beforehand or by the child as part of the activity.) Encourage the child to match the shapes.

Listening Further extension may be accomplished with picture flashcards that display objects, such as: a mop, a boat, some girls, the sun, and a box. Ask the child to listen carefully as you name a word that rhymes with the name of one of these pictures, such as: *fox, gun, top, coat, curls*. After you repeat the word twice, have the child point to the picture with the name that rhymes with the word that you said. Encourage the child to name additional words that rhyme with the names of the pictures.

Family Involvement Activity Duplicate the Family Letter on page 103 of this Teacher's Edition. Send it home with the children.

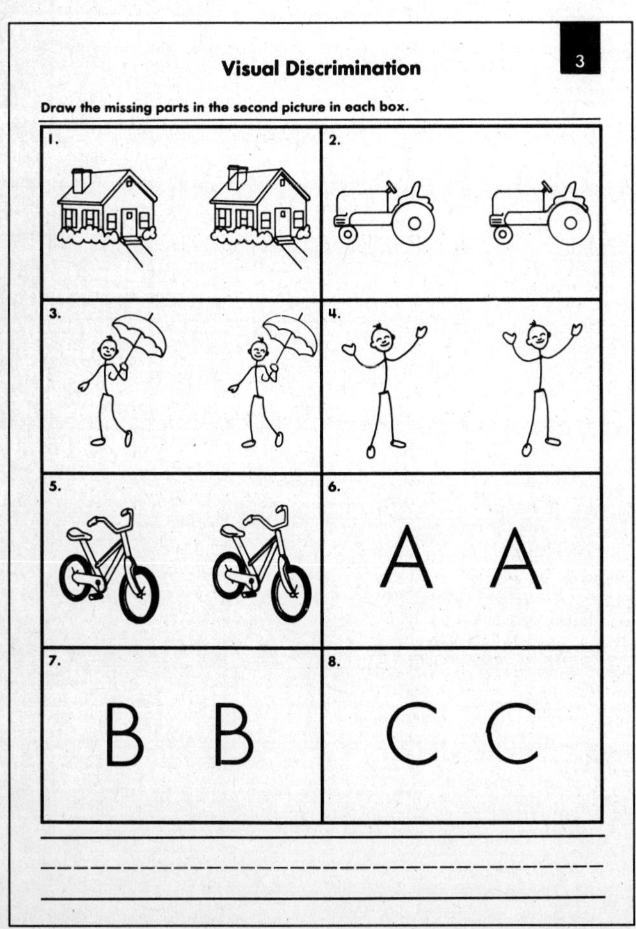

Lesson 2

The Alphabet *A* Through *F* (pages 4–7)

Objective The child will identify capital and small letters *A* through *F*.

Teaching Ideas

Matching Game Challenge the children to play the Matching Game. Use prepared alphabet letter cards or ask the children to print individual capital letters on tagboard cards and individual small letters on tagboard cards. (The letter cards may be prepared beforehand or as part of the activity. You will want to save these materials for future lessons.) Display in the correct sequence the letter cards for letters *A* through *F*, both capital and small letters, on the ledge of the chalkboard or in a pocket chart. When a capital letter appears with its corresponding small letter, refer to the pair as *partner letters*. Distribute another set of matching letter cards among the children. Invite the children to match their letter cards with those on display and to tell whether their letters are capital or small letters. To encourage children who give a wrong response, point out similarities in the two letters.

Alphabet-Train Game A variation of this game is the Alphabet-Train Game. Distribute the letter cards to the children. Invite a child who is holding a capital *A* card to be the engine of the train by standing at the front of the classroom. Ask a child who holds a small *a* to stand as the next "car." Continue the sequence, and when the train is complete, challenge the children to say the names of their letter cards in the correct order. Acknowledge the children for their participation as well as for accuracy.

Are-You-My-Partner? Game Another approach would be to play Are You My Partner? by distributing the letter cards to the children. Explain to the children that they are to seek out and stand with another child who holds their partner letter. Encourage and draw aside standing partners as they form to make the selection easier for the children who remain unmatched.

Writing Finally, you may wish to print the partner letters *Aa* through *Ff* on the chalkboard. Invite children to trace over the letters with chalk and to name them. Print the following rows of letters on the chalkboard.

F F E F E B F F B E E F E F B

f h b f e f t d b f i t f e b

Call on a child to circle in chalk the partner letters. You may use different colors of chalk for the various partner letters. Invite hesitant children to choose from your hand a favorite color of chalk.

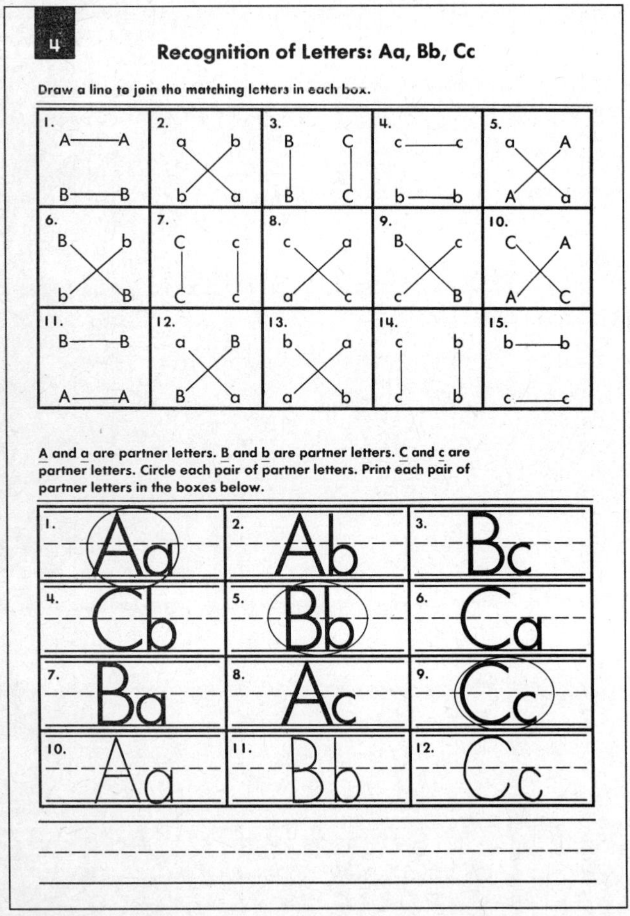

4
Recognition of Letters: Aa, Bb, Cc
Draw a line to join the matching letters in each box.
A and a are partner letters. B and b are partner letters. C and c are partner letters. Circle each pair of partner letters. Print each pair of partner letters in the boxes below.
Aa Ab Bc
Cb Bb Ca
Ba Ac Cc
Aa Bb Cc

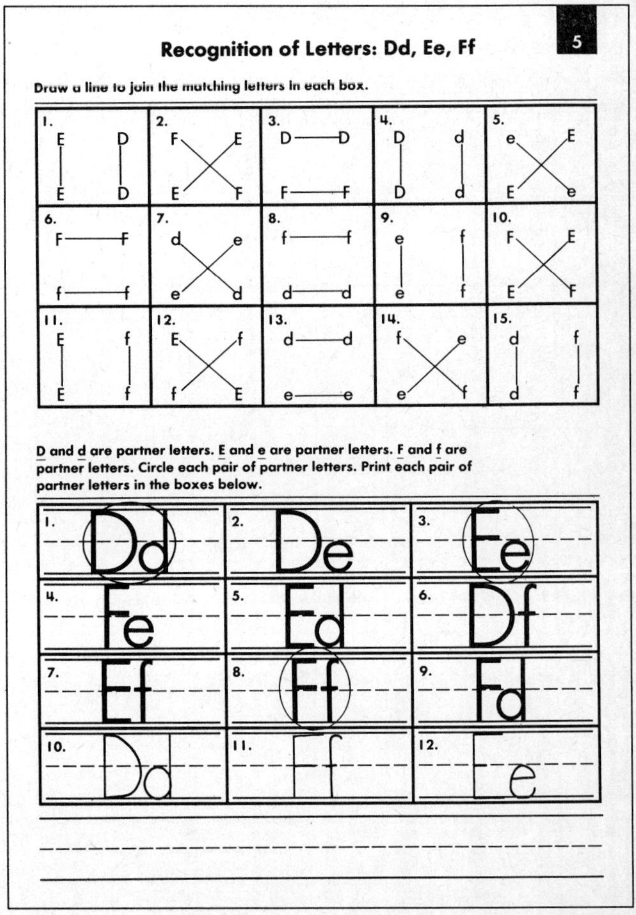

5
Recognition of Letters: Dd, Ee, Ff
Draw a line to join the matching letters in each box.
D and d are partner letters. E and e are partner letters. F and f are partner letters. Circle each pair of partner letters. Print each pair of partner letters in the boxes below.
Dd De Ee
Fe Ed Df
Ef Ff Fd
Dd Ff Ee

Extension

Writing Print the following words on the chalkboard: *dad, bad, cab, Ed, fed*. Point to each word, saying it as you point. Challenge the child to name the letters in each word. Suggest that the child print the letters *Aa* through *Ff* on the chalkboard or write other words that are comprised of the letters *a* through *f*. Reinforce, especially, attempts to form additional words.

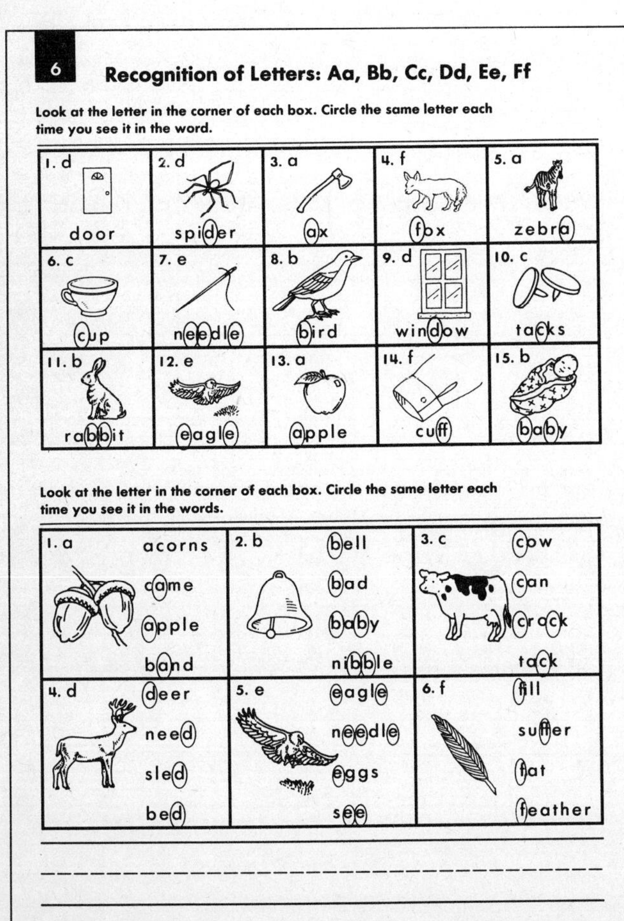

6 **Recognition of Letters: Aa, Bb, Cc, Dd, Ee, Ff**

Look at the letter in the corner of each box. Circle the same letter each time you see it in the word.

1. d door	2. d spider	3. a ax	4. f fox	5. a zebra
6. c cup	7. e needle	8. b bird	9. d window	10. c tacks
11. b rabbit	12. e eagle	13. a apple	14. f cuff	15. b baby

Look at the letter in the corner of each box. Circle the same letter each time you see it in the words.

1. a acorns came apple band	2. b bell bad baby nibble	3. c cow can crack tack
4. d deer need sled bed	5. e eagle needle eggs see	6. f fill suffer flat feather

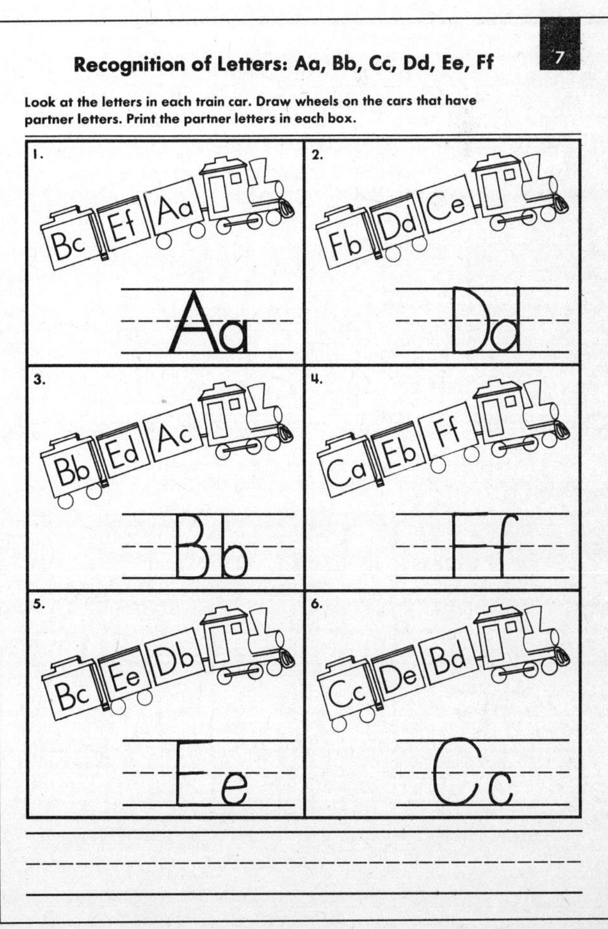

Recognition of Letters: Aa, Bb, Cc, Dd, Ee, Ff 7

Look at the letters in each train car. Draw wheels on the cars that have partner letters. Print the partner letters in each box.

1. Bc Ef Aa — Aa	2. Fb Dd Ce — Dd
3. Bb Ed Ac — Bb	4. Ca Eb Ff — Ff
5. Bc Ee Db — Ee	6. Cc De Bd — Cc

Lesson 3
The Alphabet *G* Through *L* (pages 8–11)

Objective The child will identify in sequence and in mixed order the letters *G* through *L*.

Teaching Ideas

What-Comes-Next? Game Challenge the children to play What Comes Next? by placing capital letter cards for *A* through *F* on the chalkboard ledge or in a pocket chart. Invite individual children to name each letter. Ask the children to tell which letter will be next in the proper sequence. After *G* is named, continue the game to introduce the letters *H* through *L*.

Next, you may print the partner letters for *Gg* through *Ll* on the chalkboard. Have the children tell the name of each letter and whether it is a capital or small letter.

Scramble Game The children will enjoy playing the Scramble Game. Place capital and small letter cards for *G* through *L* on the chalkboard. Using the letter cards, invite several children to arrange on the chalkboard ledge in the correct sequence both the capital and small letter cards. You may wish to remind the children that partner letters are to be placed side-by-side. Ask the children to close their eyes while you scramble the order of the letter cards. Challenge one group of children to rearrange the letter cards in the correct sequence. Permit this group to scramble the letter cards for their classmates, and repeat the unscrambling activity with another group of children.

Matching Game Finally, play the Matching Game by distributing another set of letter cards, *Gg* through *Ll*, among the children. Invite children to match their capital or small letter cards with those on the chalkboard ledge.

Reteaching

Tactile You may wish to use the letters *A* through *L* from a textured alphabet for the child. Sandpaper letters, felt letters, and wooden puzzle letters will provide the appropriate experience.

Have the child trace a letter with a finger while blindfolded. Encourage the child to guess the letter name. Have the child remove the blindfold for confirmation of the correct choice. Continue with additional letters. If you wish, the child may identify the traced letter from among the letter cards.

Writing Write the partner letters for *Aa* through *Ll* on the chalkboard. Invite the child to trace over the letter with chalk.

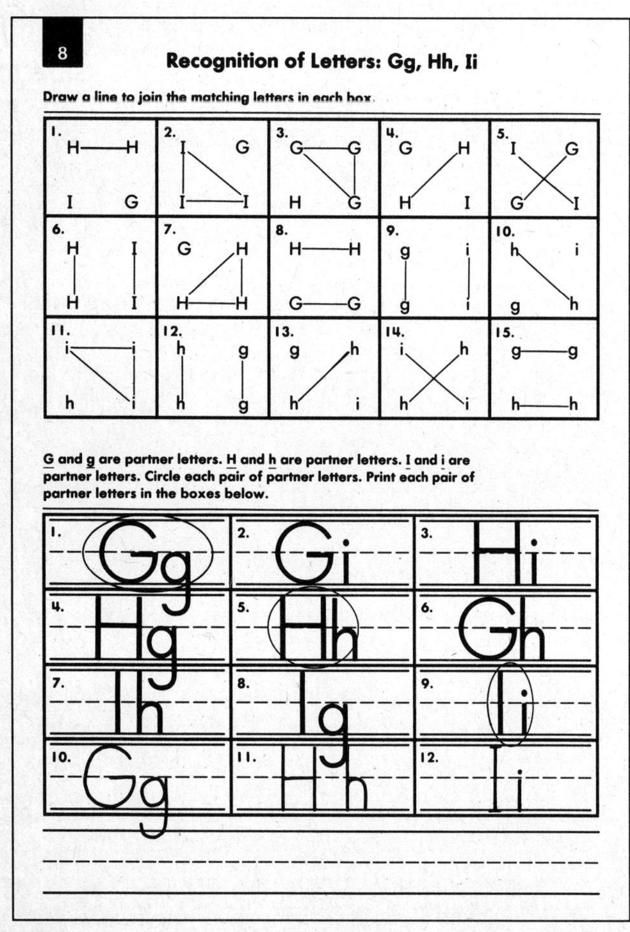

8

Recognition of Letters: Gg, Hh, Ii

Draw a line to join the matching letters in each box.

G and g are partner letters. H and h are partner letters. I and i are partner letters. Circle each pair of partner letters. Print each pair of partner letters in the boxes below.

1. Gg	2. Gi	3. Hi
4. Hg	5. Hh	6. Gh
7. Ih	8. Ig	9. Ii
10. Gg	11. Hh	12. Ii

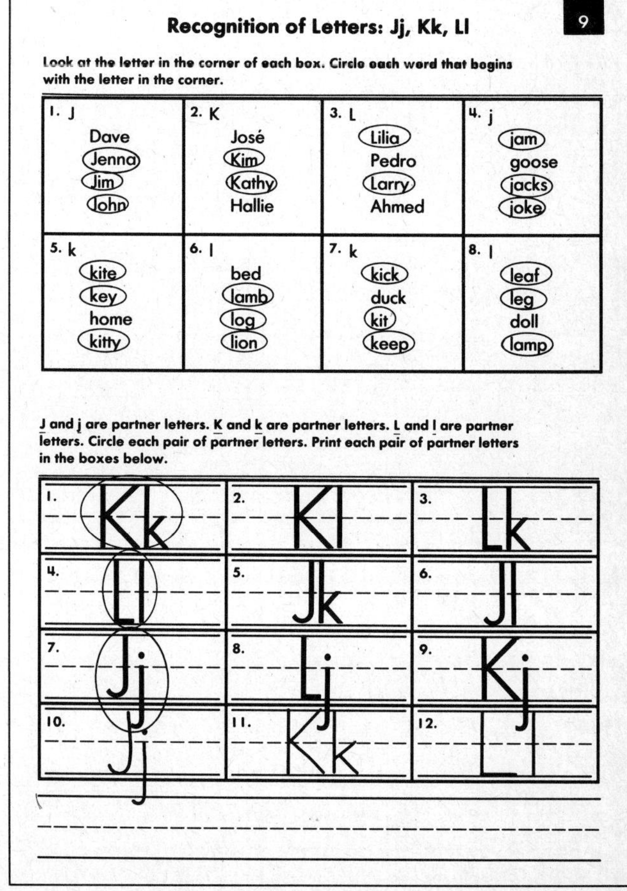

9

Recognition of Letters: Jj, Kk, Ll

Look at the letter in the corner of each box. Circle each word that begins with the letter in the corner.

1. J	2. K	3. L	4. j
Dave Jenna Jim John	José Kim Kathy Hallie	Lilia Pedro Larry Ahmed	jam goose jacks joke
5. k	**6. l**	**7. k**	**8. l**
kite key home kitty	bed lamb log lion	kick duck kit keep	leaf leg doll lamp

J and j are partner letters. K and k are partner letters. L and l are partner letters. Circle each pair of partner letters. Print each pair of partner letters in the boxes below.

1. Kk	2. Kl	3. Lk
4. Ll	5. Jk	6. Jl
7. Jj	8. Lj	9. Kj
10. Jj	11. Kk	12. Ll

Extension

Writing Print the letters *G* through *L* on the chalkboard, leaving space beside each letter for the child to copy the letter. You may wish to have the child trace over the letter with chalk before copying.

Write the following words on the chalkboard: *hide, if, egg, big, did, fed, back, Jill*. Challenge the child to name the letters, in left-to-right progression, in each word. Tell the child the word that the letters spell. Save asking the child to blend the letters till later.

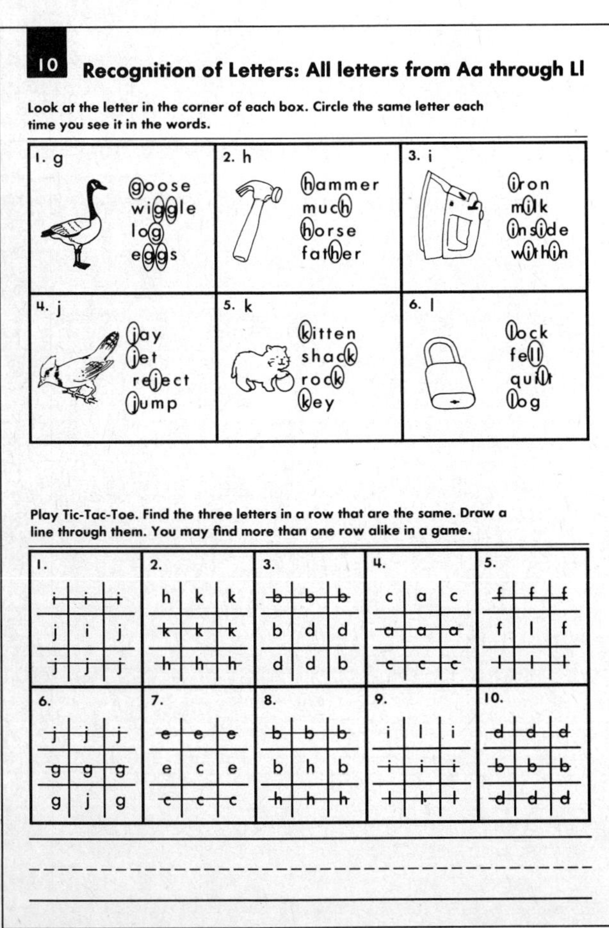

10 **Recognition of Letters: All letters from Aa through Ll**

Look at the letter in the corner of each box. Circle the same letter each time you see it in the words.

1. g	2. h	3. i
goose wiggle log eggs	hammer much horse father	iron milk inside within

4. j	5. k	6. l
jay jet reject jump	kitten shack rock key	lock fell quilt log

Play Tic-Tac-Toe. Find the three letters in a row that are the same. Draw a line through them. You may find more than one row alike in a game.

1.	2.	3.	4.	5.
i i i	h k k	b b b	c a c	f f f
j i j	k k k	b d d	a a a	f l f
j j j	h h h	d d b	c c c	l l l

6.	7.	8.	9.	10.
j j j	e e e	b b b	i l i	d d d
g g g	e c e	b h b	i i i	b b b
g j g	c c c	h h h	l l l	d d d

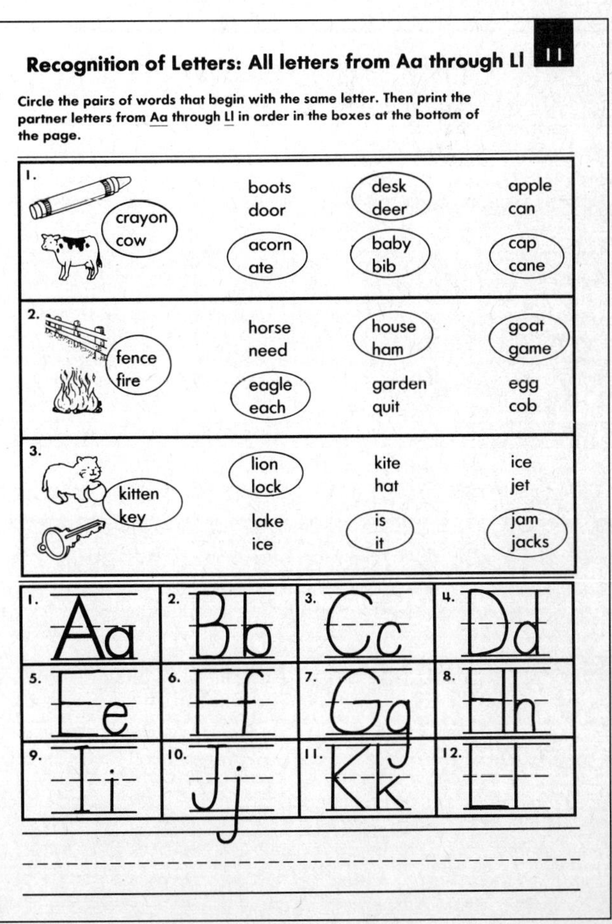

Recognition of Letters: All letters from Aa through Ll 11

Circle the pairs of words that begin with the same letter. Then print the partner letters from Aa through Ll in order in the boxes at the bottom of the page.

1. crayon cow — boots door — desk deer — apple can — acorn ate — baby bib — cap cane

2. fence fire — horse need — house ham — goat game — eagle each — garden quit — egg cob

3. kitten key — lion lock — kite hat — ice jet — lake ice — is it — jam jacks

1. Aa	2. Bb	3. Cc	4. Dd
5. Ee	6. Ff	7. Gg	8. Hh
9. Ii	10. Jj	11. Kk	12. Ll

Lesson 4

The Alphabet *M, N,* and *O* (page 12)

Objective The child will identify the letters *M, N,* and *O* in sequence and in mixed order.

Review

Listening To review auditory discrimination, challenge the children to identify rhyming words through the following activity.

Read aloud the three words in each column. Invite the children to identify the two words that rhyme.

mouse	*mail*	*wing*	*barn*	*jam*
house	*pail*	*work*	*bird*	*ham*
merry	*party*	*sing*	*yarn*	*jelly*

Speaking You may wish to continue the review with the following exercise.

Choose a word from the previous activity. Write it on the chalkboard, followed by a line (for example: *mouse/* ________). Say the written word aloud, and invite the children to name a rhyming word.

Teaching Ideas

Writing Print the partner letters for *M, N,* and *O* on the chalkboard. Say the name of each letter, discriminating between the capital and small letters. Invite the children to trace over the letters with chalk. The children may also wish to write the letters on their own papers.

You may also want to print the following rows of letters on the chalkboard.

M M N M L M M M N M M W A N M
O o o d o o a c o O o a b o a
n n N m n M n h u m n o n u m

Encourage the children to identify the capital and small letters by drawing a square around each *Nn* and by drawing a triangle around each *Oo*. Different colored chalk may be used for capital and small letters.

Extension

Find-the-Letter Game Invite the child to play Find the Letter. Display prepared letter cards for the letters *G* through *O* and their partner letters in the correct sequence. Challenge the child to find and hold up the letter you name. You may want to emphasize the partner letters for *M, N,* and *O*. If you wish, the game can be expanded to include all the letters of the alphabet.

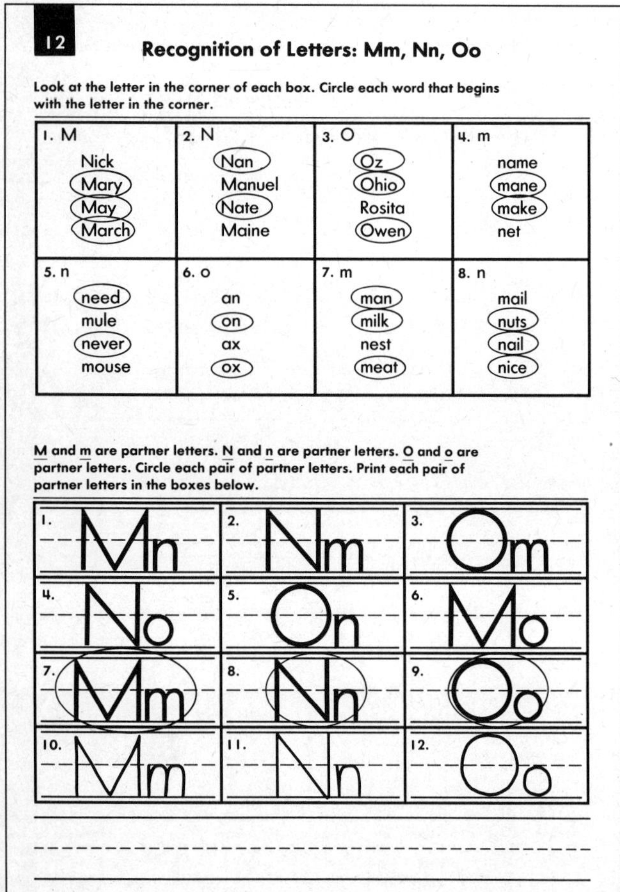

12

Recognition of Letters: Mm, Nn, Oo

Look at the letter in the corner of each box. Circle each word that begins with the letter in the corner.

1. M	2. N	3. O	4. m
Nick, Mary, May, March	Nan, Manuel, Nate, Maine	Oz, Ohio, Rosita, Owen	name, mane, make, net
5. n	**6. o**	**7. m**	**8. n**
need, mule, never, mouse	an, on, ax, ox	man, milk, nest, meat	mail, nuts, nail, nice

M and m are partner letters. N and n are partner letters. O and o are partner letters. Circle each pair of partner letters. Print each pair of partner letters in the boxes below.

1. Mn	2. Nm	3. Om
4. No	5. On	6. Mo
7. Mm	8. Nn	9. Oo
10. Mm	11. Nn	12. Oo

Lesson 5

The Alphabet *P* and *Q* (pages 13–14)

Objective The child will identify the alphabet letters *P* and *Q* in sequence and in mixed order.

Review

Matching Game To practice recognition of the alphabet letters *A* through *O*, you may wish to play the Matching Game as described in Lesson 2 in this unit.

Teaching Ideas

Touch and See Using prepared letter cards, display the cards for *P* and *Q*. Say the name of each letter. Invite the children to study each letter and to trace each one with their fingers. (This may be done on their desks, in the air, or on each card.) Encourage the children to name each letter as they are tracing it.

Writing To extend the activity above, you may want to challenge the children to write the partners for the letters *P* and *Q* on the chalkboard or on their own sheets of paper.

Scramble Game Invite the children to play the Scramble Game described in Lesson 3 in this unit. Using prepared letter cards for capital and small letters, place the cards in the correct sequence on the chalkboard ledge or in a pocket chart. Ask the children to close their eyes. Change the position of two of the letter cards. (For example, you may wish to switch the position of the *M* and the *N*.) Ask the children to open their eyes. Challenge them to find the two letters that have been mixed up. Then ask them to return each letter to its correct position. Encourage all of the children to participate.

Extension

Tactile The following activity can be used to increase the child's tactile awareness of the letters being taught in this lesson.

You may wish to provide clay for the child to mold capital and small letters of the alphabet. Trays of sand can also be provided in which the child could trace the letters of the alphabet. (Small plastic meat trays may be used for this activity.) Letters could also be preprinted on primary writing paper for the child to trace and copy.

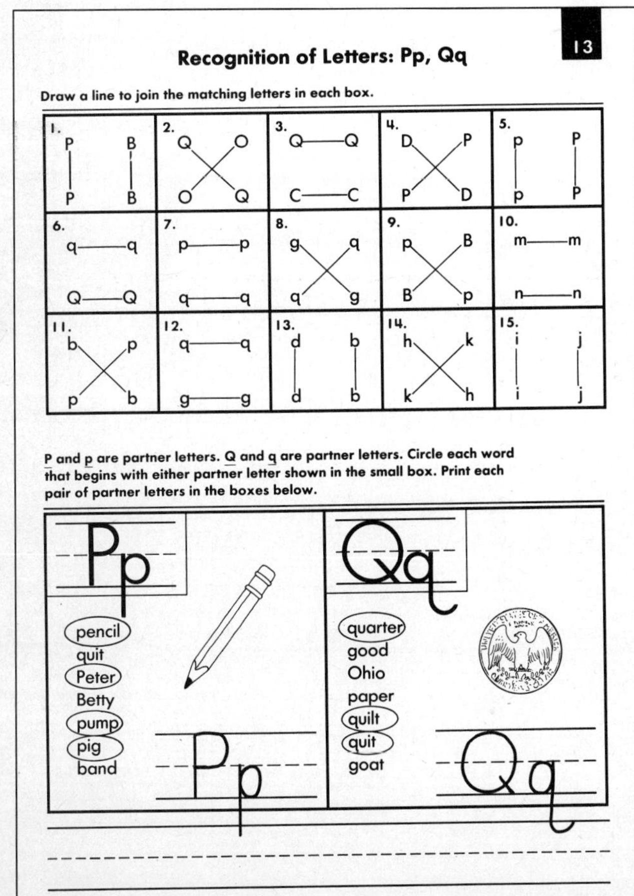

13

Recognition of Letters: Pp, Qq

Draw a line to join the matching letters in each box.

1. P B / P B	2. Q O / O Q	3. Q—Q / C—C	4. D P / P D	5. p P / p P
6. q—q / Q—Q	7. p—p / q—q	8. g q / q g	9. P B / B p	10. m—m / n—n
11. b p / p b	12. q—q / g—g	13. d b / d b	14. h k / k h	15. i j / i j

P and p are partner letters. Q and q are partner letters. Circle each word that begins with either partner letter shown in the small box. Print each pair of partner letters in the boxes below.

Pp: pencil, quit, Peter, Betty, pump, pig, band — Pp

Qq: quarter, good, Ohio, paper, quilt, quit, goat — Qq

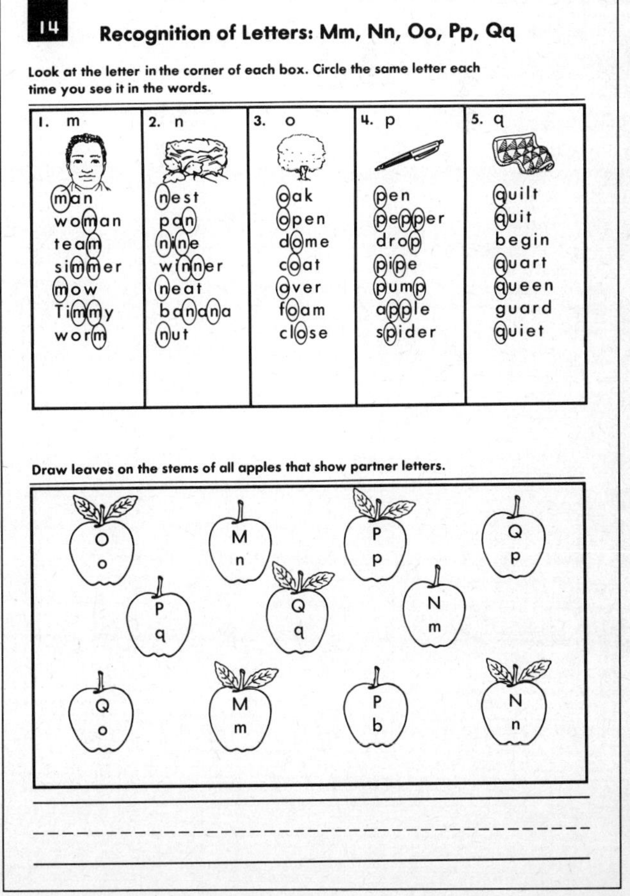

14

Recognition of Letters: Mm, Nn, Oo, Pp, Qq

Look at the letter in the corner of each box. Circle the same letter each time you see it in the words.

1. m	2. n	3. o	4. p	5. q
man	nest	oak	pen	quilt
woman	pan	open	pepper	quit
team	nine	dome	drop	begin
simmer	winner	coat	pipe	quart
mow	neat	over	pump	queen
Timmy	banana	foam	apple	guard
worm	nut	close	spider	quiet

Draw leaves on the stems of all apples that show partner letters.

Lesson 6

The Alphabet *R* Through *W* (pages 15–16)

Objective The child will identify the letters *R* through *W* in sequence and in mixed order.

Review

Writing To reinforce visual discrimination of the letters *A* through *Q*, you may want to preprint these letters on primary writing paper. Invite the children to trace the letters with their pencils. Encourage them to copy these letters on their own sheets of paper.

Matching Game Play the Matching Game, as described in Lesson 2 in this unit, to reinforce visual discrimination of the letters *A* through *Q*.

Teaching Ideas

Find-the-Letter-Game Invite the children to play Find the Letter, as described in Lesson 4 in this unit, using prepared letter cards *A* through *W*.

Card-Relay Game You may also wish to play the Card-Relay Game. Divide the children into two teams. Arrange prepared letter cards *A* through *W* and their partner letters on the chalkboard ledge or in a pocket chart. (You may want to review the concept of partner letters with the children.) Scramble the order of the letters. Challenge the first member of each team to name and take a letter, discriminating between capital and small letters. Reinforce a correct response by giving a point to the team. Continue the game by encouraging each child to take a turn. The team getting the most points wins.

Extension

Giant-Step Game Invite the child to play the Giant-Step Game. Using strips of masking tape, place parallel lines on the floor about two feet apart for a distance of twelve feet. Designate the starting line and the goal. Ask the child to stand at the starting line. Stand at the goal line. Flash one of the prepared letter cards *A* through *W*. Ask the child to name the letter presented. Invite the child to advance one line for each correct response. Continue until the child reaches the goal line.

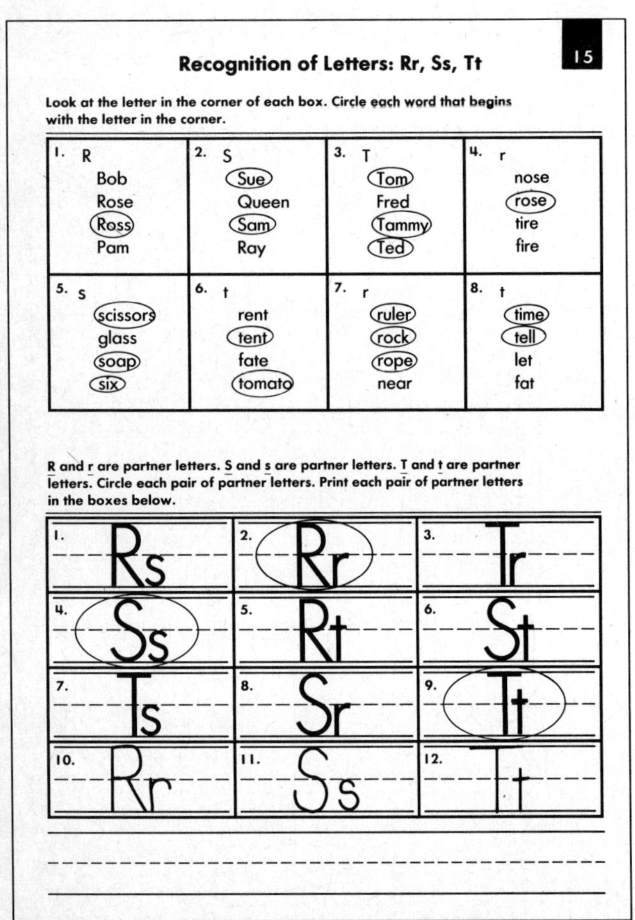

15

Recognition of Letters: Rr, Ss, Tt

Look at the letter in the corner of each box. Circle each word that begins with the letter in the corner.

1. R	2. S	3. T	4. r
Bob Rose Ross Pam	Sue Queen Sam Ray	Tom Fred Tammy Ted	nose rose tire fire
5. s	**6. t**	**7. r**	**8. t**
scissors glass soap six	rent tent fate tomato	ruler rock rope near	time tell let fat

R and r are partner letters. S and s are partner letters. T and t are partner letters. Circle each pair of partner letters. Print each pair of partner letters in the boxes below.

1. Rs	2. Rr	3. Tr
4. Ss	5. Rt	6. St
7. Ts	8. Sr	9. Tt
10. Rr	11. Ss	12. Tt

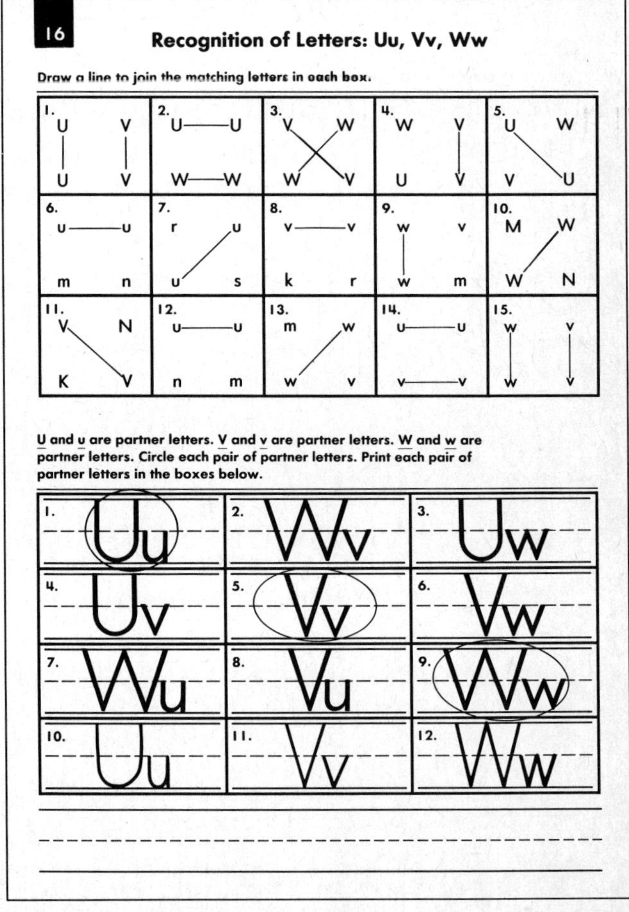

16

Recognition of Letters: Uu, Vv, Ww

Draw a line to join the matching letters in each box.

1.	2.	3.	4.	5.
U V U V	U—U W—W	V W W V	W V U V	U W V U
6.	**7.**	**8.**	**9.**	**10.**
u—u m n	r u u s	v—v k r	w v w m	M W W N
11.	**12.**	**13.**	**14.**	**15.**
V N K V	u—u n m	m w w v	u—u v—v	w v w v

U and u are partner letters. V and v are partner letters. W and w are partner letters. Circle each pair of partner letters. Print each pair of partner letters in the boxes below.

1. Uu	2. Wv	3. Uw
4. Uv	5. Vv	6. Vw
7. Wu	8. Vu	9. Ww
10. Uu	11. Vv	12. Ww

Lesson 7

The Alphabet *X*, *Y*, and *Z* (pages 17–18)

Objective The child will identify in sequence and in mixed order the letters *X*, *Y*, and *Z*.

Review

Listening To review auditory discrimination, challenge the children to suggest rhymes. Ask the children to find pictures of the following objects in magazines: *cap*, *star*, *boat*, *horn*, *sock*, *sun*, *tie*, *cake*, *book*. Have the children cut the pictures out and paste them on a piece of tagboard or construction paper. Challenge the children to name their pictures and suggest words that rhyme with the name of the object in each picture. (These pictures may be saved for future use.)

Teaching Ideas

Writing Write the partner letters for *X*, *Y*, and *Z* on the chalkboard. Ask the children to say the name of each letter and tell whether it is capital or small. Encourage the children to trace over the letters on the chalkboard or practice writing the letters on primary paper at their desks.

Write the following letters in columns on the chalkboard.

K	*j*	*Q*	*z*
J	*x*	*U*	*g*
L	*k*	*Z*	*y*
H	*l*	*G*	*q*
X	*h*	*Y*	*u*

Invite the children to draw a line from each capital letter to its partner letter. Encourage children to print the partner letters on primary paper. You may want to preprint the letters beforehand on primary paper for the children to trace. If you wish, extend the activity to include other letters.

Reteaching

Art Using paints, markers, or crayons, invite the child to make a personal set of letter cards on small squares of tagboard. Direct the child to include both capital and small letters on each card.

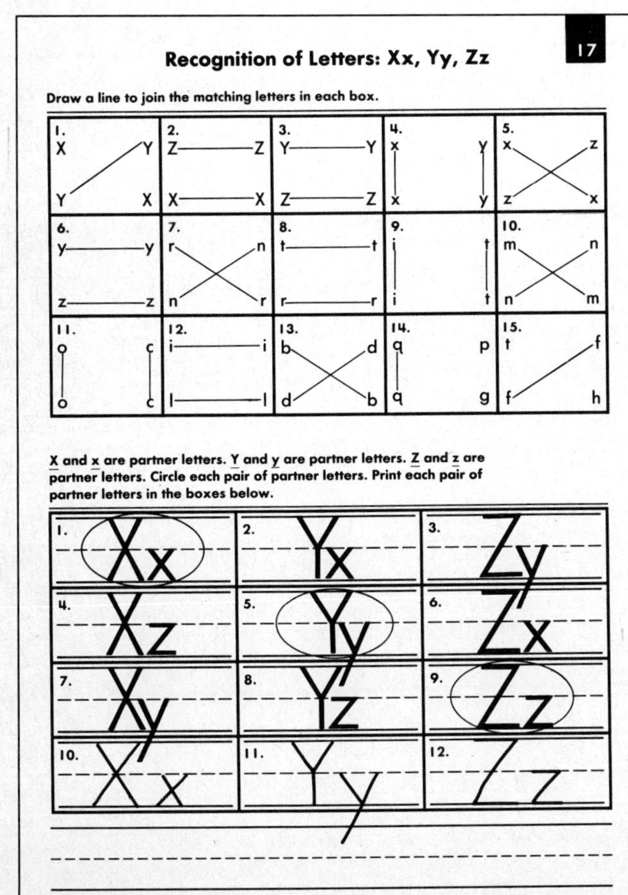

17

Recognition of Letters: Xx, Yy, Zz

Draw a line to join the matching letters in each box.

X and x are partner letters. Y and y are partner letters. Z and z are partner letters. Circle each pair of partner letters. Print each pair of partner letters in the boxes below.

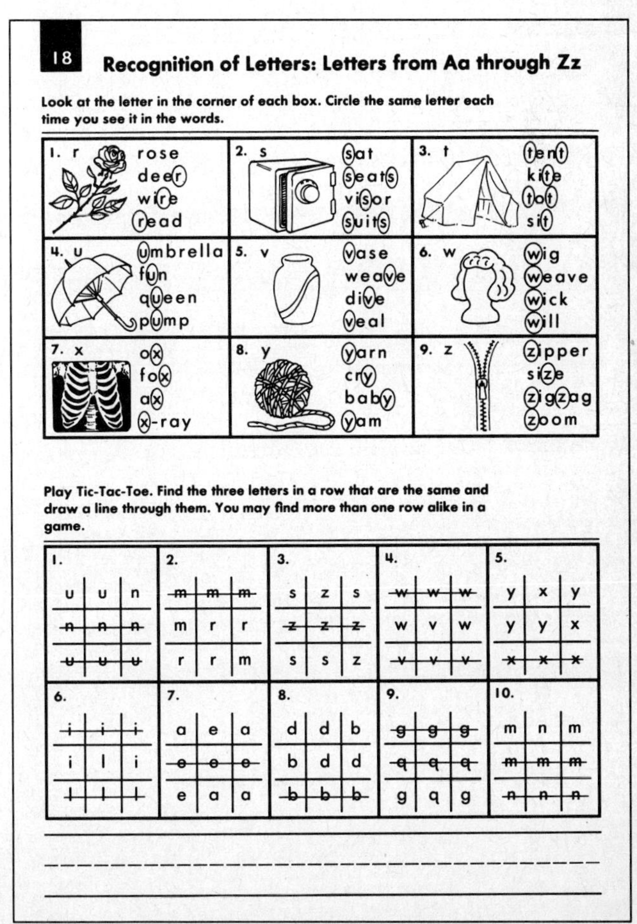

18

Recognition of Letters: Letters from Aa through Zz

Look at the letter in the corner of each box. Circle the same letter each time you see it in the words.

1. r — rose, deer, wire, read
2. s — sat, seats, visor, suits
3. t — tent, kite, tot, sit
4. u — umbrella, fun, queen, pump
5. v — vase, weave, dive, veal
6. w — wig, weave, wick, will
7. x — ox, fox, ax, x-ray
8. y — yarn, cry, baby, yam
9. z — zipper, size, zigzag, zoom

Play Tic-Tac-Toe. Find the three letters in a row that are the same and draw a line through them. You may find more than one row alike in a game.

Unit 2 Consonants

Lesson 8

Consonant Sound *S* (page 19)

Objective The child will identify the name and sound of the letter *S*.

Review

Card-Relay Game Using prepared letter cards *A* through *Z*, play the Card-Relay Game as described in Lesson 6.

Teaching Ideas

Listening Challenge the children to listen to the beginning sounds of words you say. Pronounce the following words, stressing the beginning sound in each: *salt, Sam, sister, six, sun, seven, sailboat, soap, salad, sandal*. Explain that the first sound in each word is the sound of the letter *S*. Invite the children to name other words that begin with the sound of *S*, praising correct responses.

Writing Draw on the chalkboard simple pictures of objects that begin with *S*: *sun, sailboat, seven, saw, soap*. Print the name of the object under each picture, underlining the beginning *S*. Invite the children to identify each picture and to listen for the beginning *S* sound. Encourage the children to come to the chalkboard and trace the letter *S* with chalk. You might choose to provide individual practice, using primary paper and pencil.

Art Invite the children to make a collage. Using old magazines, ask the children to cut out pictures of objects with names that begin with the *S* sound. Direct the children to paste the pictures on pieces of tagboard or construction paper. You might display the collages in the classroom.

Extension

Art List the following *S* words on the chalkboard: *saw, sun, seal, sock, sandwich*. Direct the child to fold a piece of blank paper into four squares and print an *S* word in each square. Challenge the child to draw a picture to illustrate each *S* word. The child may enjoy working with different media such as paints, chalk, or brightly colored markers.

Listening Invite the child to listen to the following words: *bus, man, horse, dress, sack, mess*. Challenge the child to identify the words that end with the *S* sound. You may wish to have the child repeat each word while listening for the *S* sound.

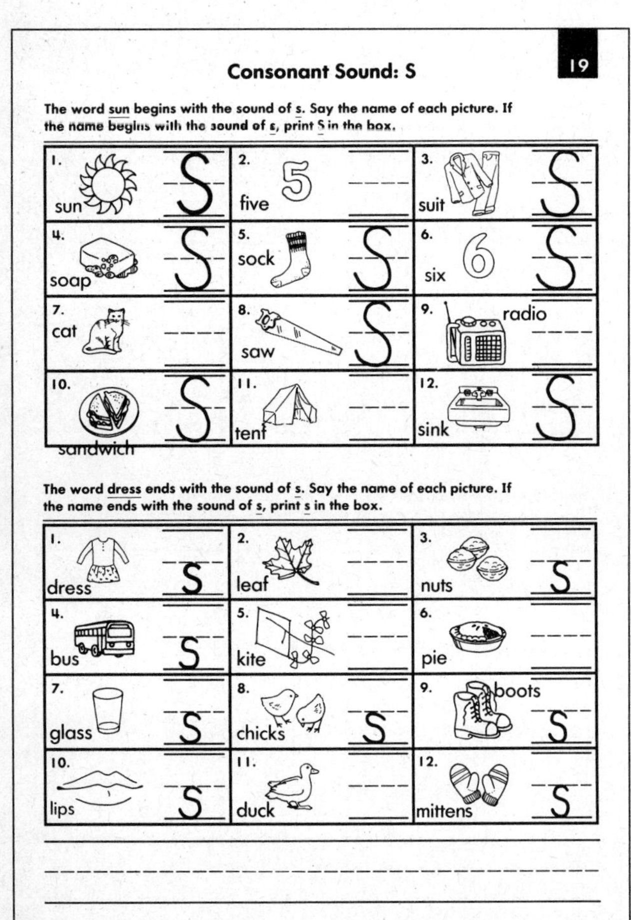

Consonant Sound: S 19

The word sun begins with the sound of s. Say the name of each picture. If the name begins with the sound of s, print S in the box.

1. sun S	2. five	3. suit S
4. soap S	5. sock S	6. six S
7. cat	8. saw S	9. radio
10. sandwich S	11. tent	12. sink S

The word dress ends with the sound of s. Say the name of each picture. If the name ends with the sound of s, print s in the box.

1. dress s	2. leaf	3. nuts s
4. bus s	5. kite	6. pie
7. glass s	8. chicks s	9. boots s
10. lips s	11. duck	12. mittens s

Lesson 9

Consonant Sound *T* (pages 20–21)

Objective The child will identify the name and sound of the letter *T*.

Teaching Ideas

Listening Introduce the sound of the letter *T* by inviting the children to listen to the beginning sound in each of the following words: *television, town, ten, ticket, tie, teeth.* Encourage the children to suggest other words that begin with the letter *T*. To provide practice in visual discrimination, write the children's responses on the chalkboard.

Continue this activity by pronouncing the following words: *hat, sit, cat, net, foot, root, pat.* Stress the ending *T* sound in each. Encourage the children to suggest other words that end with the letter *T*. Write their responses on the chalkboard. Save both lists of words for the next activity.

Writing Refer the children to the two lists of words you printed on the chalkboard during the previous activity. Invite the children to circle each letter *T*. Have them trace the letters on the chalkboard, or write them at their desks. If you provide primary paper that has been color coded to designate the top, the middle, and the bottom writing lines, ask the children to verbalize the writing process. Have the children describe the point where the letter is started, continuing the description to the letter's completion.

Extension

Art Cut out large tagboard shapes of the letter *S* and the letter *T*. Make sure the shapes are large enough so smaller pictures can be pasted on them. Invite the child to find pictures in magazines of objects with names that start with the letter *S*. Direct the child to paste those pictures on the large letter *S*, creating a collage-type effect. Encourage the child to create a similar collage for the letter *T*. If you wish, ask the child to name the pictures on each collage.

Listening Provide the child with the letter cards *S* and *T*. Challenge the child to hold up the letter *S* when the *S* sound is heard and the letter *T* when the *T* sound is heard. Pronounce the following words: *sun, tent, tire, sink, top, sorry, seven, ten, tape*. If you wish, expand this activity to include other consonants.

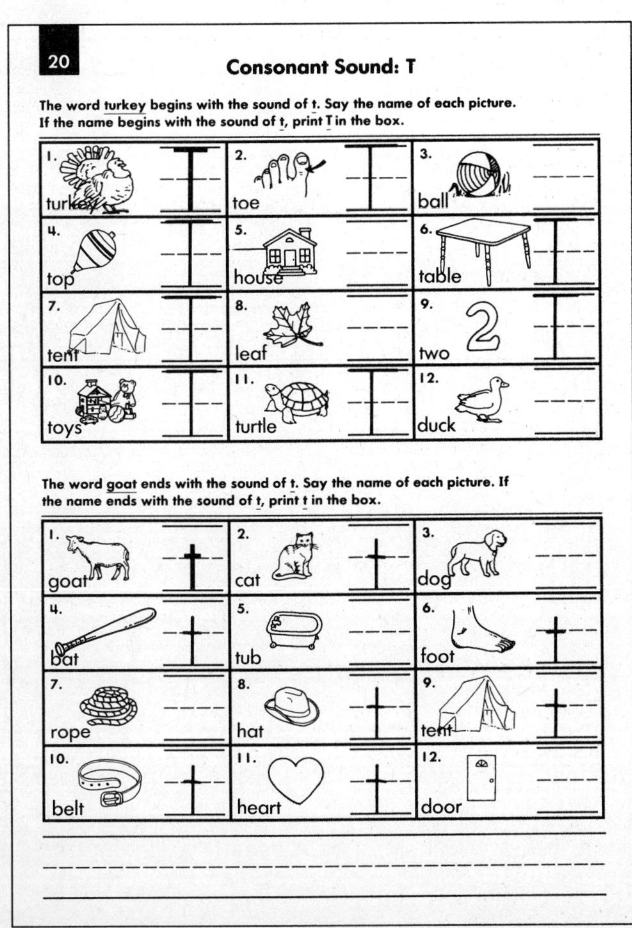

20

Consonant Sound: T

The word turkey begins with the sound of t. Say the name of each picture. If the name begins with the sound of t, print T in the box.

1. turkey — T	2. toe — T	3. ball
4. top — T	5. house	6. table — T
7. tent — T	8. leaf	9. two — T
10. toys — T	11. turtle — T	12. duck

The word goat ends with the sound of t. Say the name of each picture. If the name ends with the sound of t, print t in the box.

1. goat — t	2. cat — t	3. dog
4. bat — t	5. tub	6. foot — t
7. rope	8. hat — t	9. tent — t
10. belt — t	11. heart — t	12. door

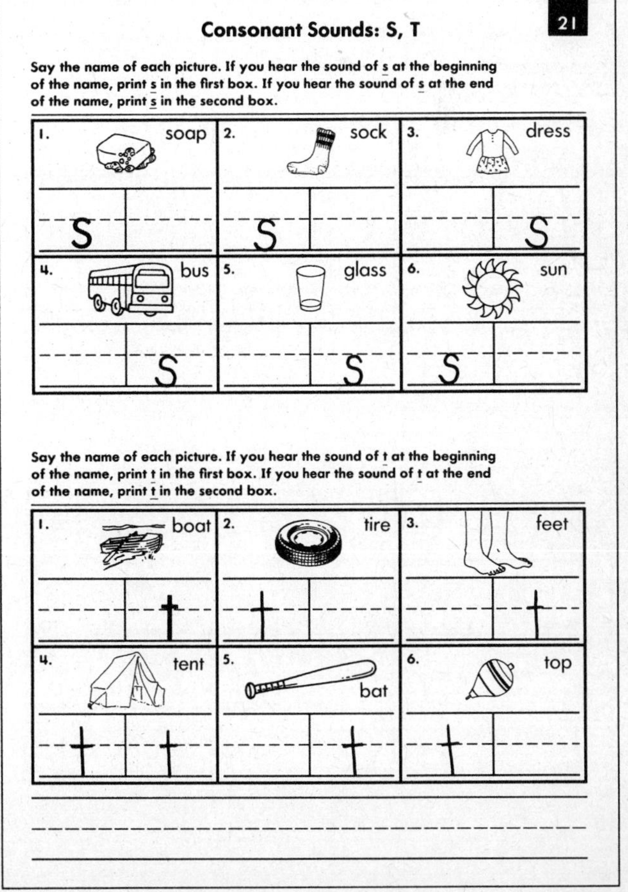

21

Consonant Sounds: S, T

Say the name of each picture. If you hear the sound of s at the beginning of the name, print s in the first box. If you hear the sound of s at the end of the name, print s in the second box.

1. soap — s	2. sock — s	3. dress — s
4. bus — s	5. glass — s	6. sun — s

Say the name of each picture. If you hear the sound of t at the beginning of the name, print t in the first box. If you hear the sound of t at the end of the name, print t in the second box.

1. boat — t	2. tire — t	3. feet — t
4. tent — t t	5. bat — t	6. top — t

Lesson 10

Consonant Sounds *B, S,* and *T* (pages 22–25)

Objective The child will associate the consonants *B, S,* and *T* with their respective sounds.

Teaching Ideas

Speaking Invite the children to repeat each of the following words after you: *bear, banana, bird, bank, box, belt, bubble, bus.* Suggest that the children feel the movement of their lips as they pronounce each word. Challenge the children to name the sound that comes at the beginning of each word.

Writing Provide the following pictures of objects with names that begin with the letter *B*: *box, bed, ball, bib, belt, bird.* Invite volunteers, in turn, to hold up the pictures and to ask the other children to identify the pictures. As the pictures are identified with various *B* words, print the words on the chalkboard. Encourage the children to use colored chalk to trace over the letter *B* at the beginning of each word.

I-Am-Thinking-of-Something Game Display pictures or picture flashcards of the following objects: *sun, turtle, suit, boat, bed, box, tape, tire, saw.* Begin the game by saying to the children, "*I am thinking of something that starts with* S." Invite the children to respond by pointing to the appropriate picture and saying the name of the object in the picture. Continue the game with the remaining pictures.

You may wish to expand the game by including objects around the room and inviting the children to guess the object.

Listening Provide the children with the letter cards *S, T,* and *B*. Challenge the children to hold up the appropriate cards when they hear the *S, T,* or *B* sounds in the following words: *bus, bell, sun, sing, tip, sew, turtle, book, bank, bird.*

Extension

Listening Encourage the child to listen to the beginning sound of each word you say for the letter *B*. Direct the child to raise a hand whenever you pronounce a word that begins with the letter *B*. Provide a series of words such as the following: *ball, tiger, Bob, boy, sock, bed, tell, bake.* If you wish, expand the activity to include the letters *S* and *T*.

Family Involvement Activity Duplicate the Family Letter on page104 of the Teacher's Edition. Send it home with the children.

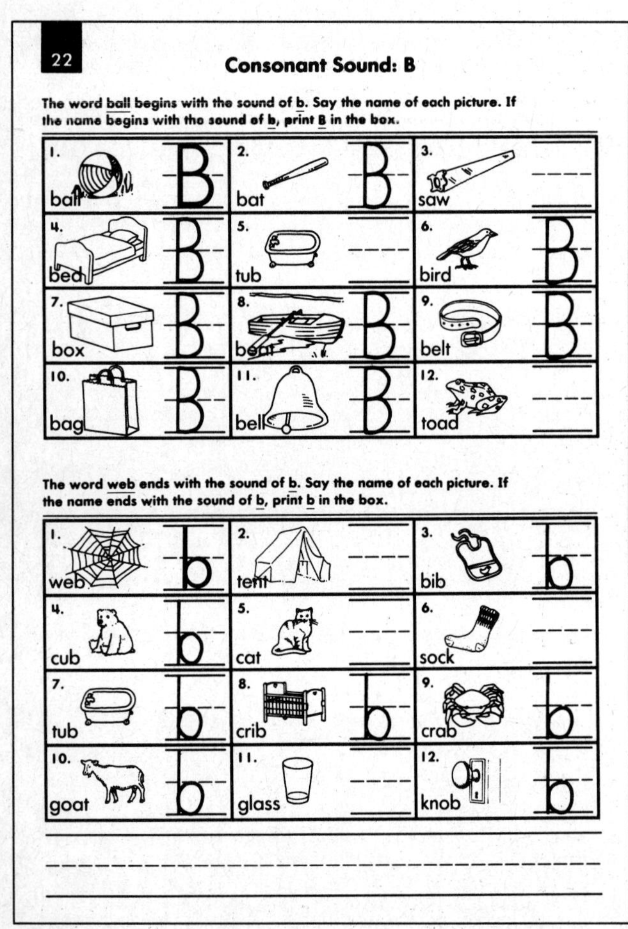

22

Consonant Sound: B

The word ball begins with the sound of b. Say the name of each picture. If the name begins with the sound of b, print B in the box.

1. ball B	2. bat B	3. saw
4. bed B	5. tub	6. bird B
7. box B	8. boat B	9. belt B
10. bag B	11. bell B	12. toad

The word web ends with the sound of b. Say the name of each picture. If the name ends with the sound of b, print b in the box.

1. web b	2. tent	3. bib b
4. cub b	5. cat	6. sock
7. tub b	8. crib b	9. crab b
10. goat b	11. glass	12. knob b

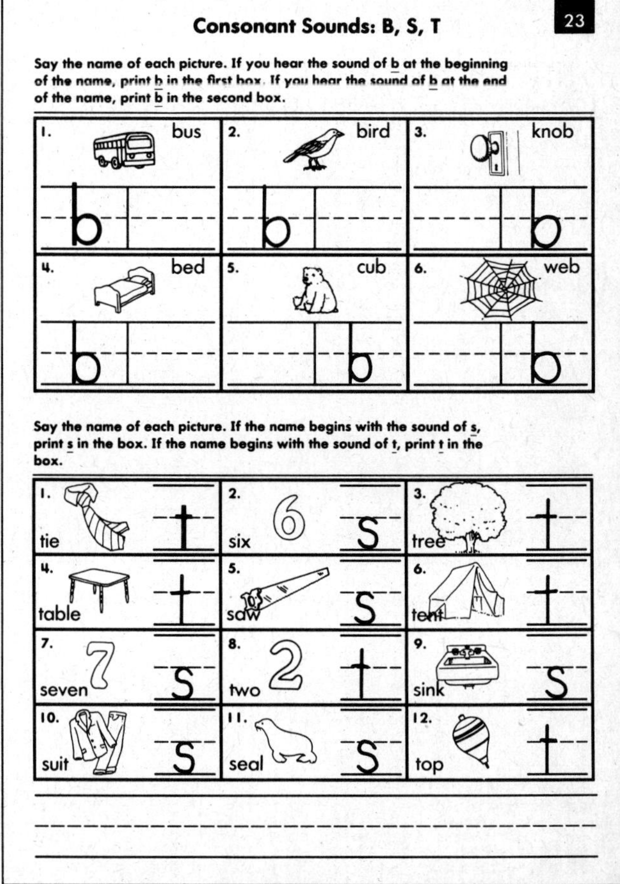

Consonant Sounds: B, S, T

23

Say the name of each picture. If you hear the sound of b at the beginning of the name, print b in the first box. If you hear the sound of b at the end of the name, print b in the second box.

1. bus b	2. bird b	3. knob b
4. bed b	5. cub b	6. web b

Say the name of each picture. If the name begins with the sound of s, print s in the box. If the name begins with the sound of t, print t in the box.

1. tie t	2. six s	3. tree t
4. table t	5. saw s	6. tent t
7. seven s	8. two t	9. sink s
10. suit s	11. seal s	12. top t

24

Consonant Sounds: B, S, T

Say the name of each picture. Circle the beginning letter.

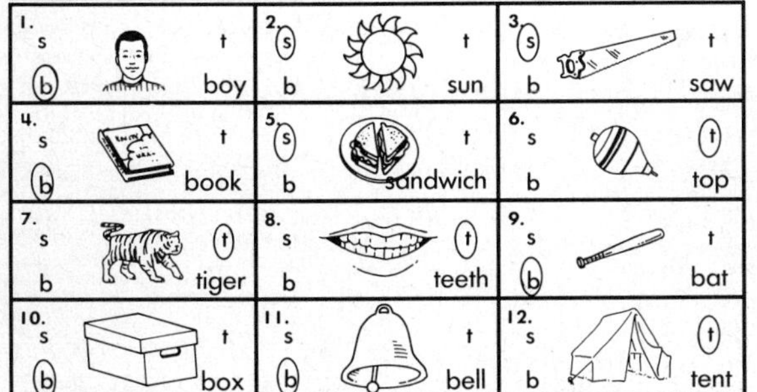

Say the name of each picture. If the name begins with the sound of the consonant shown, print the consonant in the first box. If the sound comes at the end, print the consonant in the last box.

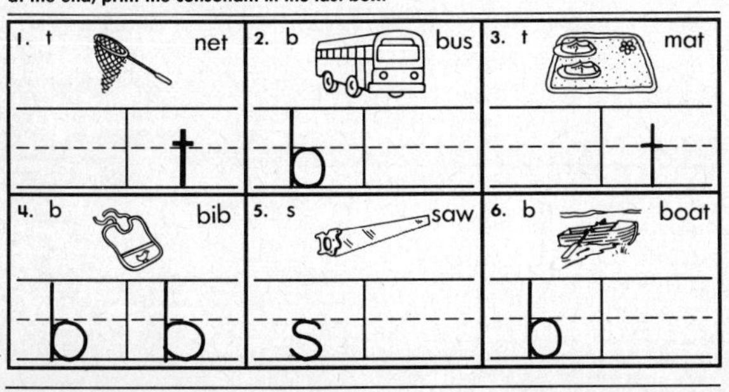

25

Consonant Sounds: B, S, T

Play Tic-Tac-Toe. Draw a line through the three pictures in a row that begin with the same sound. You may find more than one row alike in a game.

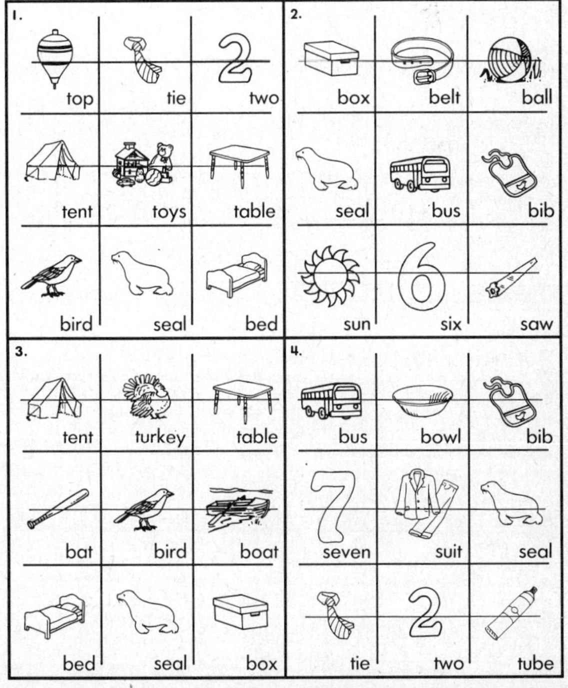

Lesson 11

Consonant Sound *H* (page 26)

Objective The child will identify the name and sound of the letter *H*.

Review

Rhyming-Riddle Game Place along the chalkboard ledge pictures or picture flashcards of the following objects: *sun, boat, bed, box, top*. (These cards may be prepared prior to the lesson, or they may be prepared by the children as part of the lesson.) Challenge the children to find the picture you will describe by using clues. For example, you might give the following clue: *The object I'm thinking of rhymes with pop and begins with T. (top)*

Continue play until all the pictures have been identified. To expand the activity, ask the children to give clues for the words. Encourage the children to formulate clues about the structure rather than the meaning of words.

Teaching Ideas

Tactile Invite the children to whisper and say the sounds *ha, has,* and *hee, hee*. Encourage them to hold a hand in front of their faces and feel their breath as they make the sound of *H*. Challenge the children to run in place for one minute. Encourage them to feel and listen to the *H* sound they are making as they pant.

Listening Invite the children to listen for the beginning sound as you say each of the following words: *hill, home, hush, hello, hammer, hide, honey, hair, house*. Pronounce the words a second time, encouraging the children to repeat the words after you. Ask the children to identify the *H* sound that begins each word.

Writing Display the following picture flashcards on the chalkboard ledge: *hammer, house, hair, honey*. For each, encourage a child to identify the picture and to name other words that begin with the sound of *H*. Write the words on the chalkboard as the children suggest them. Invite the children to trace the letter *H* that begins each word. You may wish to provide additional practice by inviting the children to trace the letter in the air with a finger.

Reteaching

Art Help the child make letter prints using old sponges, clothespins, tempera paint, and paper. Cut the sponges into specific letter shapes. Clip a clothespin onto the sponge to serve as a handle. Place a small amount of tempera (no deeper than 1/4") in a shallow container. Encourage the child to dip a sponge into the paint, wiping off the excess on the edge of the pan. Direct the child to "print" the letter by gently pressing the painted side of the sponge onto the paper. The letter may be printed several times, giving the child several prints of the same letter. Repeat the procedure using other sponge letters.

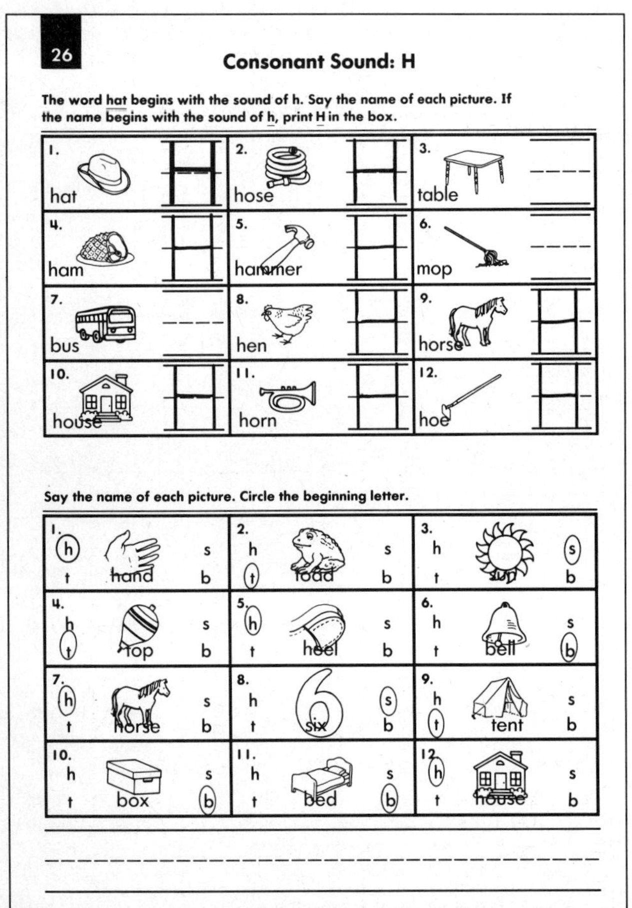

Lesson 12

Consonant Sound *M* (pages 27–28)

Objective The child will identify the name and sound of the letter *M*.

Review

Speaking To review beginning consonant sounds *S*, *T*, *B*, and *H*, write the following words on the chalkboard and encourage the children to name the beginning consonants: *hat, heel, sun, box, tent, house, bed, six, top*. You may wish to record their responses on the chalkboard by underlining the beginning consonant in each word and identifying the sound the consonant makes.

Teaching Ideas

Listening Encourage the children to listen for the beginning sound in each of the following words: *mop, monkey, Mopsy, merry, money, movie, may, morning*. Ask the children to repeat each word after you and identify the sound they hear at the beginning of the word. Point out that the beginning sound they hear is the sound of the letter *M*. Suggest that the children feel their lips while they are making the sound of *M*.

Next, ask the children to listen closely to the ending sound in each of the following words: *Sam, ham, Jim, from, gum*. Encourage the children to identify the sound heard at the end of each word.

Art Help the children to make *M* flashcards. Ask the children to work in pairs to find pictures in magazines showing objects with names that begin with the letter *M*. Have the children paste the pictures on small squares of tagboard. The partners may then take turns identifying the pictures on their flashcards.

Speaking Challenge the children to create sentences using as many words that start with *M* as possible. You may wish to give the following example: *Mr. Mills made mincemeat in the microwave*. Point out that the sentences can be silly or serious. You may wish to record the children's creations on strips of paper or the chalkboard.

Extension

I-Am-Thinking-of-Something Game Invite the child to play I Am Thinking of Something as described in Lesson 10 in this unit. Expand the game to include the letters *H* and *M*.

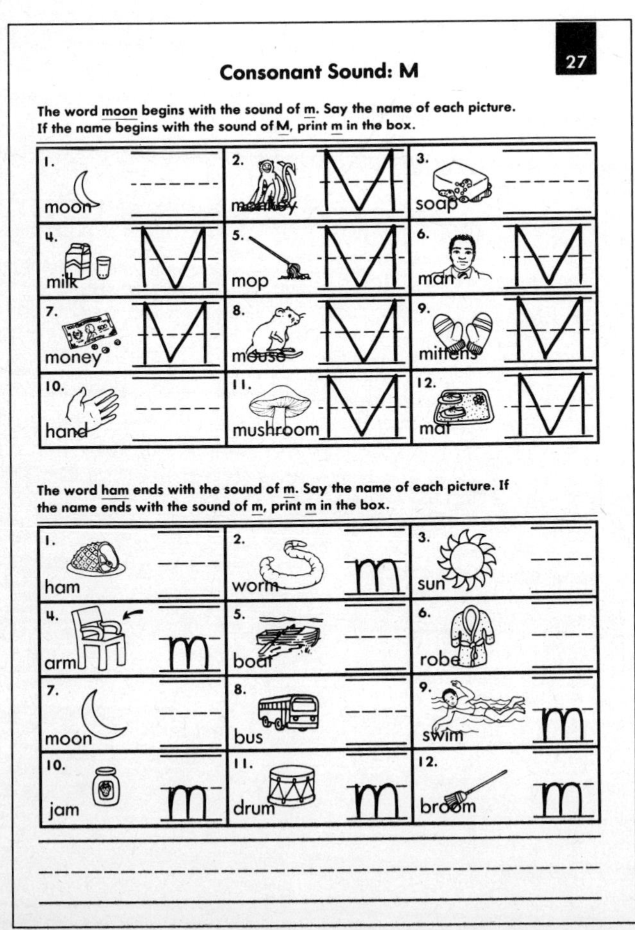

Consonant Sound: M 27

The word moon begins with the sound of m. Say the name of each picture. If the name begins with the sound of M, print m in the box.

1. moon	2. monkey M	3. soap
4. milk M	5. mop M	6. man M
7. money M	8. mouse M	9. mittens M
10. hand	11. mushroom M	12. mat M

The word ham ends with the sound of m. Say the name of each picture. If the name ends with the sound of m, print m in the box.

1. ham	2. worm m	3. sun
4. arm m	5. boat	6. robe
7. moon	8. bus	9. swim m
10. jam m	11. drum m	12. broom m

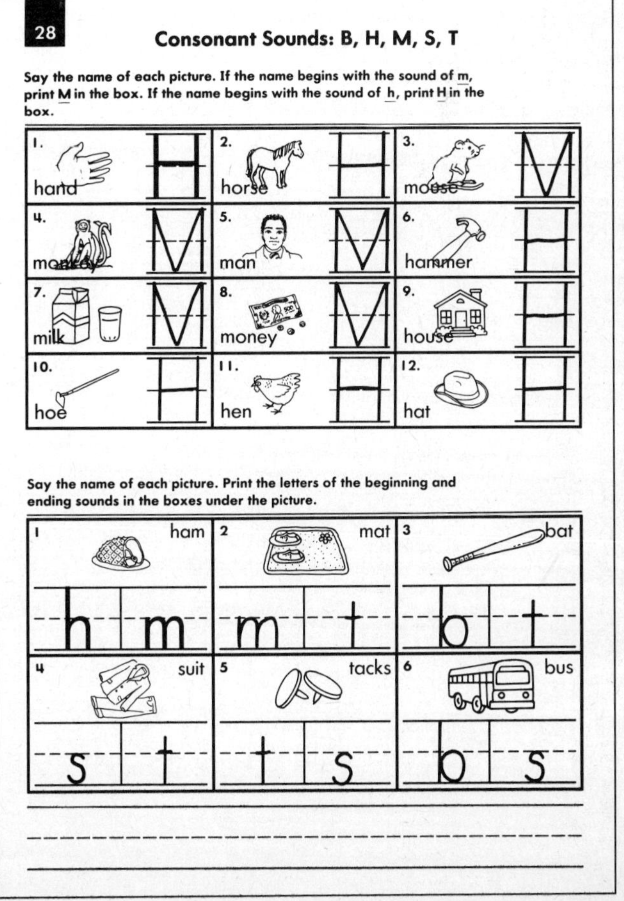

28 **Consonant Sounds: B, H, M, S, T**

Say the name of each picture. If the name begins with the sound of m, print M in the box. If the name begins with the sound of h, print H in the box.

1. hand H	2. horse H	3. mouse M
4. monkey M	5. man M	6. hammer H
7. milk M	8. money M	9. house H
10. hoe H	11. hen H	12. hat H

Say the name of each picture. Print the letters of the beginning and ending sounds in the boxes under the picture.

1 ham: h m	2 mat: m t	3 bat: b t
4 suit: s t	5 tacks: t s	6 bus: b s

Lesson 13
Consonant Sound *K* (pages 29–32)

Objective The child will identify the name and sound of the letter *K*, and review the names and sounds of *S, T, B, H,* and *M*.

Teaching Ideas

Listening Encourage the children to listen carefully as you pronounce the following words: *kitchen, kind, kit, kick, keep*. Ask the children what sound they hear at the beginning of each word. Explain that the sound they hear is the sound of the letter *K*. Invite the children to repeat the words after you, listening for the *K* sound.

Speaking Display on the chalkboard ledge the following picture flashcards: *key, kettle, kite, kitten, king*. Invite the children to name each picture and identify the *K* sound that begins each word. As the children identify each picture, write the word on the chalkboard. Encourage the children to underline and say the letter *K* that begins each word. If you wish, have the children come to the chalkboard and trace the letter *K* at the beginning of a word. You might provide additional practice by using color-coded primary paper as explained in Lesson 9 of this unit.

Beginning-Sound Game Arrange on the chalkboard ledge pictures or picture flashcards of the following objects: *balloon, basket, heart, horn, jail, man, moon, key, kite, seal, seven, turkey, tiger*. (These cards may be prepared beforehand by the children as part of the lesson.) Point to a picture and challenge one of the children to name the object in the picture and identify the beginning sound. If the child answers correctly, allow the child to challenge a classmate. To include as many children as possible, encourage the children to choose classmates that have not yet had a turn. Continue play until the remaining pictures have been identified.

Boston Game Using the letter cards *S, T, B, H, M,* and *K*, invite the children to imagine packing suitcases for a trip to Boston. Hold up the *S* letter card and say, "*I am going to Boston, and with me I will take a suit.*" Encourage each child, in turn, to add another *S* word to your sentence, for example: *I am going to Boston, and with me I will take a suit and a sandwich.* Remind the children that they must mention the items already in the suitcase before adding another *S* word. Continue the game until the children cannot think of any more *S* words. If you wish, go on to the next letter card, and continue the game.

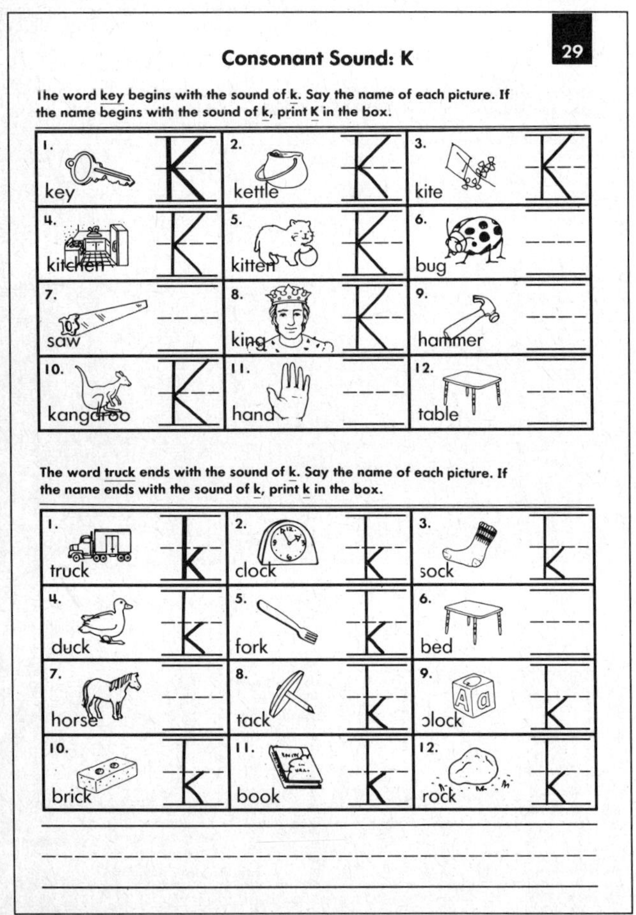

29

Consonant Sound: K

The word key begins with the sound of k. Say the name of each picture. If the name begins with the sound of k, print K in the box.

1. key K	2. kettle K	3. kite K
4. kitchen K	5. kitten K	6. bug
7. saw	8. king K	9. hammer
10. kangaroo K	11. hand	12. table

The word truck ends with the sound of k. Say the name of each picture. If the name ends with the sound of k, print k in the box.

1. truck k	2. clock k	3. sock k
4. duck k	5. fork k	6. bed
7. horse	8. tack k	9. block k
10. brick k	11. book k	12. rock k

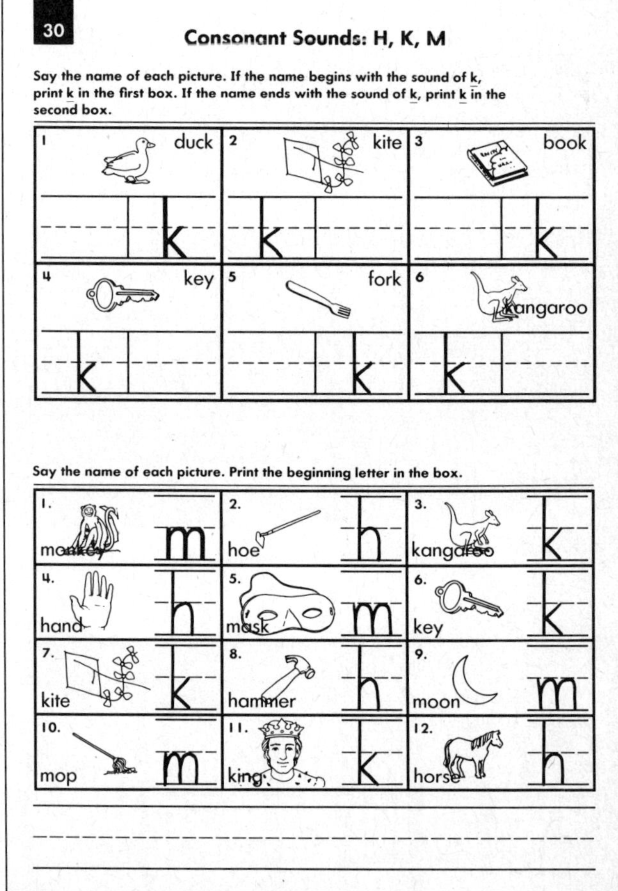

30

Consonant Sounds: H, K, M

Say the name of each picture. If the name begins with the sound of k, print k in the first box. If the name ends with the sound of k, print k in the second box.

1 duck — k (second box)	2 kite — k (first box)	3 book — k (second box)
4 key — k (first box)	5 fork — k (second box)	6 kangaroo — k (first box)

Say the name of each picture. Print the beginning letter in the box.

1. monkey m	2. hoe h	3. kangaroo k
4. hand h	5. mask m	6. key k
7. kite k	8. hammer h	9. moon m
10. mop m	11. king k	12. horse h

Extension

Mail-a-Letter Game Place two boxes on a table at the front of the classroom. Indicate to the child that one box will contain pictures with names beginning with the *K* sound, and the other box will contain pictures with names ending with the *K* sound. Invite the child to create "mail" for the boxes by finding pictures in magazines of objects with names that begin or end with the *K* sound. Have the child tell whether a picture begins or ends with the *K* sound, and then "mail" it in the appropriate box. You may then wish to repeat the game with the letters *S*, *T*, *B*, and *M*. If the child has difficulty distinguishing between those words that begin and end with a letter, print a key word on a label for each box. If the child has difficulty finding appropriate pictures, you may want to encourage the child to draw pictures.

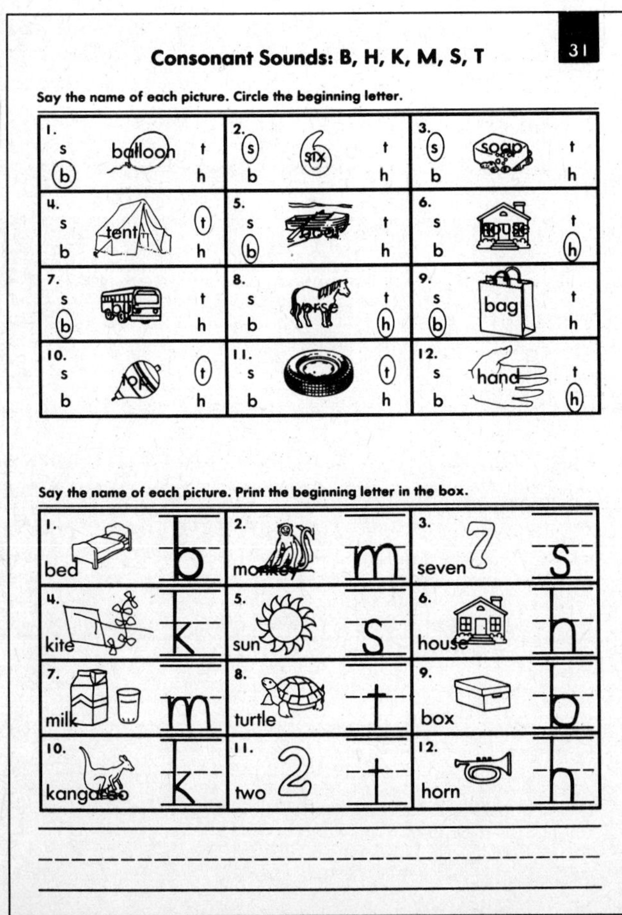

31

Consonant Sounds: B, H, K, M, S, T

Say the name of each picture. Circle the beginning letter.

1. s t b h balloon	2. s t b h six	3. s t b h soap
4. s t b h tent	5. s t b h boat	6. s t b h house
7. s t b h	8. s t b h horse	9. s t b h bag
10. s t b h top	11. s t b h	12. s t b h hand

Say the name of each picture. Print the beginning letter in the box.

1. bed b	2. monkey m	3. seven s
4. kite k	5. sun s	6. house h
7. milk m	8. turtle t	9. box b
10. kangaroo k	11. two t	12. horn h

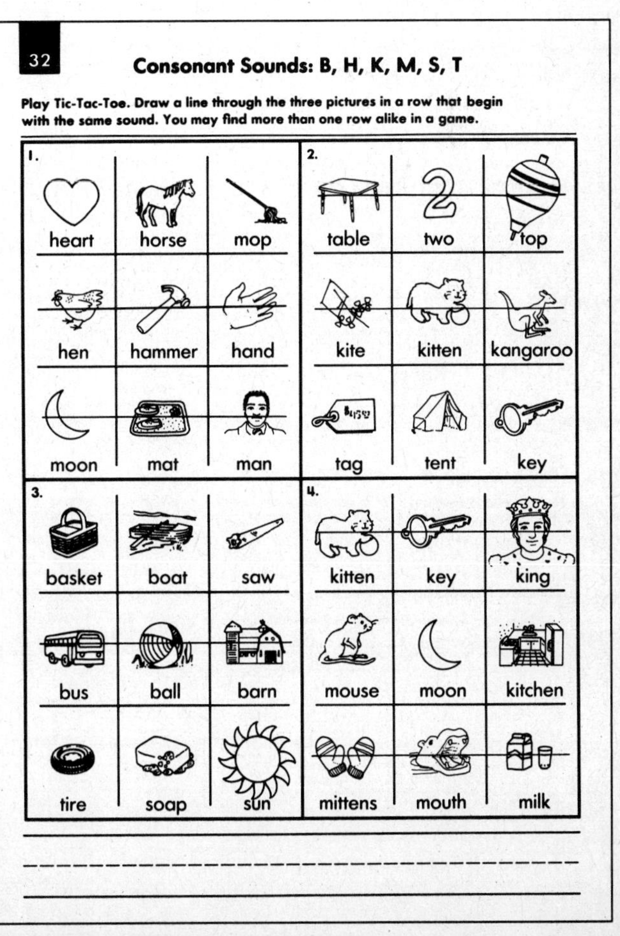

32

Consonant Sounds: B, H, K, M, S, T

Play Tic-Tac-Toe. Draw a line through the three pictures in a row that begin with the same sound. You may find more than one row alike in a game.

1.

heart	horse	mop
hen	hammer	hand
moon	mat	man

2.

table	two	top
kite	kitten	kangaroo
tag	tent	key

3.

basket	boat	saw
bus	ball	barn
tire	soap	sun

4.

kitten	key	king
mouse	moon	kitchen
mittens	mouth	milk

Lesson 14

Consonant Sound *J* (page 33)

Objective The child will identify the name and sound of the letter *J*.

Review

Rhyming-Riddle Game You may wish to practice auditory discrimination skills by playing the Rhyming-Riddle Game described in Lesson 11 in this unit. Provide riddles for the following rhyming word pairs.

bear/chair	*more/door*	*fade/shade*
looks/books	*ball/wall*	*walk/chalk*
bag/flag	*curls/girls*	*toys/boys*

As a variation, offer context clues or challenge the children to create clues for their classmates.

Teaching Ideas

Listening Invite the children to listen for the beginning sound in each of the following words: *Jack, jolly, Jim, Joe, job, juice, jigsaw, just, joy.* Encourage the children to repeat each word after you and to identify the beginning sound. Explain that the sound the children heard at the beginning of each word was the *J* sound. Then, you may wish to invite the children to name additional words that begin with the *J* sound. If you wish, record their suggestions on the chalkboard.

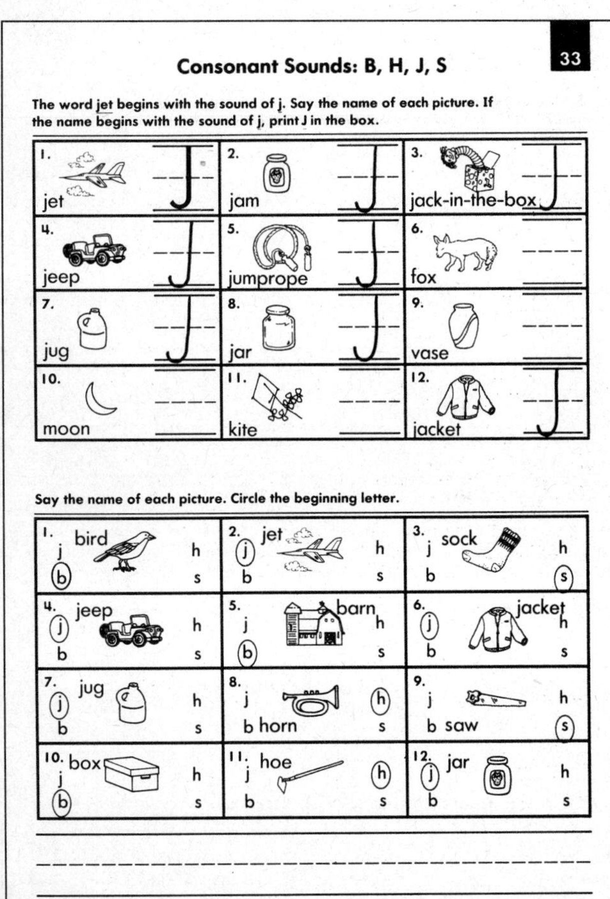

33

Consonant Sounds: B, H, J, S

The word jet begins with the sound of j. Say the name of each picture. If the name begins with the sound of j, print J in the box.

1. jet — J	2. jam — J	3. jack-in-the-box — J
4. jeep — J	5. jumprope — J	6. fox
7. jug — J	8. jar — J	9. vase
10. moon	11. kite	12. jacket — J

Say the name of each picture. Circle the beginning letter.

1. bird j h (b) s	2. jet (j) h b s	3. sock j h b (s)
4. jeep (j) h b s	5. barn j h (b) s	6. jacket (j) h b s
7. jug (j) h b s	8. horn j (h) b s	9. saw j h b (s)
10. box j h (b) s	11. hoe j (h) b s	12. jar (j) h b s

Art Draw a large *J* shape (in the form of a block-type letter) on a piece of construction paper or tagboard. Duplicate this paper for each child in the class. By cutting and pasting pictures from magazines, challenge the children to fill their *J*s with pictures of words that begin with the *J* sound. Invite the children to share their pictures with the class, and name some of the *J* pictures they found. You may then wish to display the finished projects in the classroom.

Writing Display the following picture flashcards on the chalkboard ledge and write the word that names the picture above each card: *jeep, jet, jar, jug, jacket.* Invite the children to identify the pictures and circle the *J* in each word. (Brightly colored chalk may entice reluctant students to participate.) To expand the activity, provide the children with a sheet of primary paper that has been preprinted with *J*s. Have the children trace the *J*s with pencils.

Extension

Riddle Game Challenge the child to respond to each of the following questions with a word that begins with the *J* sound.

1. *What is a name of a very fast airplane? (jet)*
2. *What month begins the year? (January)*
3. *What is something sweet we might put on our sandwich with peanut butter? (jelly)*
4. *What is something that makes us laugh? (joke)*

If the child has difficulty solving the riddles, add details to make the clues more specific. After the riddles have been solved, you may wish to encourage the child to create riddles for you to solve. If you wish, expand this game to include other consonant sounds.

Lesson 15
Consonant Sound *F* (pages 34–35)

Objective The child will identify the name and sound of the letter *F*.

Review

Listening To review auditory discrimination, challenge the students to name the beginning sound in each of the following words: *teapot, sun, Kenneth, joke, keep, jaw, jolly, Mary, basement, melon.*

Teaching Ideas

Listening Say the following words, encouraging the children to listen for the beginning sound in each: *fork, fireman, foot, father, feather, for, face.* Explain to the children that the sound they hear at the beginning of each word is the sound of the letter *F*. Invite the children to repeat each word after you, listening for the *F* sound.

Continue by asking the children to identify the middle sound in the following words: *coffee, puffing, huffy, puffy.*

Finally, ask the children to locate the *F* sounds in the following words: *loaf, leaf, muff, cuff.* Point out that the sound of *F* is heard at the end of the words in this group. Invite the children to repeat the words again after you, listening for the *F* sound. Keep the words on the chalkboard for the following activity.

Draw the following configurations on the chalkboard.

F__________ _____F____ __________F

Pronounce the words from the previous activity and invite volunteers to point to the line that shows the letter *F* in the correct position. If you say the word *foot*, for example, the child's response would be to point to the first configuration.

Complete-the-Sentence Game Display the following picture flashcards on the chalkboard ledge: *finger, feet, fish, four, forehead.* Ask the children to identify the object in each picture. Then direct the children to refer to the picture flashcards to help them complete the following sentences after you say each one.

1. *The number that follows three is* _______ .
2. *A part of a hand is called a* _______ .
3. *When we walk we step with our* _______ .
4. *Something that lives in an aquarium is a* _______ .
5. *The part of the face above the eyes is the* _______ .

Reteaching

Writing Write the following words on the chalkboard: *kite, key, mittens, moon, jacks, five, fire, jelly.* Ask the child to listen to each word and identify the beginning sound. Challenge the child to write or trace the letter that makes the beginning sound of each word.

Boston Game Play the Boston Game as described in Lesson 13 in this unit, using the letter *F*.

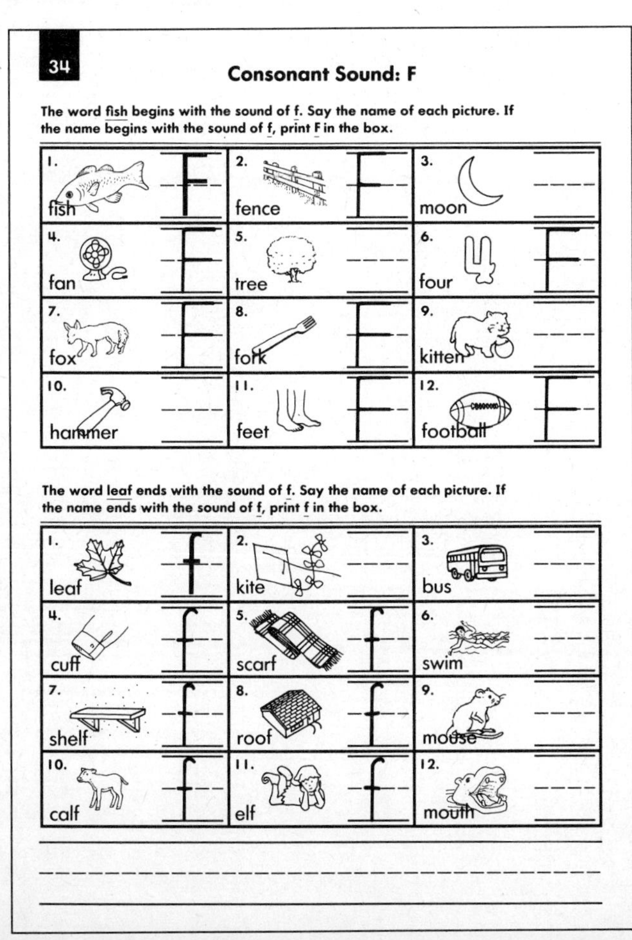

34

Consonant Sound: F

The word fish begins with the sound of f. Say the name of each picture. If the name begins with the sound of f, print F in the box.

1. fish F	2. fence F	3. moon
4. fan F	5. tree	6. four F
7. fox F	8. fork F	9. kitten
10. hammer	11. feet F	12. football F

The word leaf ends with the sound of f. Say the name of each picture. If the name ends with the sound of f, print f in the box.

1. leaf f	2. kite	3. bus
4. cuff f	5. scarf f	6. swim
7. shelf f	8. roof f	9. mouse
10. calf f	11. elf f	12. mouth

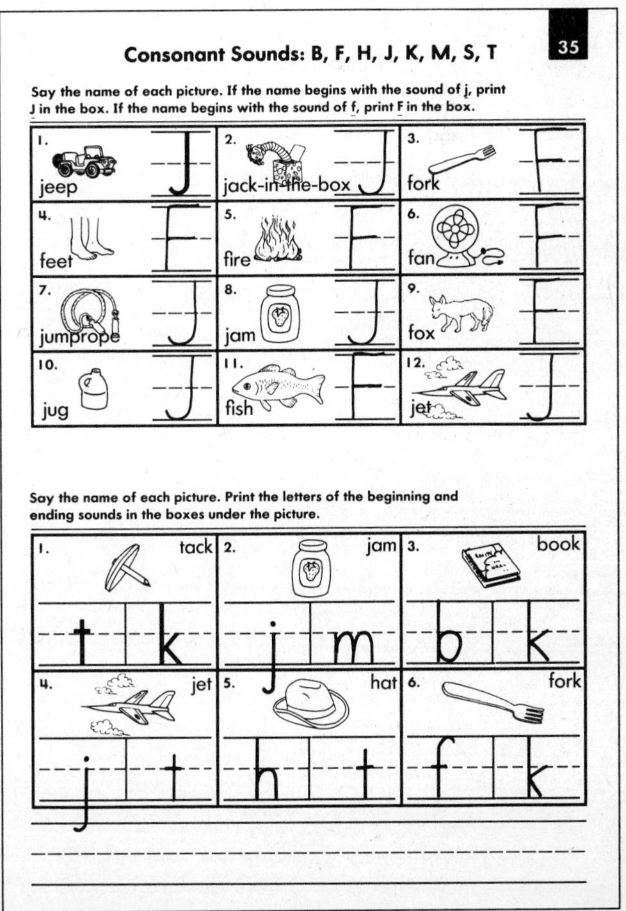

Consonant Sounds: B, F, H, J, K, M, S, T

35

Say the name of each picture. If the name begins with the sound of j, print J in the box. If the name begins with the sound of f, print F in the box.

1. jeep J	2. jack-in-the-box J	3. fork F
4. feet F	5. fire F	6. fan F
7. jumprope J	8. jam J	9. fox F
10. jug J	11. fish F	12. jet J

Say the name of each picture. Print the letters of the beginning and ending sounds in the boxes under the picture.

1. tack — t k	2. jam — j m	3. book — b k
4. jet — j t	5. hat — h t	6. fork — f k

Lesson 16

Consonant Sound *G*; Consonant Sound Review (pages 36–39)

Objective The child will identify the name and the sound of the letter *G* and review the letter/sound associations that have been learned in previous lessons.

Review

Matching Game To review letter/sound associations, have the children play the Matching Game. Distribute the small letter cards, *A* through *Z*. Place the capital letter cards on the chalkboard ledge in alphabetical order. Invite each child to place the small letter card next to its partner letter on the chalkboard ledge. Have each child say the name of the letter and give its associated sound.

Teaching Ideas

Speaking Display large pictures of objects with names beginning with the letter *G*. Encourage the children to say the names of these objects with you. Ask the children to place their fingers under their chins to feel the muscles move when they say the following words: *guardian, guard, goose, garden, goat, gum.*

Listening Ask the children to raise their hands when they hear a word that begins with the *G* sound. Slowly read the following sentences.

1. *The goldfish are in a gold goblet.*
2. *Guy plays a good game of golf.*
3. *Gus will go to get gobs of gum.*
4. *Gail began to giggle.*
5. *Our goat is a very good guy.*

Writing Write the following words on the chalkboard and have the children circle the *G* in each: *tag, flag, girl, gate, goat, pig, rug, gum.* Then have the children read each word aloud.

Explain to the children that the letter *G* may be seen and heard at the beginning, the middle, or the end of a word. Use split boxes to demonstrate this concept.

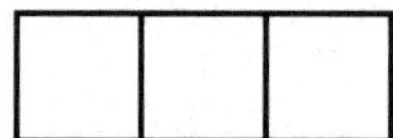

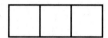

Complete the boxes to show that in the following words, *G* can be found at the beginning, as in *go;* in the middle, as in *wiggle;* and at the end, as in *dog.*

Use a letter card for *G* and two blank cards to model the split-box concept. Have the children arrange the cards on the chalkboard ledge, placing the *G* card in the beginning, the middle, or the ending position for each of the following words: *jiggle, tag, wagon, jug, flag, juggle, goat, game, bag, girl.*

Draw a split box above each of the following picture

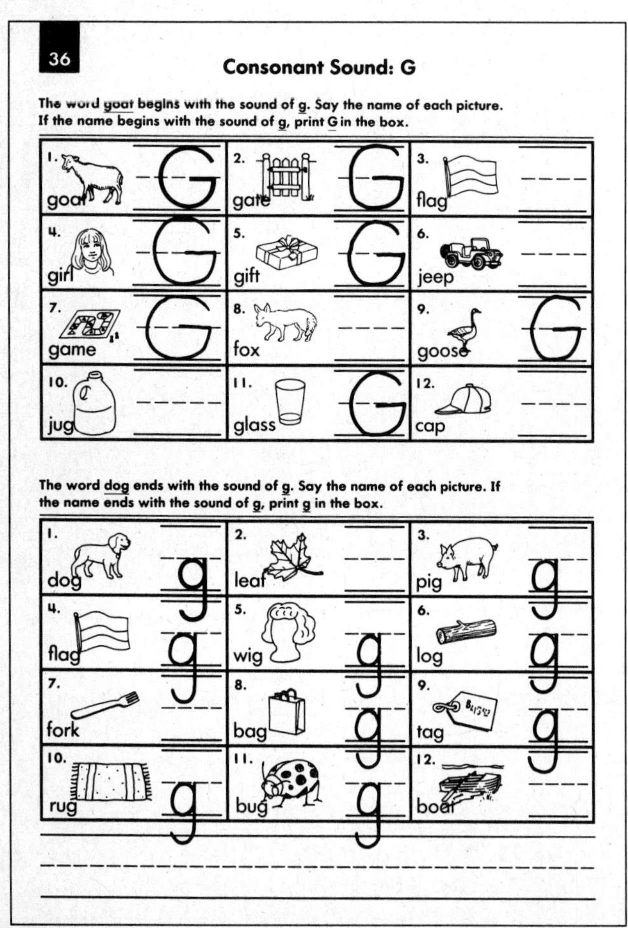

36

Consonant Sound: G

The word goat begins with the sound of g. Say the name of each picture. If the name begins with the sound of g, print G in the box.

1. goat 2. gate 3. flag 4. girl 5. gift 6. jeep 7. game 8. fox 9. goose 10. jug 11. glass 12. cap

The word dog ends with the sound of g. Say the name of each picture. If the name ends with the sound of g, print g in the box.

1. dog 2. leaf 3. pig 4. flag 5. wig 6. log 7. fork 8. bag 9. tag 10. rug 11. bug 12. boat

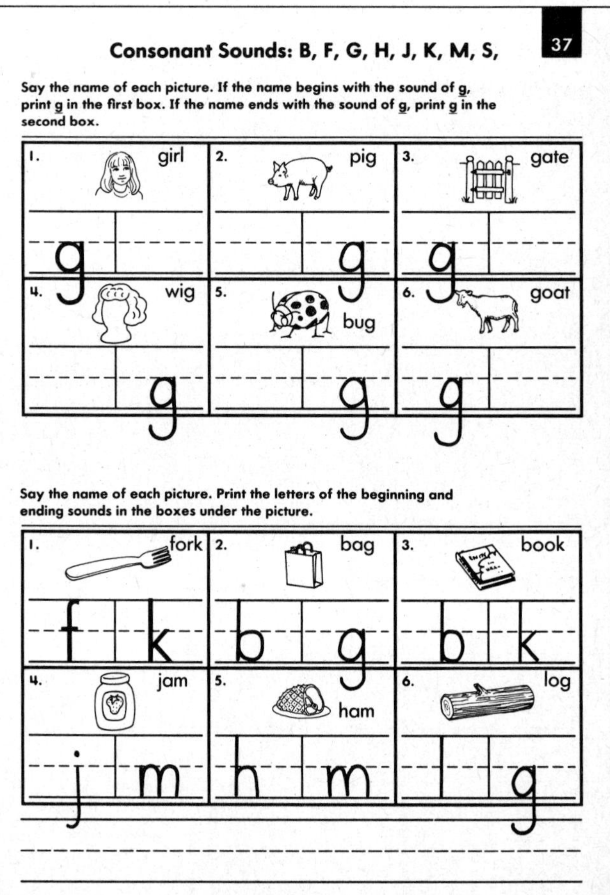

37

Consonant Sounds: B, F, G, H, J, K, M, S,

Say the name of each picture. If the name begins with the sound of g, print g in the first box. If the name ends with the sound of g, print g in the second box.

1. girl 2. pig 3. gate 4. wig 5. bug 6. goat

Say the name of each picture. Print the letters of the beginning and ending sounds in the boxes under the picture.

1. fork 2. bag 3. book 4. jam 5. ham 6. log

flashcards on the chalkboard ledge: *hat, book, jug, mitt, gate.* Encourage the children to print the beginning and ending sound above each picture.

Present the following letter cards, encouraging the children to say a word beginning with each letter: *G, S, T, B, H, M, K, J, F.*

Have the children listen for the ending sound as you pronounce the following words: *wig, bug, frog, leg, log, tag, jug.* Ask the children to repeat each word after you and to identify the ending sound.

Boston Game Challenge the children to play the Boston Game, described in Lesson 13 in this unit, with the letter *G.*

Extension

Sorting Game Give the child three manila envelopes, each marked with a letter between *A* and *K.* Provide a variety of magazine pictures or picture flashcards to sort. Show the child how to classify the pictures for each of the three envelopes. For example, the letter *S* envelope might include pictures of the following objects: *sun, sundae, soda, soup, scissors, seven, saw, soap.*

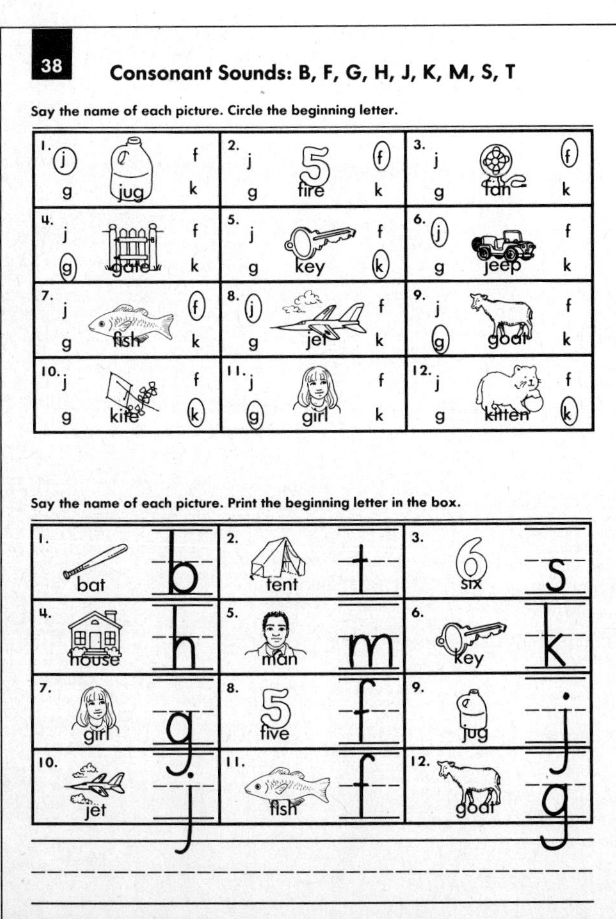

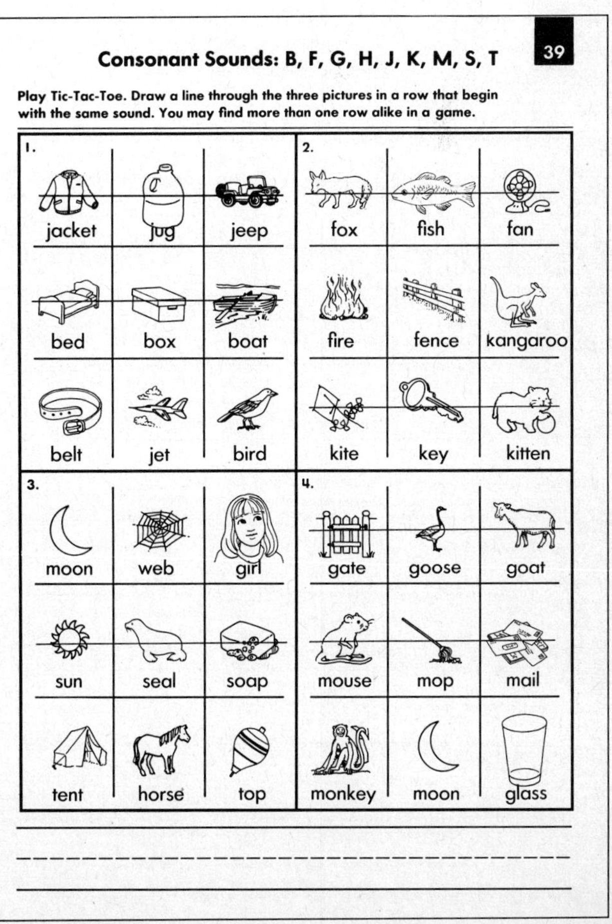

Lesson 17

Consonant Sound *D* (page 40)

Objective The child will identify the name and the sound of the letter *D*.

Review

Listening To review the letters and the sounds that the children have learned, encourage the children to identify the beginning sounds in the names of the following picture flashcards: *book, goat, horse, jack-in-the-box, mittens, seal, turkey, key.*

Teaching Ideas

Art Have the children sort through magazine pictures to find pictures of objects that begin with the letter *D*. Have each child find at least four pictures. On a large sheet of paper, ask each child to write the partner letters *Dd*. Then have the children cut and paste the pictures around the letters *Dd*, creating a collage effect.

Listening Place picture flashcards for the following words that begin with the letter *D* on the chalkboard ledge: *duck, dog, doctor, dentist, daddy, desk, doughnut, donkey, dish.* Have the children say the name of each picture.

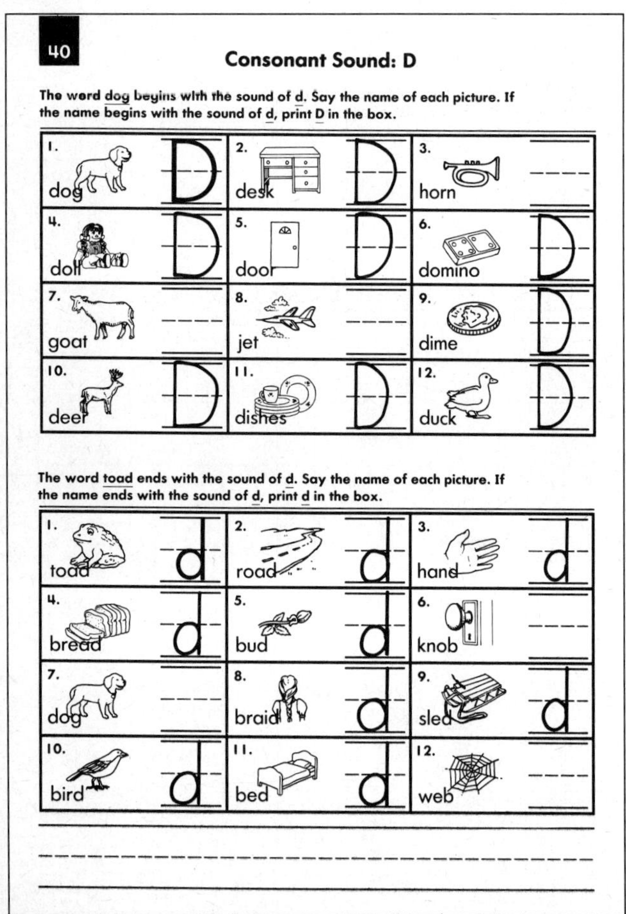

40

Consonant Sound: D

The word dog begins with the sound of d. Say the name of each picture. If the name begins with the sound of d, print D in the box.

1. dog D	2. desk D	3. horn
4. doll D	5. door D	6. domino D
7. goat	8. jet	9. dime D
10. deer D	11. dishes D	12. duck D

The word toad ends with the sound of d. Say the name of each picture. If the name ends with the sound of d, print d in the box.

1. toad d	2. road d	3. hand d
4. bread d	5. bud d	6. knob
7. dog	8. braid d	9. sled d
10. bird d	11. bed d	12. web

Encourage the children to listen to the following sentences and to raise their hands when they hear a word that begins with the letter *D*.

1. *I did not eat my dessert at dinner.*
2. *Daddy bought a doll for Dorothy.*
3. *The doctor gave Dave a dime.*
4. *Did you go to the dentist?*
5. *Daisies and dandelions are spring flowers.*

Draw the following split boxes on the chalkboard.

Say the following words, and encourage the children to tell you if they hear *D* at the beginning or the ending position: *doll, domino, sled, bud, dime, lid, deer, pad.*

Extension

Boston Game Play the Boston Game described in Lesson 13 in this unit, using the letter *D*.

Writing Distribute the small letter cards *A* through *G*, encouraging the child to match the letters with capital letter cards on the chalkboard ledge. Ask the child to write the partner letters *Aa, Bb, Cc, Dd, Ee, Ff, Gg* on a sheet of paper.

Lesson 18

Consonant Sound *L* (pages 41–42)

Objective The child will identify the name and the sound of the letter *L*.

Teaching Ideas

Listening Challenge the children to identify and to pronounce names of picture flashcards depicting words such as the following: *lake, laugh, ladder, lion, lock, lollipop.* Identify other *L* words on a phonics picture chart or on picture flashcards.

Write the following on the chalkboard as example words with *L* as the ending sound: *bell, gill, mail, nail, pencil, ball.* Have the children pronounce these words and circle the final *L* in each.

Writing Draw the following split boxes on the chalkboard.

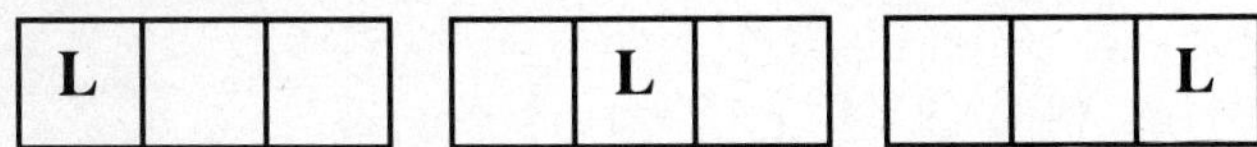

Ask the children to listen as you pronounce the following words listed on the chalkboard or on a phonics word chart: *Lillian, bell, pail, pal, log, lily, lion, leaf, lollipop, pencil.* Challenge the children to identify the position of the letter *L* as the beginning, middle, or ending sound. Point out that the *L* might occur in more than one place in some words. Ask the children to write the letter *L* in the correct position in the appropriate split box on the chalkboard. Encourage the children to write some of these *L* words or others that they know on sheets of paper.

Extension

Boston Game Challenge the child to play the Boston Game described in Lesson 13 in this unit using the letter *L*.

Art Invite the child to create an original drawing or painting from the shape of the letter *L*. Begin by having the child draw or paint a large bold *L* on a blank sheet of drawing paper. Suggest that the child turn the paper different ways to study the shape of the letter before beginning the drawing. You might display completed drawings in the classroom.

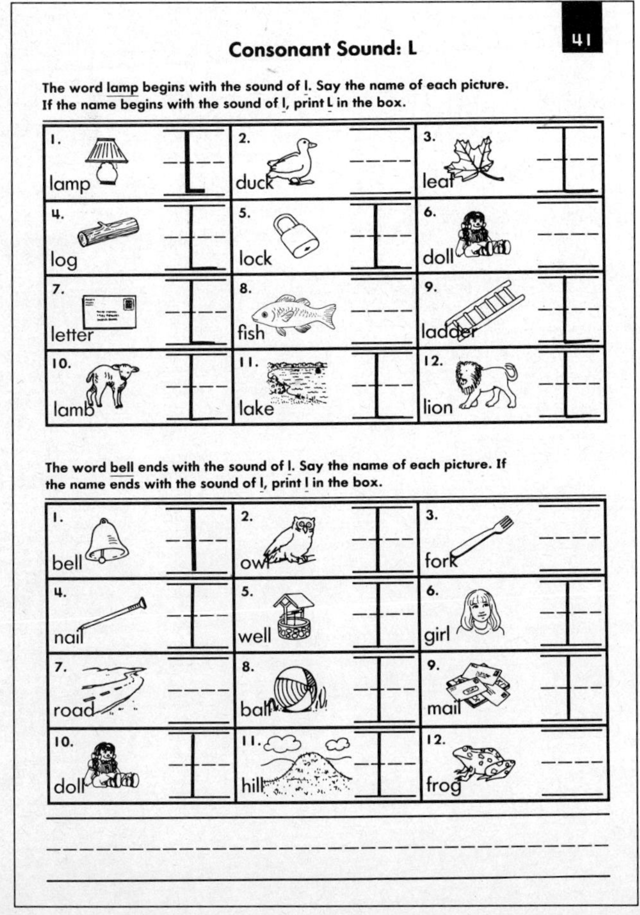

41

Consonant Sound: L

The word lamp begins with the sound of l. Say the name of each picture. If the name begins with the sound of l, print L in the box.

1. lamp — L	2. duck —	3. leaf — L
4. log — L	5. lock — L	6. doll —
7. letter — L	8. fish —	9. ladder — L
10. lamb — L	11. lake — L	12. lion — L

The word bell ends with the sound of l. Say the name of each picture. If the name ends with the sound of l, print l in the box.

1. bell — l	2. owl — l	3. fork —
4. nail — l	5. well — l	6. girl — l
7. road —	8. ball — l	9. mail — l
10. doll — l	11. hill — l	12. frog —

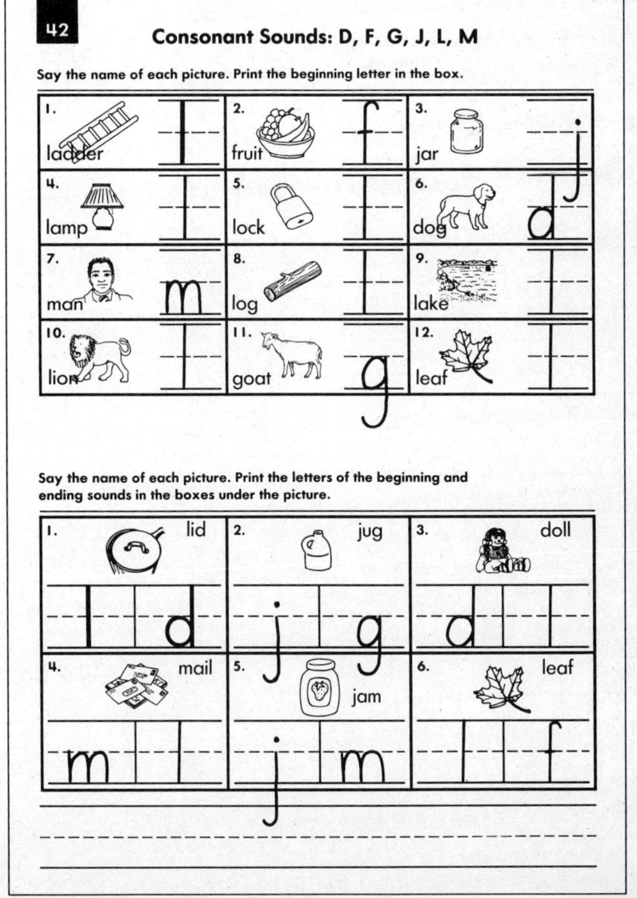

42

Consonant Sounds: D, F, G, J, L, M

Say the name of each picture. Print the beginning letter in the box.

1. ladder — l	2. fruit — f	3. jar — j
4. lamp — l	5. lock — l	6. dog — d
7. man — m	8. log — l	9. lake — l
10. lion — l	11. goat — g	12. leaf — l

Say the name of each picture. Print the letters of the beginning and ending sounds in the boxes under the picture.

1. lid — l, d	2. jug — j, g	3. doll — d, l
4. mail — m, l	5. jam — j, m	6. leaf — l, f

Lesson 19

Consonant Sound *N*; Consonant Sound Review (pages 43–46)

Objective The child will identify the name and the sound of the letter *N* and review the letter/sound association of the letters *B, D, F, G, H, J, K, L, M, N, S, T.*

Teaching Ideas

Listening Encourage the children to listen for the *N* sound in the following words: *needle, nurse, nut, noon, newspaper, nose, nine, neck, pen, on, spoon, train, in, ten.* Ask whether the *N* is heard at the beginning or the end of each word. You might point out that the *N* occurs in more than one place in some words.

Dictionary Game Encourage the children to say words in which they hear the sound of the letter *N*. As each child volunteers a word, ask whether the *N* is at the beginning, the middle, or the ending position in the word. Create a list of *N* words on the chalkboard.

Art The children will enjoy the challenge of creating a picture page for the letter *N*. After writing a letter *N* in the left-hand corner of a sheet of paper, have the children draw objects that begin with the letter *N*. Ideas can be taken from the words listed in the Dictionary Game, a primary level dictionary, or the child's own vocabulary. Examples include the following: *nickel, nail, nine.*

Listening Encourage the children to name a rhyming word for each of the following riddles.

1. *rhymes with* sold *and begins with* G
2. *rhymes with* make *and begins with* L
3. *rhymes with* go *and begins with* N
4. *rhymes with* luck *and begins with* D

Reinforce successful responses by challenging the children to create additional rhyming riddles for words that begin with the letters *B, D, F, G, H, J, K, L, M, N, S,* or *T.*

Reteaching

Tactile The child may enjoy using the letter templates or sandpaper letters to trace the shape of the following letters: *B, D, F, G, H, J, K, L, M, N, S, T.* Encourage the child to say each letter name and to identify the sound of each letter as it is traced.

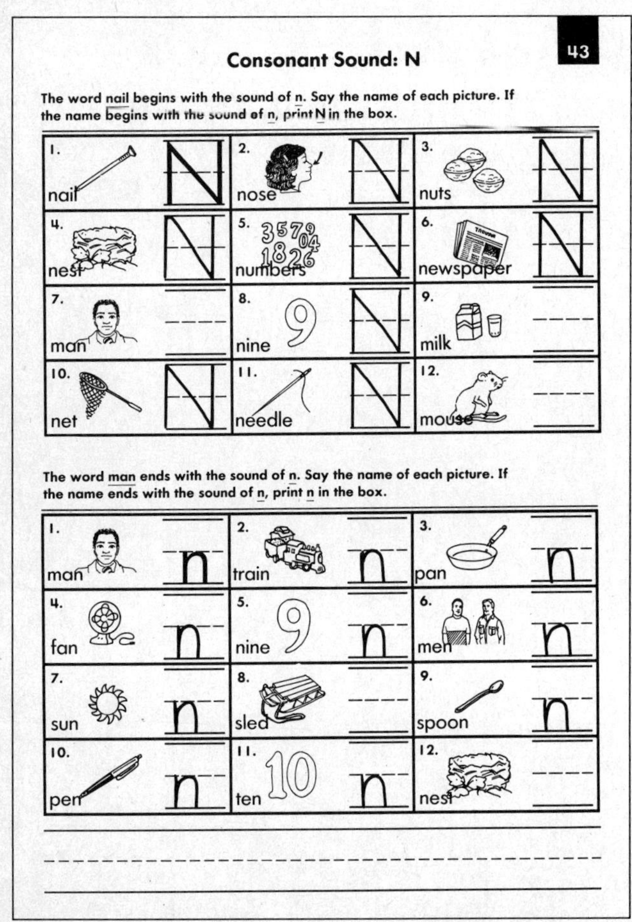

43
Consonant Sound: N
The word nail begins with the sound of n. Say the name of each picture. If the name begins with the sound of n, print N in the box.
1. nail
2. nose
3. nuts
4. nest
5. numbers
6. newspaper
7. man
8. nine
9. milk
10. net
11. needle
12. mouse
The word man ends with the sound of n. Say the name of each picture. If the name ends with the sound of n, print n in the box.
1. man
2. train
3. pan
4. fan
5. nine
6. men
7. sun
8. sled
9. spoon
10. pen
11. ten
12. nest

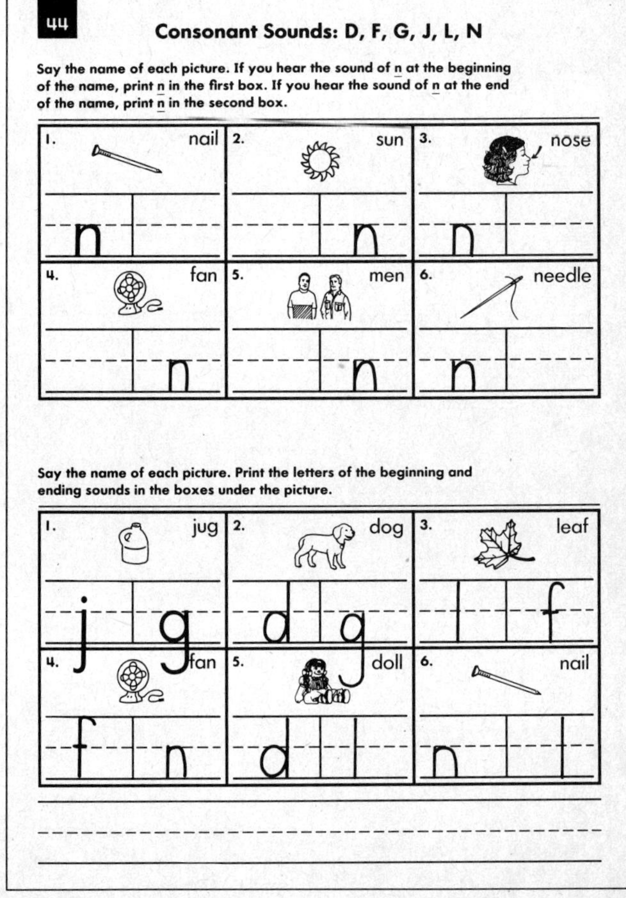

Writing Encourage the child to trace and practice writing all of the letters in the alphabet. You may wish to provide dot-to-dot outlines of the letters, on either the chalkboard or on paper, or letter stencils to help the child focus on the contour of the letters.

Extension

Boston Game Play the Boston Game, described in Lesson 13 in this unit, using the letters *G, L, D,* and *N.*

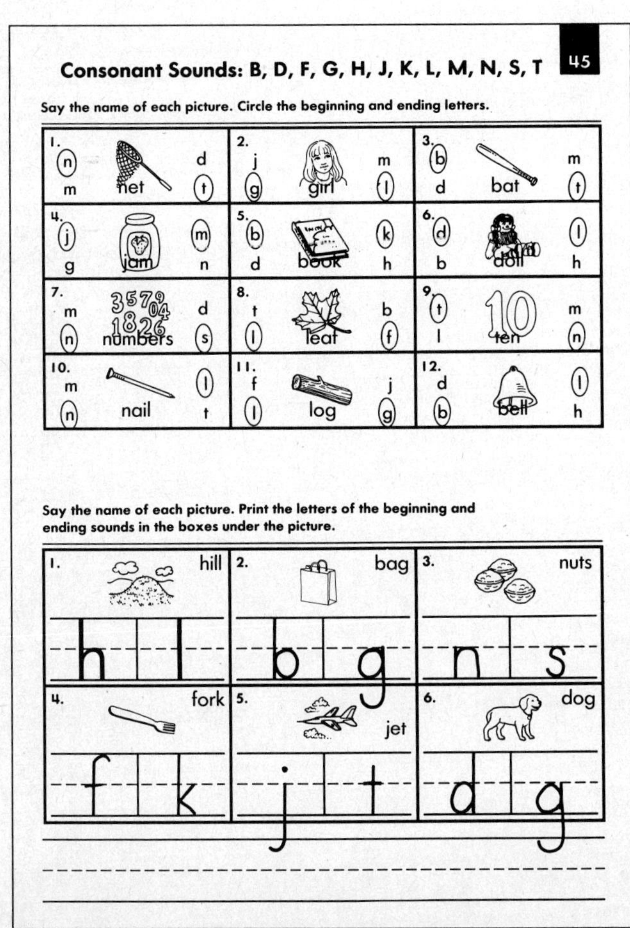

45

Consonant Sounds: B, D, F, G, H, J, K, L, M, N, S, T

Say the name of each picture. Circle the beginning and ending letters.

1. n m net d t
2. j g girl m l
3. b d bat m t
4. j g jam m n
5. b d book k h
6. d b doll l h
7. m n numbers d s
8. t l leaf b f
9. t l ten m n
10. m n nail l t
11. f l log j g
12. d b bell l h

Say the name of each picture. Print the letters of the beginning and ending sounds in the boxes under the picture.

1. hill h l
2. bag b g
3. nuts n s
4. fork f k
5. jet j t
6. dog d g

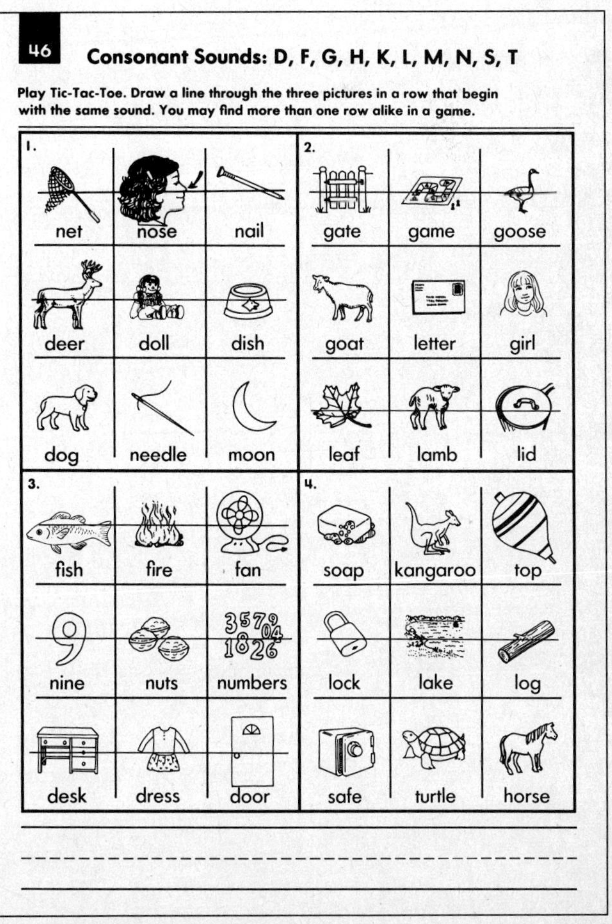

46

Consonant Sounds: D, F, G, H, K, L, M, N, S, T

Play Tic-Tac-Toe. Draw a line through the three pictures in a row that begin with the same sound. You may find more than one row alike in a game.

1.

net	nose	nail
deer	doll	dish
dog	needle	moon

2.

gate	game	goose
goat	letter	girl
leaf	lamb	lid

3.

fish	fire	fan
nine	nuts	numbers
desk	dress	door

4.

soap	kangaroo	top
lock	lake	log
safe	turtle	horse

Lesson 20

Consonant Sound *W* (page 47)

Objective The child will identify the name and the sound of the letter *W*.

Review

Listening Display prepared letter cards for *S, T, B, H, M, K, J, F, G, L, N.* Invite the children to say words that begin with each letter.

Matching Game Play this version of the Matching Game described in Lesson 16 in this unit. Provide pictures of words that begin with the following letters: *S, T, B, H, M, K, J, F, G, L, N.* Display the pictures and letter cards on the chalkboard ledge. For each, have a child identify the picture and match its beginning sound with the correct letter.

Teaching Ideas

Listening Encourage the children to listen carefully as you say the following list of *W* words: *wiggle, wall, wind, wolf, were, water, well, will, we, winter, wire.* Ask the children to repeat each word and to be aware of the position of their lips as they say each *W* word. Present additional words on picture cards, encouraging the children to say each word with you. Suggest that the children name other familiar *W* words.

What-Is-Missing? Game Present additional *W* words on a phonics picture chart. Write the following incomplete sentences on the chalkboard. Encourage the children to identify the missing words by referring to the picture chart.

1. *You can tell time with a* _______ . *(watch)*
2. *Some sweaters are made of* _______. *(wool)*
3. *One of the largest fruits is a* _______ . *(watermelon)*
4. *A spider spins a* _______ . *(web)*

As the children respond, write each correct response in the appropriate space. Invite the children to provide additional incomplete sentences.

Writing Ask the children to practice writing the *W* words listed on the chalkboard during the previous activity.

Extension

Writing Draw split boxes above the following picture flashcard set on the chalkboard ledge: *windmill, web, wagon, lion, dog.* Invite the child to print the beginning and ending sounds for each word above its picture. Continue the writing activity with additional picture flashcards suggested by the child.

Consonant Sounds: B, G, L, M, N, W 47

The word wagon begins with the sound of w. Say the name of each picture. If the name begins with the sound of w, print W in the box.

1. wagon W	2. web W	3. window W
4. wing W	5. house	6. wheel W
7. mouse	8. watch W	9. hat
10. windmill W	11. well W	12. worm W

Say the name of each picture. Print the letters of the beginning and ending sounds in the boxes under the picture.

1. worm w m	2. well w l	3. wagon w n
4. windmill w l	5. web w b	6. log l g

Lesson 21

Consonant Sound C; Consonant Sound Review (pages 48–49)

Objective The child will identify the name and the hard consonant sound of the letter *C* and review the letter/sound associations of the letters *D, G, L, M, N,* and *W.*

Teaching Ideas

Listening Using appropriate picture flashcards or a phonics picture chart, invite the children to listen carefully as you pronounce each of the following words: *cat, candy, cake, cab, cookie, cartoon.* Pronounce each word again, asking the children to repeat each word after you. Introduce the hard consonant sound of *C*, and invite the children to identify the hard *C* sound in each of the above words.

Dictionary Game Play the Dictionary Game, as described in Lesson 19 in this unit. Encourage the children to think of as many words as possible that begin with the hard consonant sound of *C*. List these words on the chalkboard.

Writing Draw a three-way split box on the chalkboard. Ask the children to write the consonant sound *C* at the beginning, middle, or ending position as they listen to you pronounce the following words: *canary, picnic, coaster, car, color, cucumber, cupboard, cape, card.* Point out that some words may have *C* in more than one position.

Art Point out that the shape of the letter *C* is found in many objects. Encourage the children to draw a large bold letter *C* in the middle of a sheet of drawing paper. After having the children turn their papers and study the shape of the letter *C*, invite them to create a drawing from the letter *C*.

Alphabetizing Display the following picture flashcards on the chalkboard ledge: *doll, girl, lion, moon, nurse, wagon.* Pronounce each word, asking the children to repeat each one. After each word is said, have the children identify the beginning sound. List the beginning consonant for each on the chalkboard. After all of the beginning sounds are listed, encourage the children to put the letters in alphabetical order.

Extend the challenge by mixing up the same picture flashcards and repeating the previous activity. You may also suggest that the children change the game by adding new picture flashcards and by deleting some of the cards previously used.

Scramble Game Play the Scramble Game, described in Lesson 3, using all of the letters of the alphabet. After the game is finished and all of the partner letters are arranged side by side on the chalkboard ledge, invite the children to write all the partner letters on sheets of paper.

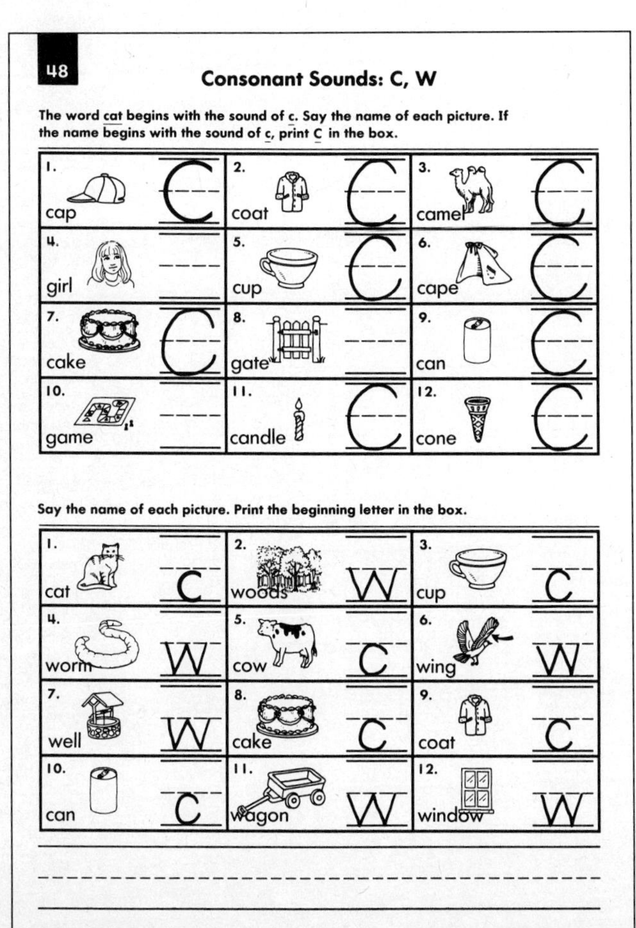

48
Consonant Sounds: C, W
The word cat begins with the sound of c. Say the name of each picture. If the name begins with the sound of c, print C in the box.
1. cap C
2. coat C
3. camel C
4. girl
5. cup C
6. cape C
7. cake C
8. gate
9. can C
10. game
11. candle C
12. cone C
Say the name of each picture. Print the beginning letter in the box.
1. cat c
2. woods W
3. cup c
4. worm W
5. cow c
6. wing W
7. well W
8. cake c
9. coat c
10. can c
11. wagon W
12. window W

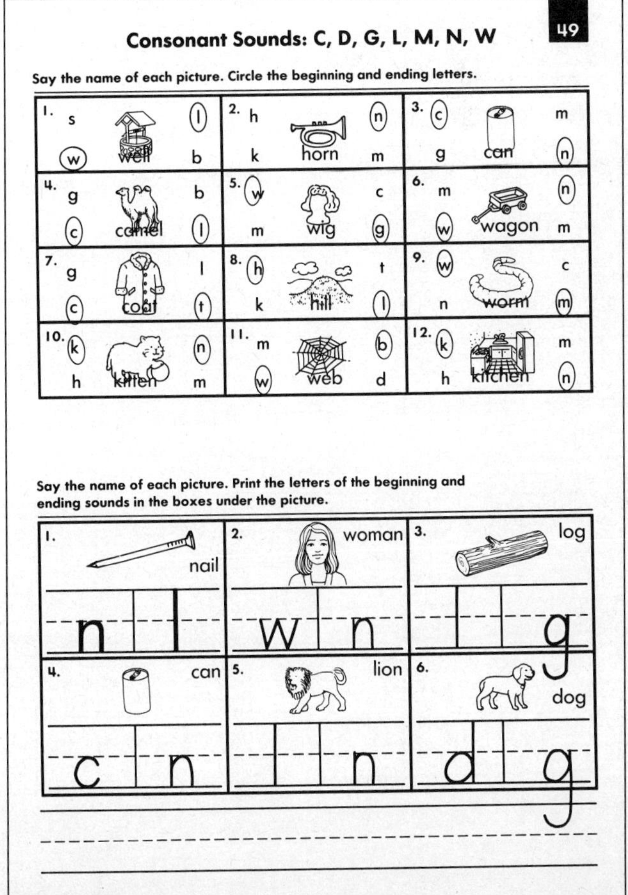

Lesson 22

Consonant Sound *R* (pages 50–51)

Objective The child will identify the name and the sound of the letter *R*.

Review

Alphabet-Train Game Distribute letter cards for the entire alphabet to the children. Call out a letter and ask the child holding that letter to come forward. Challenge the children to identify the next letter of the alphabet. Invite the child with that letter to stand behind the first child. For example, call out the letter *K* and ask what letter comes after *K*. The child with the letter *L* should come forward to form a "train" that looks like *K-L*. Continue calling out letters of the alphabet, making trains with two, three, four, or five letters.

Teaching Ideas

Listening Using a phonics picture chart or picture flashcards, introduce the following words that begin with the letter *R*: *red, record, rocket, robin, river, round, rose, rabbit, rooster, roof, ribbon.* Encourage the children to name each picture and to identify the beginning *R* sound.

Writing Place the picture flashcards on the chalkboard ledge, and write the name of each *R* word on the chalkboard above the picture. Ask the children to repeat each word after you. Have volunteers circle the letter *R* as each word is repeated.

Write the following sentences on the chalkboard. Encourage the children to complete the sentences by writing the missing *R* word for each.

1. *The shape of a ball is _______. (round)*
2. *One of the bright colors is _______. (red)*
3. *Every house must have a _______. (roof)*
4. *Girls like to wear _______ (ribbons) in their hair.*
5. *Did you hear the bell _______? (ring)*
6. *That is a beautiful red _______. (rose)*
7. *The _______ (rabbit) has a white bushy tail.*

Help the children fold writing paper into thirds, draw lines along the folds, and number writing lines from 1 to 10. Say the following words slowly, directing the children to listen and to record the beginning or the ending position of the letter *R* for each word in the correct column: *rake, pear, rat, fire, tire, ear, radio, ring, bear, rocket.*

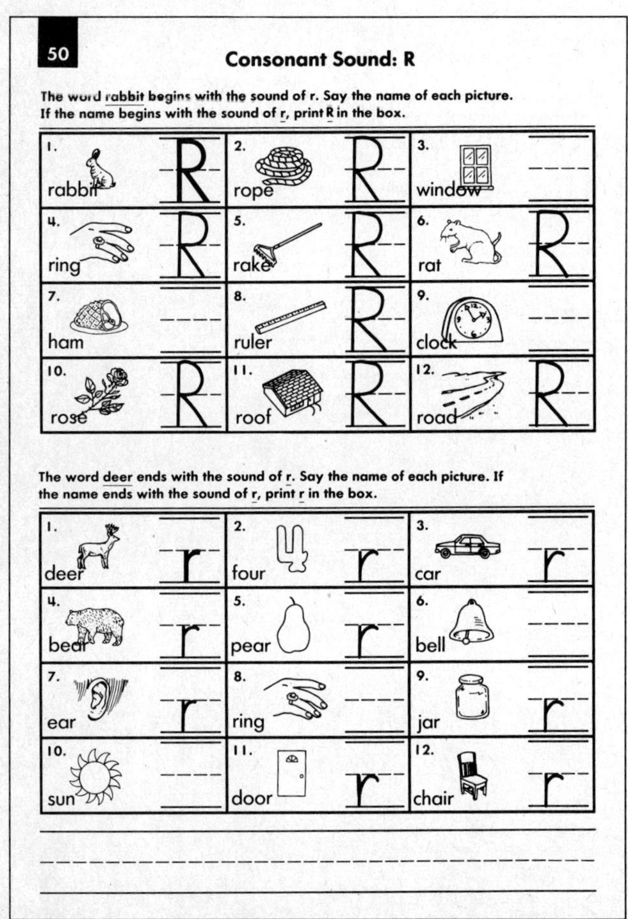

50

Consonant Sound: R

The word rabbit begins with the sound of r. Say the name of each picture. If the name begins with the sound of r, print R in the box.

1. rabbit R	2. rope R	3. window
4. ring R	5. rake R	6. rat R
7. ham	8. ruler R	9. clock
10. rose R	11. roof R	12. road R

The word deer ends with the sound of r. Say the name of each picture. If the name ends with the sound of r, print r in the box.

1. deer r	2. four r	3. car r
4. bear r	5. pear r	6. bell
7. ear r	8. ring	9. jar r
10. sun	11. door r	12. chair r

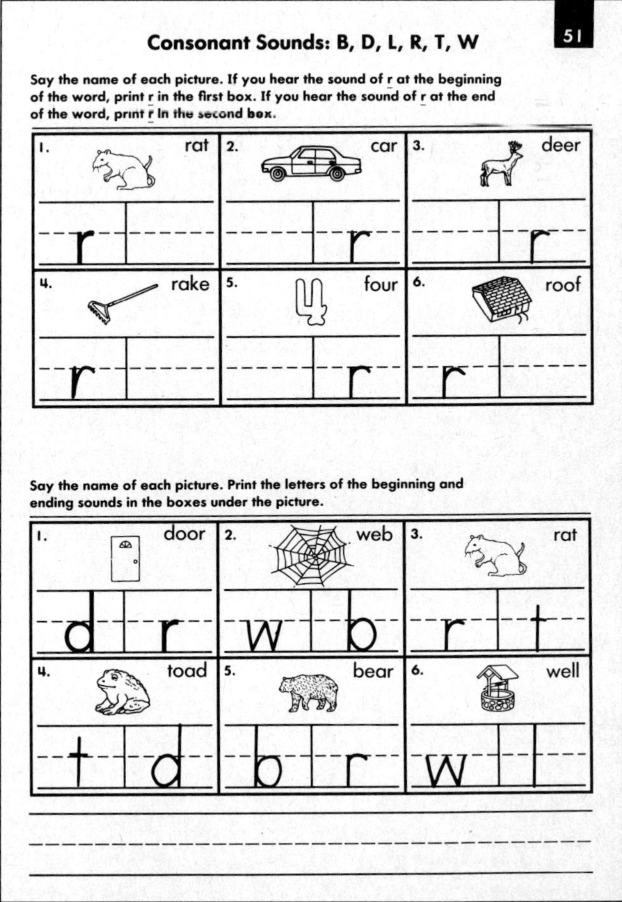

Consonant Sounds: B, D, L, R, T, W

51

Say the name of each picture. If you hear the sound of r at the beginning of the word, print r in the first box. If you hear the sound of r at the end of the word, print r in the second box.

1. rat — r /	2. car — / r	3. deer — / r
4. rake — r /	5. four — / r	6. roof — r /

Say the name of each picture. Print the letters of the beginning and ending sounds in the boxes under the picture.

1. door — d / r	2. web — w / b	3. rat — r / t
4. toad — t / d	5. bear — b / r	6. well — w / l

Lesson 23

Consonant Sound Review (pages 52–53)

Objective The child will review the letter/sound associations of the consonants *B, C, D, L, N, R, W.*

Teaching Ideas

Listening Display picture flashcards for the following words: *book, camel, doctor, lips, napkin, rug, dog, web.* Encourage the children to repeat each word after you and to identify the beginning and the ending sounds. Add other picture flashcards and continue the activity.

Pantomime Game Play a game that combines action, listening, and the application of sounds the children have learned. Invite volunteers to each perform an action word that starts with a specified letter. For example, the child might act out *dive* for the letter *D*. Challenge the group to guess the action word. Continue the game by encouraging children who respond correctly to provide the next pantomime clue. You may wish to suggest the following.

B: batting a ball, boxing
C: coloring, cutting
D: dancing, diving
L: looking, listening
N: nailing, nodding
R: running, reading
W: washing, walking

Reteaching

Tactile Encourage the child to trace all of the letters of the alphabet by using sandpaper letters, dot-to-dot letters, or letter stencils.

Art If the child needs to develop the letter/sound relationship of a particular letter, making a picture page may help. Directions can be found in the Art activity in Lesson 19 in this unit.

Listening Invite the child to listen to a tape recording you have made or have available that reinforces the letter/sound relationships that have been studied. A tape recording that involves the child repeating what is said may provide extra practice with letter/sound relationships.

Extension

Listening Display a list of words containing the letters *B, C, D, L, N, R, W* on the chalkboard. Examples might include the following words.

big	*car*	*dog*	*lap*	*no*	*ride*	*we*
bat	*cow*	*down*	*lay*	*not*	*real*	*went*

Ask the child to repeat each word after you. Challenge the child to rhyme a few words with each of these words. For example: *Big* rhymes with or sounds like _______, _______.

Writing Encourage the child to write the partner letters for the beginning sound of each word on the chalkboard.

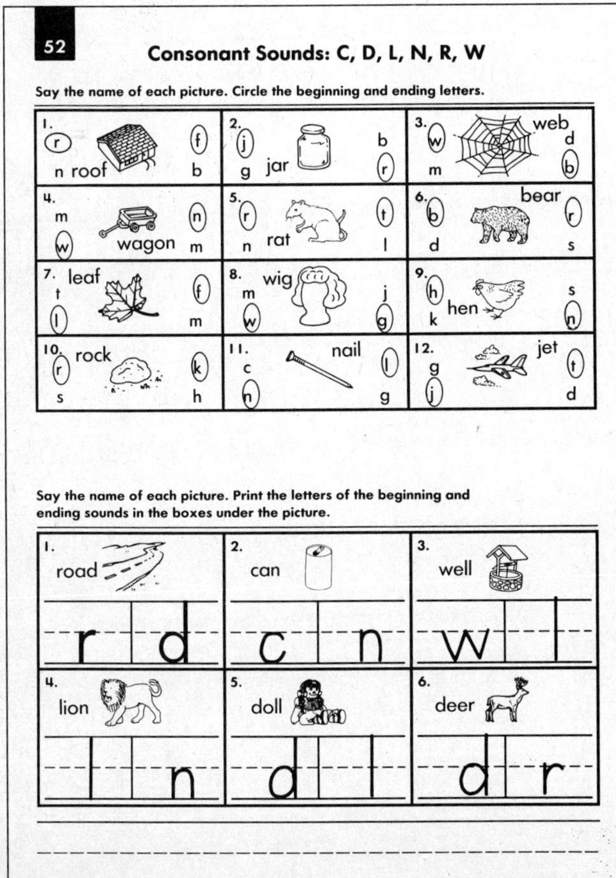
52

Consonant Sounds: C, D, L, N, R, W

Say the name of each picture. Circle the beginning and ending letters.

1. roof 2. jar 3. web 4. wagon 5. rat 6. bear 7. leaf 8. wig 9. hen 10. rock 11. nail 12. jet

Say the name of each picture. Print the letters of the beginning and ending sounds in the boxes under the picture.

1. road — r d 2. can — c n 3. well — w l 4. lion — l n 5. doll — d l 6. deer — d r

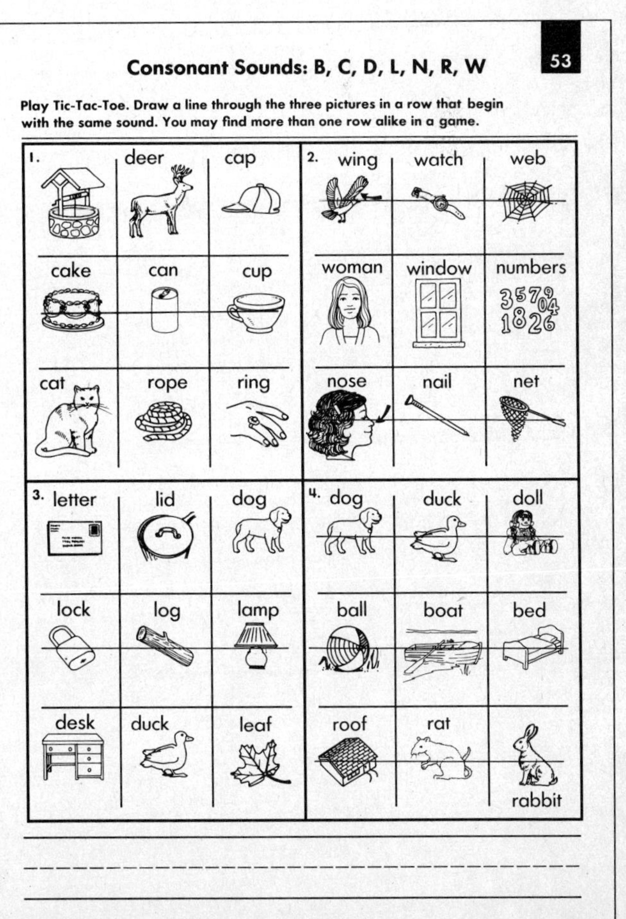
Consonant Sounds: B, C, D, L, N, R, W

53

Play Tic-Tac-Toe. Draw a line through the three pictures in a row that begin with the same sound. You may find more than one row alike in a game.

1. deer, cap, cake, can, cup, cat, rope, ring
2. wing, watch, web, woman, window, numbers, nose, nail, net
3. letter, lid, dog, lock, log, lamp, desk, duck, leaf
4. dog, duck, doll, ball, boat, bed, roof, rat, rabbit

Lesson 24

Consonant Sound *P* (page 54)

Objective The child will identify the name and the sound of the letter *P*.

Review

Listening To practice auditory discrimination, have the children identify the beginning sounds of the following words by repeating them after you: *cap, door, girls, jacks, ladder, web, newspaper, rabbit, balloon.* You might challenge the children to identify the ending sounds of these words as well.

Teaching Ideas

Listening Pronounce the following words to introduce the consonant sound *P: package, pancake, parade, peanuts, popcorn, paper, parakeet, piano, pickles, potato.* Point out the sound of the letter *P* in each word, asking the children to repeat each word after you. Challenge the children to identify the words having *P* in more than one place.

You might display picture flashcards or a phonics picture chart with other words that begin with the *P* sound. Write the name of each word on the chalkboard. As the children repeat each word, have them circle the beginning *P* sound on the chalkboard.

54

Consonant Sound: P

The word pig begins with the sound of p. Say the name of each picture. If the name begins with the sound of p, print P in the box.

1. pig P	2. pan P	3. girl
4. paw P	5. pillow P	6. jug
7. pencil P	8. pie P	9. pitcher P
10. pot P	11. pen P	12. parrot P

The word cap ends with the sound of p. Say the name of each picture. If the name ends with the sound of p, print p in the box.

1. cap p	2. mop p	3. soap p
4. top p	5. cup p	6. pear
7. paw	8. map p	9. pan
10. rabbit	11. trap p	12. jeep p

Encourage the children to identify the sound of the letter *P* by having them raise their hands when they hear you say a word with a *P* sound, as in the following sentences.

1. *Dad gave Peter a pen and pencil set.*
2. *The princess gave a party for the people.*
3. *The principal gave Pam a prize.*
4. *Pam loved the pair of pajamas that was in the package.*
5. *Polly loved her pet parakeet.*

Dictionary Game Play the Dictionary Game as described in Lesson 19 in this unit. As the children think of more words that have *P* in them, add these words to the list on the chalkboard.

Writing Help the children fold writing paper into thirds, draw lines along the folds, and number writing lines from 1 to 10. As they hear you say each of the words, ask them to write the letter *P* in the beginning, middle, or ending column for each of the following.

captain	*mop*	*popcorn*	*pillow*	*stamp*
sweep	*pickle*	*cape*	*supper*	*Paul*
cup	*potato*	*apple*	*top*	*soap*

Acknowledge, especially, those children who are able to identify the *P* in *popcorn* as being in two positions.

Extension

Art Provide a variety of pictures from old magazines and catalogs. Ask the child to print a bold letter *P* on a sheet of paper. Invite the child to choose pictures of *P* words, cutting and pasting them on the paper in collage form.

Lesson 25

Consonant Sound *V* (pages 55–56)

Objective The child will identify the name and the sound of the letter *V*.

Review

Listening Invite the children to suggest rhyming words for each of the following words: *book, cap, fun, girls, horn, mittens, hand, rake, rose.* Write the pairs of rhyming words on the chalkboard as they are suggested. You might encourage the children to write the rhyming words from the previous activity on a sheet of paper.

Teaching Ideas

Listening Encourage the children to repeat the following *V* words: *violet, vase, vacuum, vacation, vest, valentine, vitamin, voice, vaccination.* Explain that the beginning sound in each word is the *V* sound. Point out the position of the lips and teeth and the vibration that is felt when saying the letter *V*. Suggest that the *V* sound is similar to the sound of an airplane or a motorboat engine.

Display picture flashcards or a phonics picture chart for the following words: *van, hive, volcano, cave, vine, vegetables, wave, dive.* Encourage the children to say these words, identifying the sound of the letter *V* at the beginning or ending position.

Encourage the children to identify the sound of the letter *V* by having them clap every time they hear the letter sound in the following sentences.

1. *Virginia ate a violet vegetable.*
2. *Victor was making a weather vane.*
3. *The village is in the valley.*
4. *Veronica wore a velvet dress.*

Challenge the children to create similar sentences of their own, using words that begin with the letter *V*.

Art Invite the children to create letter pictures using the letter *V*. After writing the letter on sheets of drawing paper, suggest that the children study the shape of the letter *V* before drawing their pictures.

Extension

Alphabet Game Invite the child to create an alphabet train, using all of the letters of the alphabet. You might provide guidance in the sequencing of the letters of the alphabet. Encourage the child to think of one word that begins with the sound of each letter. Help the child write each word on the chalkboard or on a sheet of paper.

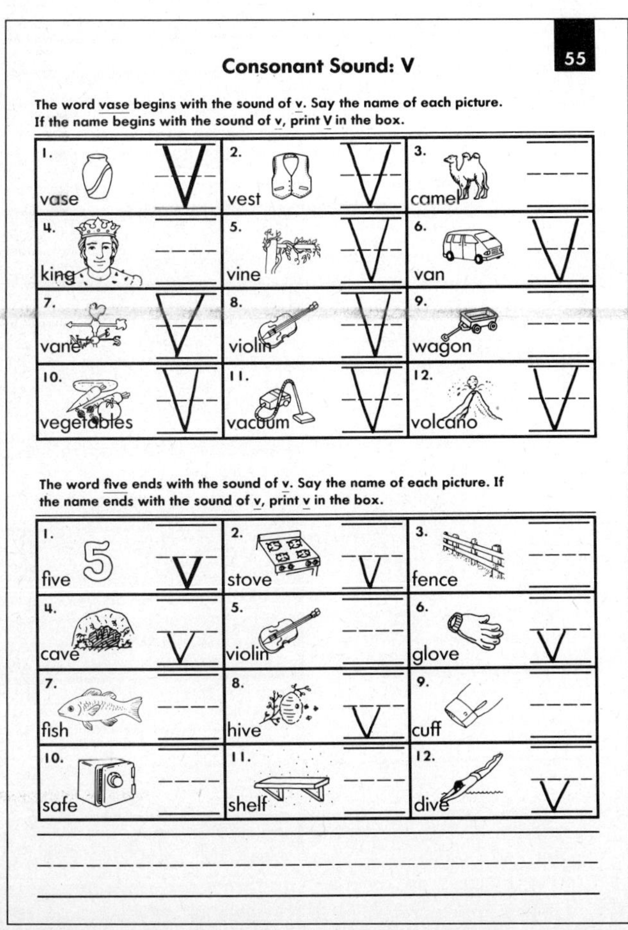

Consonant Sound: V 55

The word vase begins with the sound of v. Say the name of each picture. If the name begins with the sound of v, print V in the box.

1. vase V	2. vest V	3. camel
4. king	5. vine V	6. van V
7. vane V	8. violin V	9. wagon
10. vegetables V	11. vacuum V	12. volcano V

The word five ends with the sound of v. Say the name of each picture. If the name ends with the sound of v, print v in the box.

1. five v	2. stove v	3. fence
4. cave v	5. violin	6. glove v
7. fish	8. hive v	9. cuff
10. safe	11. shelf	12. dive v

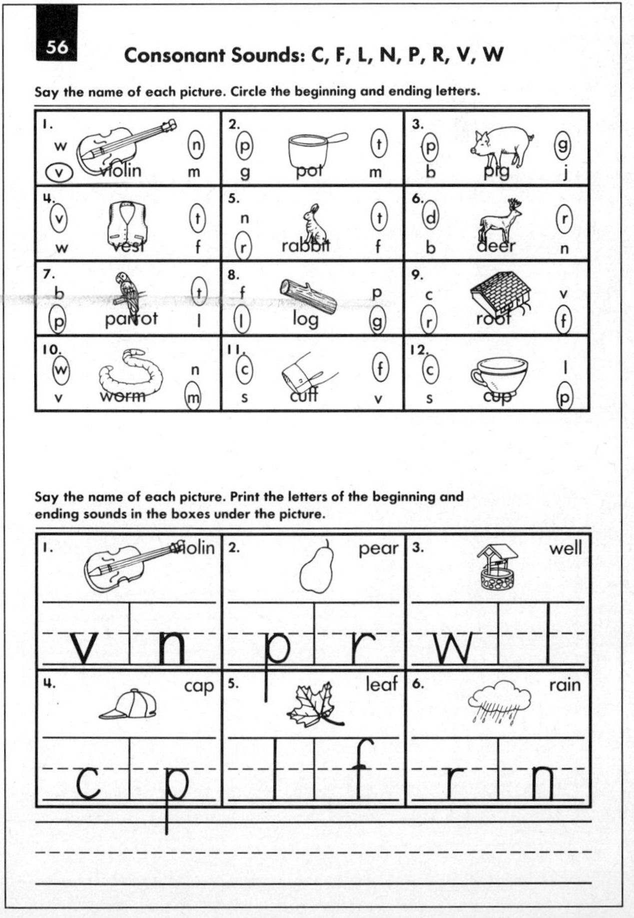

56 **Consonant Sounds: C, F, L, N, P, R, V, W**

Say the name of each picture. Circle the beginning and ending letters.

1. w (v) violin (n) m	2. (p) g pot (t) m	3. (p) b pig (g) j
4. (v) w vest (t) f	5. n (r) rabbit (t) f	6. (d) b deer (r) n
7. b (p) parrot (t) l	8. f (l) log p (g)	9. c (r) roof v (f)
10. (w) v worm n (m)	11. (c) s cuff (f) v	12. (c) s cup l (p)

Say the name of each picture. Print the letters of the beginning and ending sounds in the boxes under the picture.

1. violin: v n	2. pear: p r	3. well: w l
4. cap: c p	5. leaf: l f	6. rain: r n

Lesson 26

Consonant Sounds *QU* and *X* (page 57)

Objective The child will identify the names and the sounds of the letters *Qu* and *X*.

Review

Boston Game To review the beginning sounds of words, play the Boston Game, described in Lesson 13 in this unit, using all of the letters of the alphabet in sequential order.

Teaching Ideas

Listening Introduce the *Qu* sound, having the children listen carefully as you pronounce the following words: *quiet, quarrel, quit, quick, quarter, quilt, quack.*

Present picture flashcards or a phonics picture chart with *Qu* words. Explain that the letter *u* always comes after *Q* in words. Invite the children to repeat the *Qu* words as they identify them on the picture chart.

Encourage the children to listen for the *Qu* sound in words in the following sentences.

1. *I heard the duck quack.*
2. *Mary asked the question quickly.*
3. *Please quit quarreling.*
4. *The queen is quietly waiting for the king.*

Encourage the children to raise their hands each time they hear the *Qu* sound.

To introduce the *X* sound, say the following words that end with *X*: *fox, mix, wax, six, ax, box, fix.* Encourage the children to repeat these words after you, identifying the ending sound in each word.

Writing Display picture flashcards or a phonics word chart showing words with the *X* sound. Write these words on the chalkboard above each picture flashcard or list the words on the chalkboard if using a phonics word chart. Encourage the children to repeat each word and to locate the *X* sound in words such as: *six, box, fox, ax, taxi, x-ray.* Invite the children to locate and to circle the letter *X* in each of these words. Ask the children to practice writing the *X* words found on the chalkboard on their own sheets of paper.

Dictionary Game Play the Dictionary Game, as described in Lesson 19 in this unit, using the letters *Qu* and *X*.

Art Suggest that the children create a picture page for either the letter *Qu* or the letter *X*. See directions for this activity in Lesson 19 in this unit.

Consonant Sounds: Qu, X 57

The word queen begins with the sound of q. Say the name of each picture. If the name begins with the sound of qu, print Qu in the box.

1. queen Qu	2. question Qu	3. kite
4. quilt Qu	5. king	6. sock

The word box ends with the sound of x. Say the name of each picture. If the name ends with the sound of x, print x in the box.

1. box x	2. six x	3. ax x

Say the name of each picture. Print the letters of the beginning and ending sounds in the boxes under the picture.

1. queen	2. fox	3. six
qu n	f x	s x
4. quilt	5. box	6. question
qu t	b x	qu n

Lesson 27

Consonant Sounds *Y* and *Z*; Consonant Sound Review (pages 58–60)

Objective The child will identify the names and the sounds of the letters *Y* and *Z* and review the letter/sound associations that have been learned in previous lessons.

Teaching Ideas

Listening Introduce the *Y* sound with the following picture flashcards: *yo-yo, yellow, yawn, yam, yard, yarn.* As you say each word, invite the children to point to the picture and to repeat the *Y* word.

Ask the children to listen carefully to each of the following sentences, raising their hands each time they hear a *Y* word.

1. *Yesterday we played in the yard.*
2. *The yolk is the yellow part of the egg.*
3. *I like to play with my yo-yo on the yellow yacht.*
4. *The yam is not baked yet.*
5. *Playing in the yard made me yawn.*
6. *You might yell if I spill the yellow paint.*

Pause after each sentence, inviting the children to tell you the *Y* words they heard. Encourage the children to make up more *Y* sentences to continue the activity.

Dictionary Game Play the Dictionary Game described in Lesson 19 in this unit, using the letter *Y*. List the words on the chalkboard as they are named.

Listening Introduce the *Z* sound with the following picture flashcards: *zebra, zoo, zipper, zero.* Invite the children to repeat each word after you, pointing out the closed position of their teeth and the vibrating, buzzing sound that the letter *Z* makes.

Writing Draw three-way split boxes on the chalkboard. Ask the children to repeat each of these words: *fuzz, zinnia, breeze, zig-zag, puzzle, lazy, zoo, bazaar, size, wizard, sneeze, zipper.* Encourage the children to identify the position of the letter *Z* in each word. Have them write *Z* in the split boxes to indicate its sound at the beginning, the middle, or the ending position of each word. Acknowledge, especially, those students identifying the *Z* at the beginnig and the middle of *zig-zag*.

Art Invite the children to make a *Y* or a *Z* picture using noodles and paint or crayons. After having the children print the letter *Z* or the letter *Y* on sheets of drawing paper, show them how they can paste noodles over the shape of the letter. Encourage them to draw crayon pictures of *Z* or *Y* words on the paper or to paint their noodles if they wish.

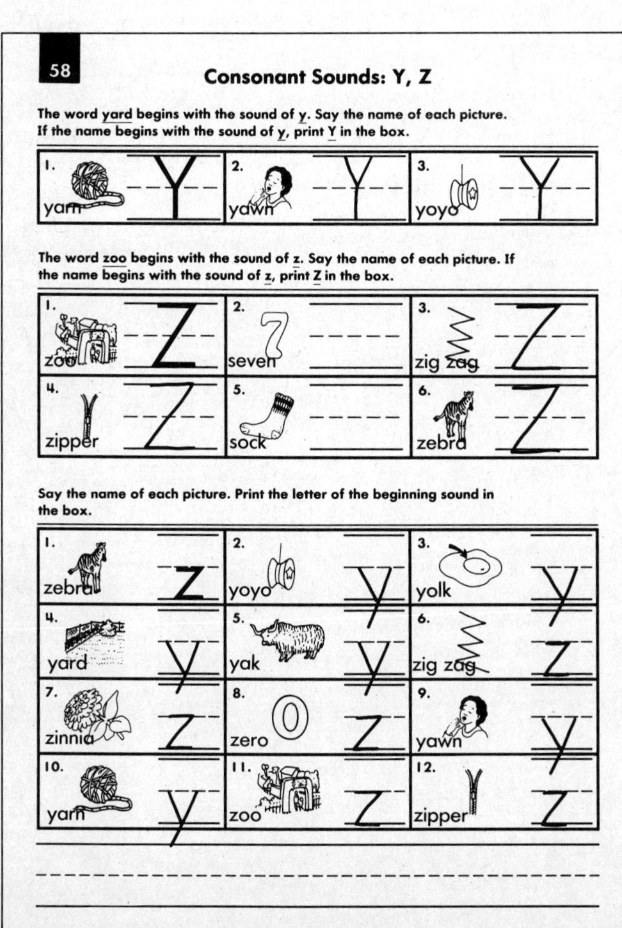

58 Consonant Sounds: Y, Z

The word yard begins with the sound of y. Say the name of each picture. If the name begins with the sound of y, print Y in the box.

1. yarn Y 2. yawn Y 3. yoyo Y

The word zoo begins with the sound of z. Say the name of each picture. If the name begins with the sound of z, print Z in the box.

1. zoo Z 2. seven 3. zig zag Z 4. zipper Z 5. sock 6. zebra Z

Say the name of each picture. Print the letter of the beginning sound in the box.

1. zebra z 2. yoyo y 3. yolk y 4. yard y 5. yak y 6. zig zag z 7. zinnia z 8. zero z 9. yawn y 10. yarn y 11. zoo z 12. zipper z

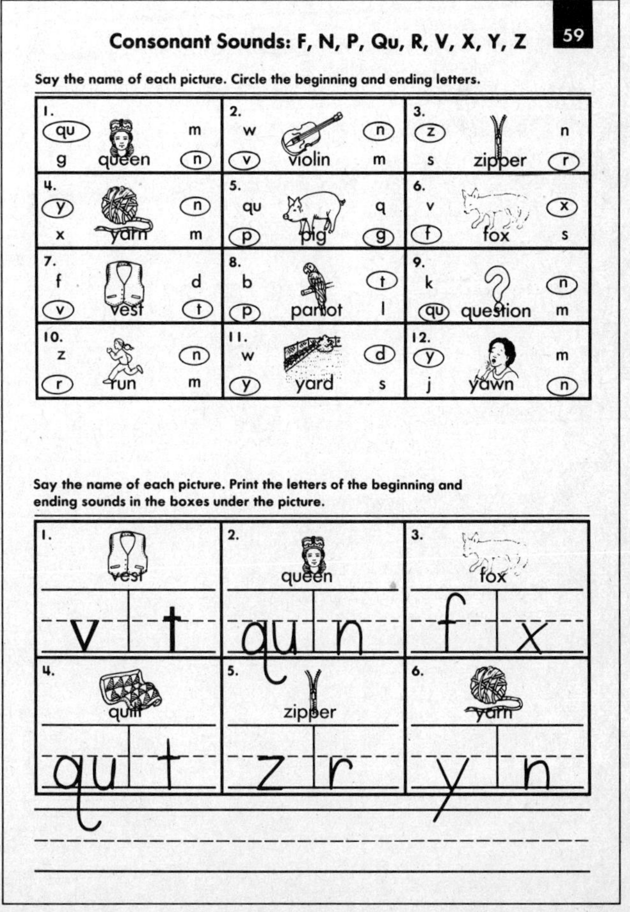

Consonant Sounds: F, N, P, Qu, R, V, X, Y, Z 59

Say the name of each picture. Circle the beginning and ending letters.

1. qu m g queen n 2. w n v violin m 3. z n s zipper r 4. y n x yarn m 5. qu q p pig g 6. v x f fox s 7. f d v vest t 8. b t p parrot l 9. k n qu question m 10. z n r run m 11. w d y yard s 12. y m j yawn n

Say the name of each picture. Print the letters of the beginning and ending sounds in the boxes under the picture.

1. vest v t 2. queen qu n 3. fox f x 4. quilt qu t 5. zipper z r 6. yarn y n

Extension

Writing Review consonant sounds by having the child listen for the beginning or the ending consonant sounds in each of the following words: *jam, bike, can, dentist, faucet, geese, house, jeep, rope, mittens, nap, peanut, queen, robot, sail, team, vase, weed, wax, yawn, zipper.* As each consonant sound is identified, encourage the child to write the partner letters for each sound heard.

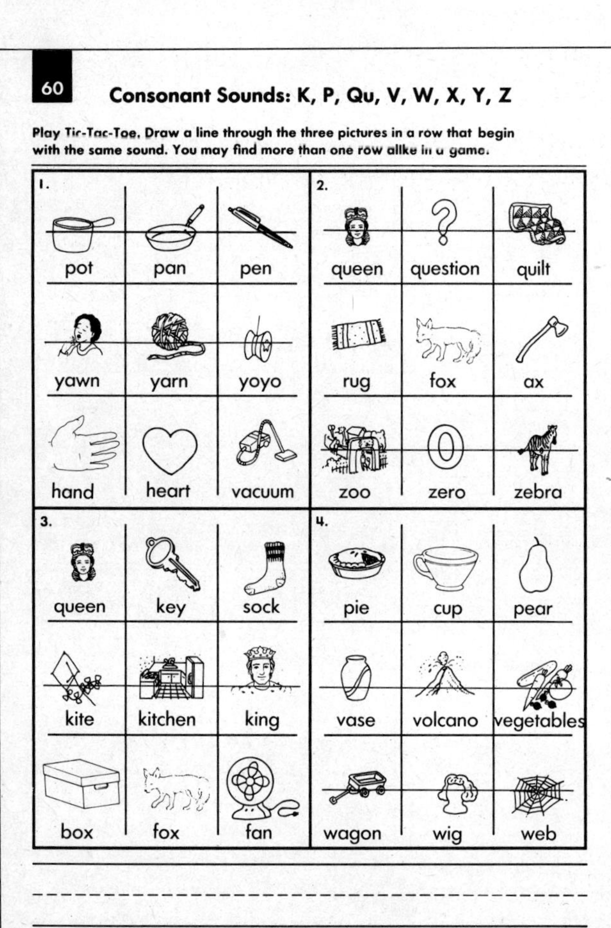

60 **Consonant Sounds: K, P, Qu, V, W, X, Y, Z**

Play Tic-Tac-Toe. Draw a line through the three pictures in a row that begin with the same sound. You may find more than one row alike in a game.

1.

pot	pan	pen
yawn	yarn	yoyo
hand	heart	vacuum

2.

queen	question	quilt
rug	fox	ax
zoo	zero	zebra

3.

queen	key	sock
kite	kitchen	king
box	fox	fan

4.

pie	cup	pear
vase	volcano	vegetables
wagon	wig	web

Unit 3 Short Vowels

Lesson 28

Short Vowel A (pages 61–63)

Objective The child will identify the letter *A* and the short *A* sound in isolation and within words.

Teaching Ideas

Listening Remind the children that they have studied all of the consonant sounds in the alphabet. Display the five letter cards for the vowel letters on the chalkboard ledge, explaining that *A, E, I, O, U* make up another group of sounds that will help the children learn to read. Invite the children to name the vowels by their letter names.

Have the children identify each of the following letters as a vowel or as a consonant: *A, C, E, F, H, I, J, L, N, O, R, S, U, V*.

Introduce the short vowel sound *A* by placing picture flashcards on the chalkboard ledge with words such as the following: *ax, ant, hat, mat, cat*. Invite the children to repeat each word and to say the short *A* sound with you.

Encourage the children to listen carefully as you read the following words with the short *A* sound: *ham, bat, pan, pat, can, mat, hand, act, glass*. Invite the children to identify where the short *A* sound occurs in each of the words.

Write the following words on the chalkboard: *fan, cap, bag*. Encourage the children to think of words that rhyme, such as the following: *fan/man/Dan/ran/tan/plan, cap/tap/rap/nap/lap/sap, bag/rag/tag/sag/wag/flag*.

Writing You may suggest that the children write the rhyming words from the previous activity on sheets of paper.

Blending Introduce the concept of blending to the children. Write *bat* on the chalkboard and draw a slide under the word as shown below.

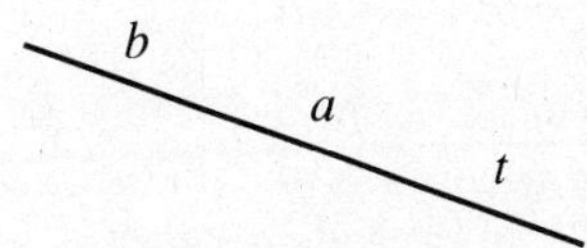

Explain to the children that these letters can be read by slowly saying the sound of each letter and slurring the sounds together. Provide an example by slowly blending the letters in *bat*. Encourage the children to repeat the blending.

Write the following words on the chalkboard: *sad, bag, fat, mat, ham, man, rap, tap, nap, wax, fan, map, sag, ran*. Blend each word, encouraging the children to repeat each one. Challenge the children to suggest additional short *A* words. List these words and invite the children to blend each one.

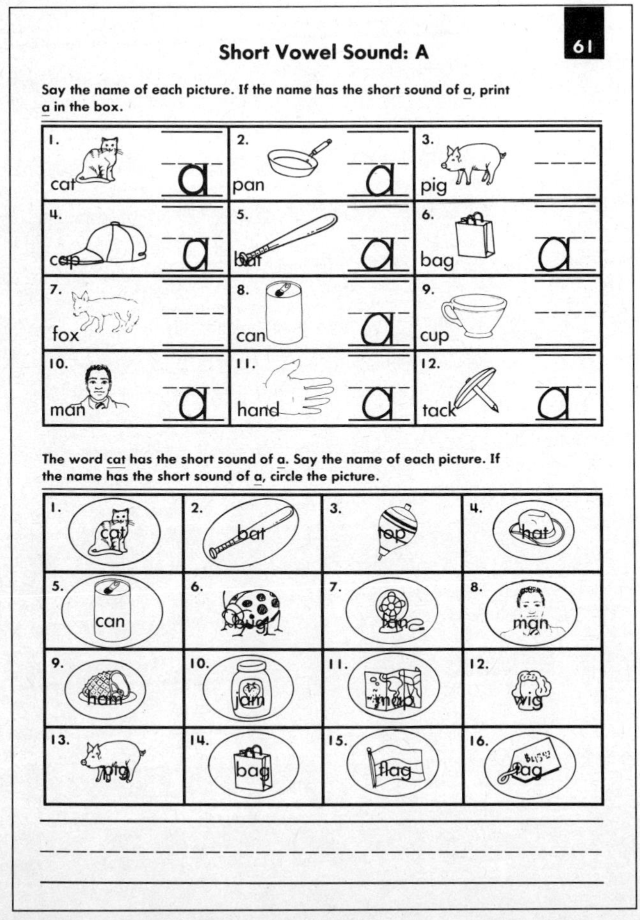

61

Short Vowel Sound: A

Say the name of each picture. If the name has the short sound of a, print a in the box.

1. cat a	2. pan a	3. pig
4. cap a	5. bat a	6. bag a
7. fox	8. can a	9. cup
10. man a	11. hand a	12. tack a

The word cat has the short sound of a. Say the name of each picture. If the name has the short sound of a, circle the picture.

1. cat	2. bat	3. top	4. hat
5. can	6. bug	7. fan	8. man
9. ham	10. jam	11. map	12. wig
13. pig	14. bag	15. flag	16. tag

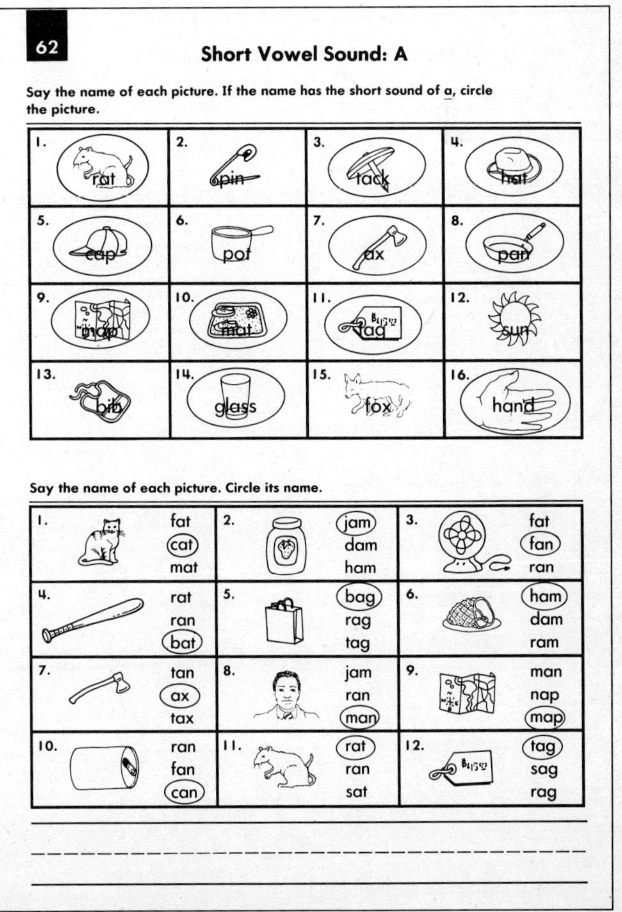

62

Short Vowel Sound: A

Say the name of each picture. If the name has the short sound of a, circle the picture.

1. rat	2. pin	3. tack	4. hat
5. cap	6. pot	7. ax	8. pan
9. map	10. mat	11. tag	12. sun
13. bib	14. glass	15. fox	16. hand

Say the name of each picture. Circle its name.

1.	fat cat mat	2.	jam dam ham	3.	fat fan ran
4.	rat ran bat	5.	bag rag tag	6.	ham dam ram
7.	tan ax tax	8.	jam ran man	9.	man nap map
10.	ran fan can	11.	rat ran sat	12.	tag sag rag

Boston Game Invite the children to imagine packing suitcases for a trip to Boston. Explain that each item to be packed in the suitcase must have a short *A* sound. Say, for example, *I am going to Boston, and with me I will take a cap.* Encourage each child, in turn, to add another short *A* word to your sentence, for example: *I am going to Boston, and with me I will take a cap and a map.* Remind the children that they must mention the items already in the suitcase before adding another short *A* word. Continue the game until all the children have had a turn or until the list of items becomes too lengthy for memory.

Listen-Look-Touch Game Display all of the letter cards on the chalkboard ledge. Tell the children to listen for the beginning, the middle, or the ending sound of a given word. For example, you might say, *Listen for the ending sound in the word* kitten. Ask them to look at the letter cards, and have a volunteer locate and touch the correct letter among those on the chalkboard ledge. Have the child identify the ending sound as the *N* sound. Encourage the child to ask a classmate to locate the beginning, the middle, or the ending sound of another word. Encourage all of the children to take turns as the game continues. You may wish to include listening for the short vowel *A* as well as the consonant sounds.

Art Have the children identify pictures from magazines with names that have the short *A* sound. Invite the children to cut and paste short *A* pictures on sheets of drawing paper. You might suggest that the children look at a short *A* picture chart or a primary level dictionary if they need help identifying short *A* words. Show the children how to trace the letter *A* with a stencil. Ask them to trace the *A* on colored paper, cut it out, and paste it on their *A* pictures.

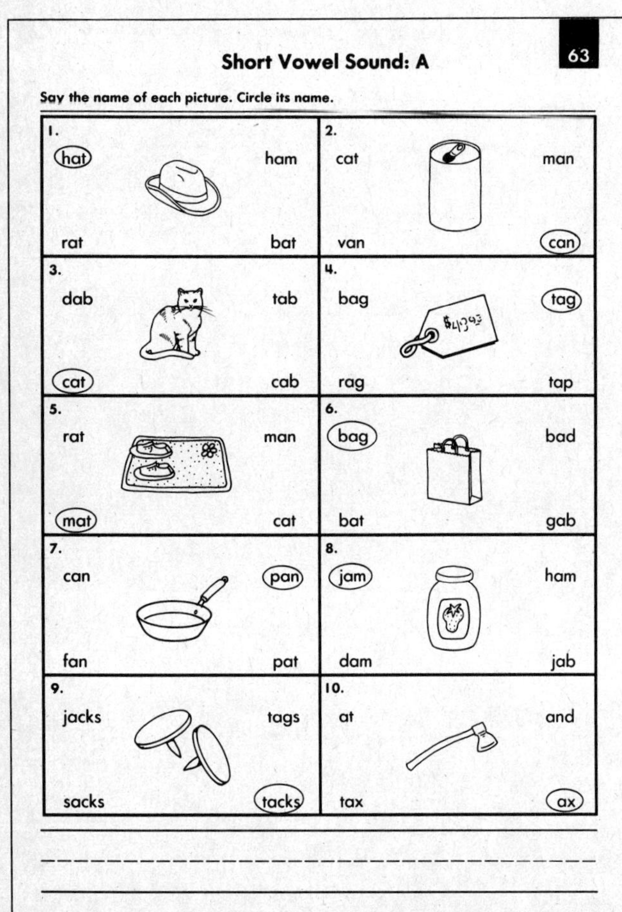

63

Short Vowel Sound: A

Say the name of each picture. Circle its name.

1. (hat) ham rat bat	2. cat man van (can)
3. dab tab (cat) cab	4. bag (tag) rag tap
5. rat man (mat) cat	6. (bag) bad bat gab
7. can (pan) fan pat	8. (jam) ham dam jab
9. jacks tags sacks (tacks)	10. at and tax (ax)

Reteaching

Matching Game The child may play this version of the Matching Game with you or with another child. Challenge the child to match letter cards for capital letters with letter cards for small letters. As the child matches each partner letter on the table, suggest that the child use the sound of the letter in a word. Encourage the child to write the letters on a sheet of paper. If the child needs help writing the letters, encourage the use of letter stencils, templates, or sandpaper letters.

Family Involvement Activity Duplicate the Family Letter on page 105 of this Teacher's Edition. Send it home with the children.

Lesson 29

Short Vowel A (pages 64–65)

Objective The child will read short *A* words appearing in isolation or within sentences.

Review

Listening To reinforce auditory skills, challenge the children to identify beginning and ending sounds in sample words you recite. Help the children fold writing paper in half, draw a line along the fold, and number writing lines. Then direct them to write the letters for the beginning and ending sounds they hear on the correct side of the paper. Choose a variety of short *A* words or picture flashcards naming words with the short *A* sound, such as the following: *bag, cap, cat, lad, hat, fan, can, man.*

Teaching Ideas

Listening Read aloud the words in the following columns. Ask the children to tell which words in each column contain the short *A* sound.

can	*bus*	*fish*	*hen*	*set*	*duck*
yes	*cub*	*cab*	*wag*	*sick*	*doll*
bid	*tap*	*Rick*	*lip*	*sat*	*sack*
Dan	*tip*	*dish*	*ham*	*lick*	*pack*

Speaking Write a list of short *A* words on the chalkboard, or create picture flashcards that name short *A* words. Invite volunteers to choose a word and to read it to the class. Then ask the children to create sentences that use each word. You might wish to use the following words: *jam, and, ran, at, dad, lap, tag, back, had.*

Acting Using the short *A* words or picture flashcards from the previous activity, encourage volunteers to choose a word and to act it out. Challenge the other children to guess the word. Invite the child who guesses the word correctly to write it on the chalkboard.

Extension

Writing Write the following sentences on the chalkboard. Ask the child to identify the short *A* words in each sentence by writing them on a sheet of paper.

1. *The lad ran.*
2. *Pass the jam.*
3. *The man has a fan.*
4. *Jack has a cat.*

Art Encourage the child to create a set of picture flashcards for words that contain the short *A* sound. You may suggest that the child draw the pictures or, alternatively, that the child paste pictures cut from old magazines.

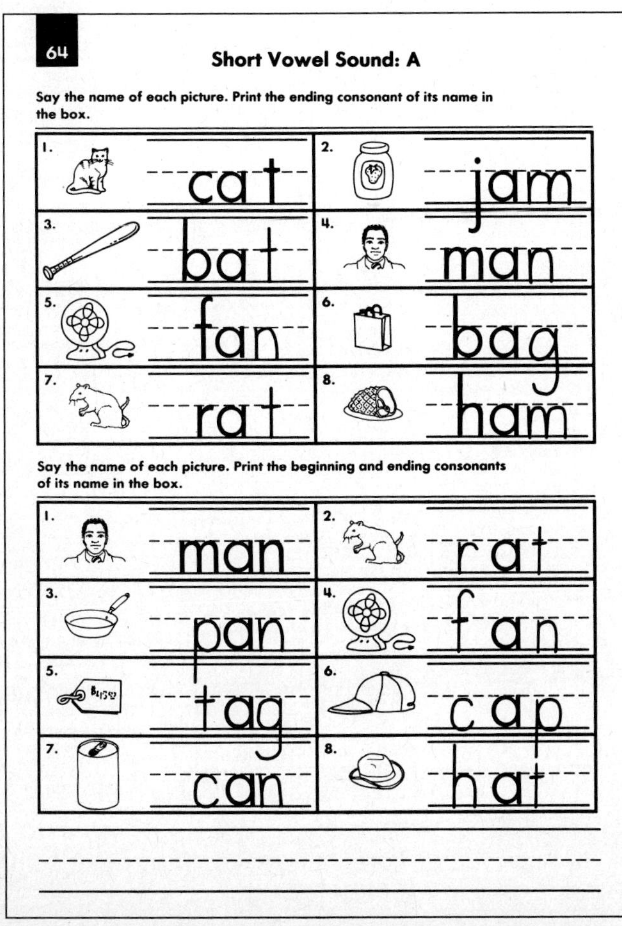

64

Short Vowel Sound: A

Say the name of each picture. Print the ending consonant of its name in the box.

1. cat
2. jam
3. bat
4. man
5. fan
6. bag
7. rat
8. ham

Say the name of each picture. Print the beginning and ending consonants of its name in the box.

1. man
2. rat
3. pan
4. fan
5. tag
6. cap
7. can
8. hat

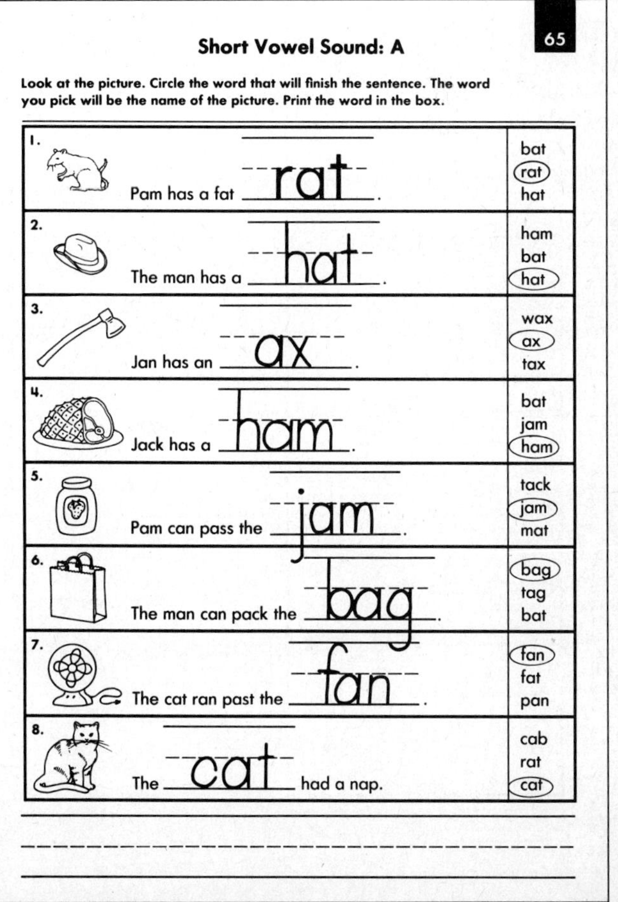

Short Vowel Sound: A

65

Look at the picture. Circle the word that will finish the sentence. The word you pick will be the name of the picture. Print the word in the box.

1.	Pam has a fat rat.	bat, (rat), hat
2.	The man has a hat.	ham, bat, (hat)
3.	Jan has an ax.	wax, (ax), tax
4.	Jack has a ham.	bat, jam, (ham)
5.	Pam can pass the jam.	tack, (jam), mat
6.	The man can pack the bag.	(bag), tag, bat
7.	The cat ran past the fan.	(fan), fat, pan
8.	The cat had a nap.	cab, rat, (cat)

Lesson 30

Short Vowel A (pages 66–67)

Objective The child will apply the Short Vowel Rule.

Short Vowel Rule: If a word or syllable has only one vowel, and it comes at the beginning of the word or between two consonants, the vowel is usually short.

Review

Listening To practice auditory skills, ask the children to listen to the following words. Invite them to tell if the consonant is heard at the beginning, the middle, or the end of each word.

M: marble, drum, camel
K: walk, kitchen, pocket
B: button, bubble, crib
S: pass, sawed, basin
T: market, town, butter

Teaching Ideas

Listening Write the following words in two columns on the chalkboard: *ax, at, as, an; rat, cap, jam, fan.* Encourage volunteers to read the words in the first column. Then ask the children the following questions.

1. *Where do you see the vowel* A *in these words?*
2. *What is the sound of* A *in these words?*
3. *When does the vowel* A *have a short sound?*

Repeat this procedure with the words in the second column. Then guide the children to make a rule, in their own words, about the sound of the short *A*.

Writing Write the following sentences on the chalkboard.

1. *Sam has the bat.*
2. *Ann ran to Jack.*
3. *Dad has an ax.*
4. *Pat and Pam ran.*

Invite volunteers to each underline the short *A* words in a sentence.

Extension

Reading Encourage the child to identify short *A* words in stories selected from books in the classroom collection.

Art Make a list of familiar short *A* words or display several picture flashcards for short *A* words. Encourage the child to use two of the words in one sentence. Have the child draw a picture to accompany the sentence. For example, the child might draw a stick figure representation of a boy running for *Sam ran.*

66

Short Vowel Sound: A

Say the name of each picture. Print its name in the box.

1.	fan	2.	can
3.	man	4.	cat
5.	mat	6.	bag
7.	rat	8.	ham
9.	tag	10.	ax
11.	map	12.	ant
13.	bag	14.	jam
15.	pan	16.	hat
17.	bat	18.	cap

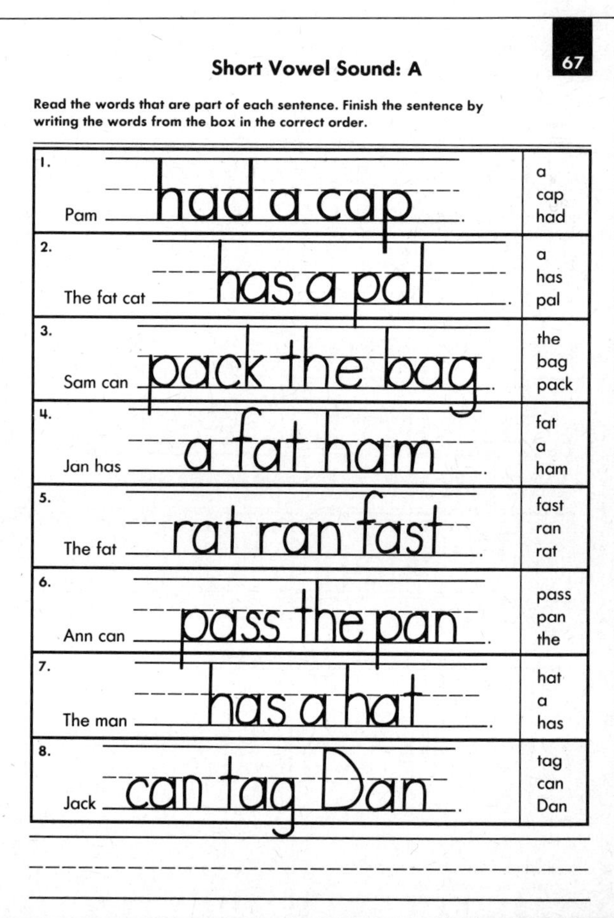

Short Vowel Sound: A 67

Read the words that are part of each sentence. Finish the sentence by writing the words from the box in the correct order.

1.	Pam had a cap.	a cap had
2.	The fat cat has a pal.	a has pal
3.	Sam can pack the bag.	the bag pack
4.	Jan has a fat ham.	fat a ham
5.	The fat rat ran fast.	fast ran rat
6.	Ann can pass the pan.	pass pan the
7.	The man has a hat.	hat a has
8.	Jack can tag Dan.	tag can Dan

Lesson 31
Short Vowel *I* (pages 68–70)

Objective The child will identify the letter *I* and its short vowel sound in isolation and in words.

Teaching Ideas

Listening Present a word card or print a word with a short *I* sound on the chalkboard, such as *bib*. Say the word for the children and ask them to repeat it. Point out the vowel, explaining to the children that the vowel sound they hear is the sound of the short *I*. Repeat the activity with the following short *I* words: *wig, mix, hid, fit, will, sip.*

Rhyming To develop recognition of the short *I* sound, you might want to present a series of rhyming words. Print the word *pin* on the chalkboard and say it aloud. Ask the children to suggest words that rhyme with *pin*. The children may volunteer such words as *tin, win, twin, fin, bin.* Write the words on the chalkboard as the children say them. Continue the activity with the words *lip, fill, it.* If you wish to create an extension activity, challenge the children to use each of the words in a sentence.

Writing Write the following short *I* words on the chalkboard: *lid, sink, milk, fill, tip, king, sit, bib, lick, rim.* Invite the children to circle the letter that makes the short *I* sound in each word.

Write the following words on the chalkboard: *lap, sack, peg, tap, wag, sat, bed.* Challenge volunteers to erase the vowel in each word and to write the vowel *I* in its place. Then lead the children to say the new word.

Riddle Game Write several short *I* words on the chalkboard, or display several word cards for the short *I* sound. Ask the children a riddle involving one of these words, such as the following for the word *mitt: I am thinking of something that helps you catch a ball. What is it?* Challenge the children to guess the answer to the riddle. Continue asking riddles for other short *I* words, or invite the children to offer riddles of their own. You may wish to use the following words: *hill, sink, bib, pin, lips, pig, six.*

Extension

Art Encourage the child to continue working with rhymes. Ask the child to choose two rhyming words from the following list and to draw a picture about them.

fix	*pig*	*Sid*	*Rick*	*fish*
mix	*wig*	*hid*	*sick*	*wish*

You might suggest that the child print the two words at the bottom of the drawing.

Writing Encourage the child to create a picture book for a short *I* riddle. Direct the child to fold a large sheet of paper in half. Have the child write the letter *I* on the front page. On the inside, have the child draw a picture clue for a short *I*

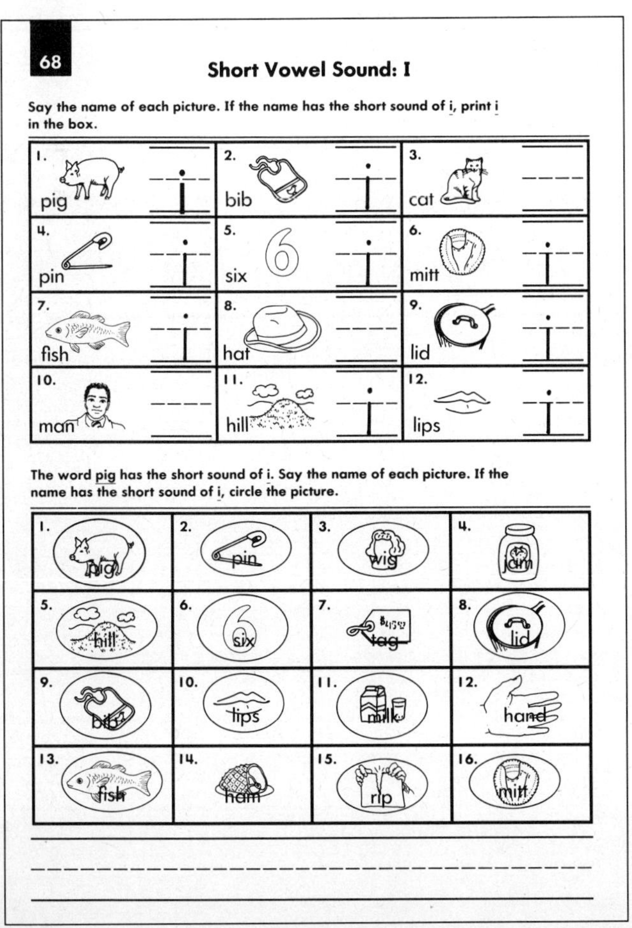

68

Short Vowel Sound: I

Say the name of each picture. If the name has the short sound of i, print i in the box.

1. pig — i
2. bib — i
3. cat
4. pin — i
5. six — i
6. mitt — i
7. fish — i
8. hat
9. lid — i
10. man
11. hill — i
12. lips — i

The word pig has the short sound of i. Say the name of each picture. If the name has the short sound of i, circle the picture.

1. pig 2. pin 3. wig 4. jam 5. hill 6. six 7. tag 8. lid 9. bib 10. lips 11. milk 12. hand 13. fish 14. ham 15. rip 16. mitt

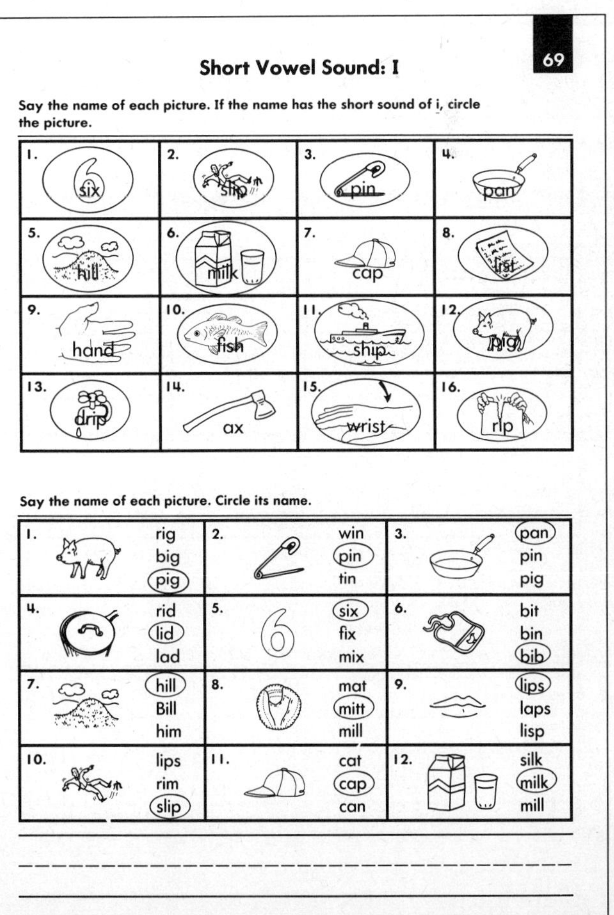

Short Vowel Sound: I

69

Say the name of each picture. If the name has the short sound of i, circle the picture.

1. six 2. slip 3. pin 4. pan 5. hill 6. milk 7. cap 8. list 9. hand 10. fish 11. ship 12. pig 13. drip 14. ax 15. wrist 16. rip

Say the name of each picture. Circle its name.

1. rig, big, pig
2. win, pin, tin
3. pan, pin, pig
4. rid, lid, lad
5. six, fix, mix
6. bit, bin, bib
7. hill, Bill, him
8. mat, mitt, mill
9. lips, laps, lisp
10. lips, rim, slip
11. cat, cap, can
12. silk, milk, mill

word. Then have the child draw blanks for each letter of the word below the picture clue. On the back page, have the child write the short *I* word for the picture in the book. Encourage the child to show the picture riddle to friends, classmates, or family members and to ask them to guess the correct word. If a child has time to complete several picture books, you might want to staple them into a larger book. Acknowledge the creativity or design of the drawings.

Rhyming-Sentences Game The child might enjoy writing rhyming sentences that contain words with the short vowel *I*. List the following words in random order on the chalkboard: *pin, lid, sit, win, kid, twin, fish, sick, lick, bin, bib, clip, sip, Rick.* Encourage the child to discover short *I* words that rhyme. Then ask the child to compose serious or silly sentences using the rhyming words.

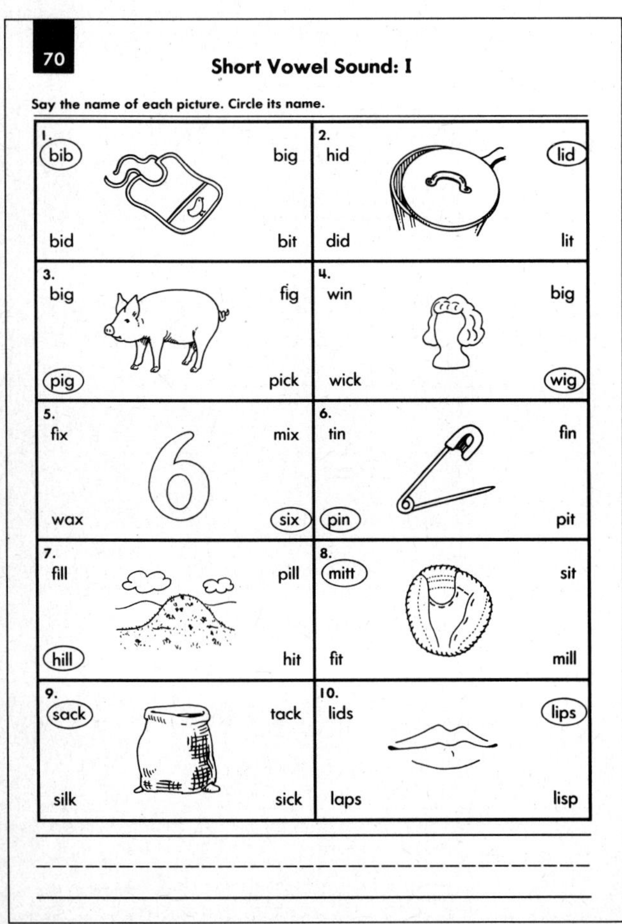

70

Short Vowel Sound: I

Say the name of each picture. Circle its name.

1. bib	big	2. hid	lid
bid	bit	did	lit
3. big	fig	4. win	big
pig	pick	wick	wig
5. fix	mix	6. tin	fin
wax	six	pin	pit
7. fill	pill	8. mitt	sit
hill	hit	fit	mill
9. sack	tack	10. lids	lips
silk	sick	laps	lisp

Lesson 32

Short Vowel *I* (pages 71–72)

Objective The child will complete sentences with appropriate short *A* and short *I* words.

Review

Listening To reinforce auditory skills, challenge the children to identify beginning and ending sounds in sample words you recite. Help the children fold writing paper in half, draw a line along the fold, and number writing lines. Then direct them to write the beginning and ending letters for the sounds they hear on the correct side of the paper. Choose a variety of words or picture flashcards for words with the short *I* sound, such as the following: *pig, tip, bib, lid, mitt.*

Teaching Ideas

Listening Pronounce each of the following words and encourage the children to identify the vowel sound they hear: *big, fit, can, miss, cap, win, pan, sip, tap, bill, pig, mat.* You might point out that each word contains a short vowel sound.

Speaking Write the following short *I* words on the chalkboard: *tip, pin, pig, bill, lid, swim, fin, miss.* Point to each word. Encourage volunteers to read each word and to use it in a sentence.

To vary this activity, you might want to provide sentences that are missing the short *I* word. For each sentence, challenge a child to supply the missing short *I* word from the words listed on the chalkboard.

Acting Write the following short *A* and short *I* words on the chalkboard, or provide a stack of word cards for the following short *A* and short *I* words: *sad, cat, wig, fat, pig, sip, swim, mitt, win, hat.* Invite volunteers to choose a word and to act it out for the other children. Encourage the children to guess the word that is being dramatized. Have the children who guess correctly write the word on the chalkboard.

Reteaching

Reading Have the child look through magazines for short *I* words appearing in isolation or in sentences. Encourage the child to cut out the words and to paste them on a sheet of paper.

Extension

Writing Print the following incomplete words on the chalkboard.

h__m *s__t* *b__g*
b__t *f__t* *s__ck*
t__n *p__n* *w__g*

Direct the child to print the letter *A* or *I* in each space to complete the word. You might suggest that the child draw a picture to accompany each word.

71

Short Vowel Sound: I

Say the name of each picture. Print the ending consonant of its name in the box.

1.	pig	2.	pin
3.	cat	4.	wig
5.	bib	6.	bag
7.	six	8.	lid

Say the name of each picture. Print the beginning and ending consonants of its name in the box.

1.	pin	2.	lid
3.	pig	4.	tag
5.	fan	6.	six
7.	bib	8.	ham

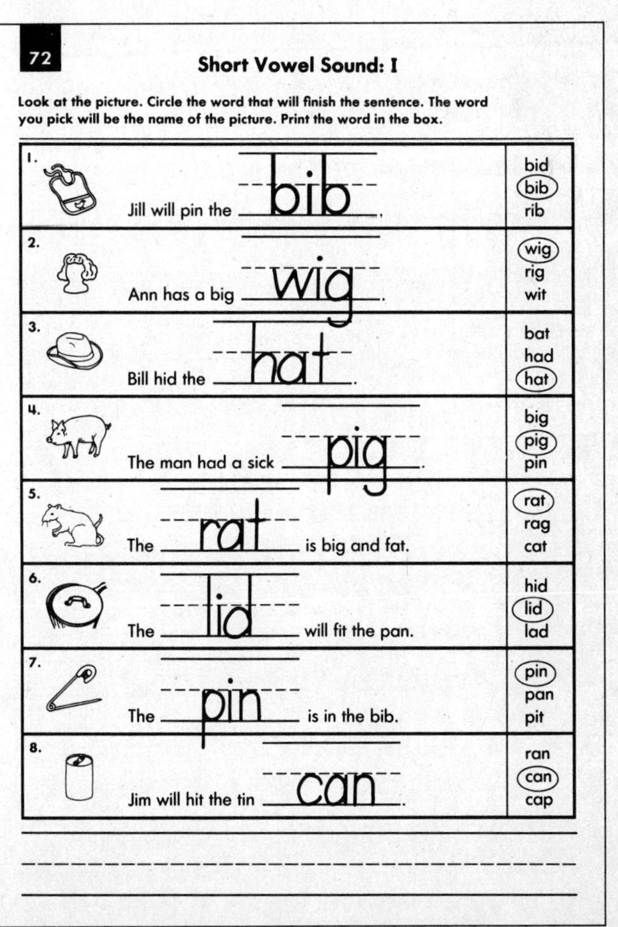

72

Short Vowel Sound: I

Look at the picture. Circle the word that will finish the sentence. The word you pick will be the name of the picture. Print the word in the box.

1.	Jill will pin the bib.	bid, (bib), rib
2.	Ann has a big wig.	(wig), rig, wit
3.	Bill hid the hat.	bat, had, (hat)
4.	The man had a sick pig.	big, (pig), pin
5.	The rat is big and fat.	(rat), rag, cat
6.	The lid will fit the pan.	hid, (lid), lad
7.	The pin is in the bib.	(pin), pan, pit
8.	Jim will hit the tin can.	ran, (can), cap

Lesson 33

Short Vowel *I* (pages 73–74)

Objective The child will apply the Short Vowel Rule.

Short Vowel Rule: If a word or syllable has only one vowel, and it comes at the beginning of the word or between two consonants, the vowel is usually short.

Review

Listening To reinforce auditory discrimination of vowel sounds, print the following words on the chalkboard. Ask children to identify the vowel sound heard in each: *in, did, Sam, pin, am, tack, slick, win, add, Lin.*

Teaching Ideas

Writing Write the following words in two columns on the chalkboard: *in, is, and, it, as; pin, pan, sit, cab, wish.* Encourage volunteers to read aloud the words in the first column and to circle the short *I*. Repeat the procedure with the second column. Keep the words on the chalkboard for the next activity.

Speaking Reinforce the Short Vowel Rule by asking the following questions about the words from the previous activity.

1. *Where do you see the vowels in these words?*
2. *What is the sound of each vowel?*
3. *When does a vowel have a short sound?*

Lead the children to state the Short Vowel Rule in their own words.

Fish-Pond Game Draw seven fish on the chalkboard and print one of the following short *A* or short *I* words on each fish: *and, is, lid, cat, it, pig, Jim.* Divide the class into two teams. Challenge the children to catch fish for their team by reading a word, naming the vowel, and explaining the Short Vowel Rule as it applies to that word. Explain that the team catching the most fish will win.

Extension

Art Encourage the child to look through old newspapers and magazines for pictures of objects with names that have the short *I* sound. Direct the child to cut out each picture and to paste it on tagboard or a large sheet of paper. You might want to display the child's poster at the front of the classroom.

Writing Give the child several picture flashcards representing words with the sound of short *I*. Encourage the child to write the name of each picture and to circle the short *I* in each. You may need to help the child identify the pictures correctly.

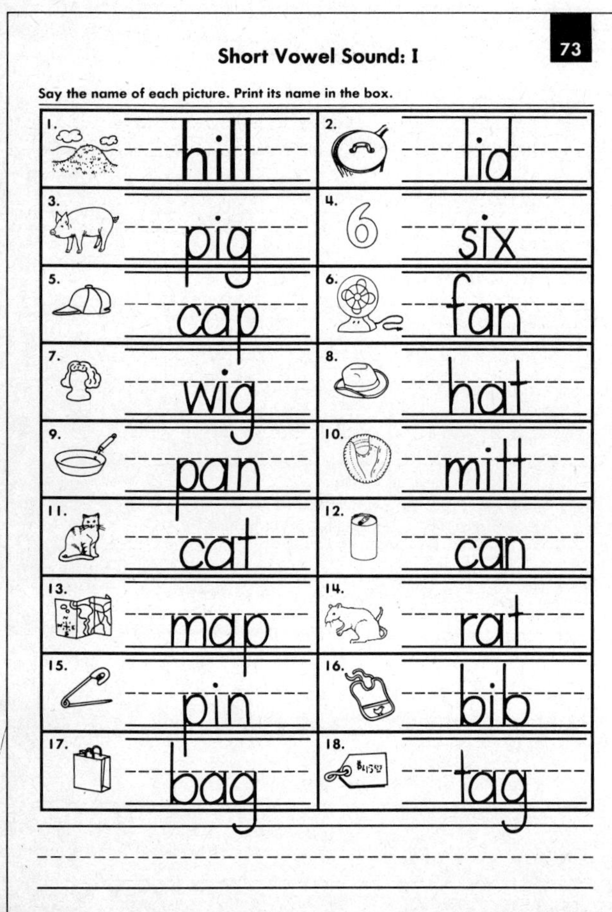

73

Short Vowel Sound: I

Say the name of each picture. Print its name in the box.

1. hill	2. lid
3. pig	4. six
5. cap	6. fan
7. wig	8. hat
9. pan	10. mitt
11. cat	12. can
13. map	14. rat
15. pin	16. bib
17. bag	18. tag

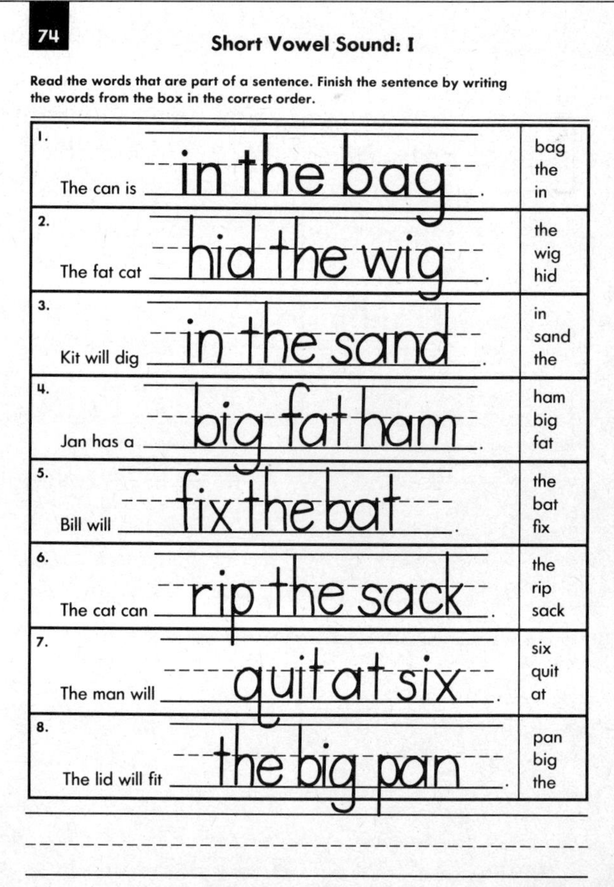

74

Short Vowel Sound: I

Read the words that are part of a sentence. Finish the sentence by writing the words from the box in the correct order.

1. The can is in the bag.	bag the in
2. The fat cat hid the wig.	the wig hid
3. Kit will dig in the sand.	in sand the
4. Jan has a big fat ham.	ham big fat
5. Bill will fix the bat.	the bat fix
6. The cat can rip the sack.	the rip sack
7. The man will quit at six.	six quit at
8. The lid will fit the big pan.	pan big the

Lesson 34
Short Vowel *U* (pages 75–77)

Objective The child will identify the letter *U* and its short vowel sound in isolation and in words.

Teaching Ideas

Listening Present a picture flashcard showing a tub. Say the word *tub* aloud and ask the children to repeat the word. Encourage the children to identify the short *U* sound.

Rhyming Game To develop an understanding of the short *U* sound, you may wish to work with rhymes. Write the following words on the chalkboard: *mug, bun, but, jump, up.* Point out the word *mug,* and encourage volunteers to name rhyming words. Encourage children who give incorrect answers by pointing out the similarities between their answers and the correct responses. List correct responses under the key word *mug*. Continue the activity with each of the key words on the chalkboard.

Speaking Display a series of pictures or picture flashcards for words that contain the short *U* sound. Encourage the children to identify each picture by naming the appropriate short *U* word. You might want to use pictures of the following objects: *sun, nut, duck, cup, truck, brush, cuff, drum, bud.*

Write a series of short *U* words on small cards and place them facedown on a desk or table at the front of the classroom. Invite the children to take a card, read the word on the card, and then use the word in a sentence. You might want to supply the following short *U* words: *cuff, bus, hum, tub, duck, gum, bug, rug, bump, rub.* Praise the children for using the words in the proper context. Save the cards for the next activity.

Riddle Game Play the Riddle Game, as described in Lesson 31 in this unit, using short *U* words. Place the cards from the previous activity facedown on the desk or table. You might invite volunteers to create the riddles for the other children. To provide an example, choose a short *U* word such as *cub* and say the following: *I am thinking of a word for baby bear. It contains short* U *and begins with the sound of* C. *What is it?* Encourage the children to guess the answer to each riddle. Invite those children who guess correctly to write the words on the chalkboard. You might want to ask other children to circle the short *U* in each word that has been written on the chalkboard.

Extension

Art Challenge the child to find short *U* words in books or magazines. Ask the child to select one word and to draw a picture for the word. Encourage the child to print the short *U* word under the picture.

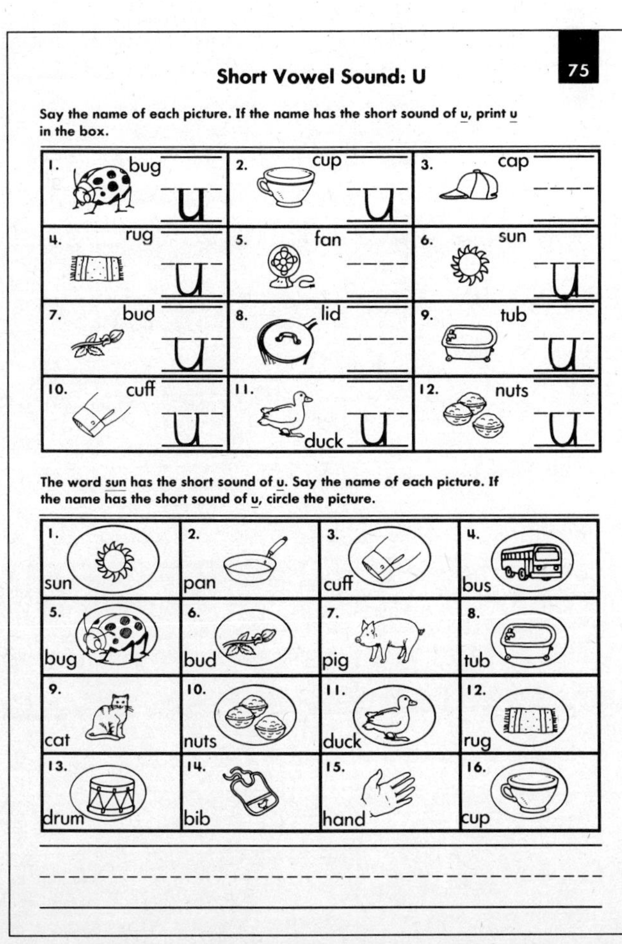
75

Short Vowel Sound: U

Say the name of each picture. If the name has the short sound of u, print u in the box.

1. bug u	2. cup u	3. cap
4. rug u	5. fan	6. sun u
7. bud u	8. lid	9. tub u
10. cuff u	11. duck u	12. nuts u

The word sun has the short sound of u. Say the name of each picture. If the name has the short sound of u, circle the picture.

1. sun	2. pan	3. cuff	4. bus
5. bug	6. bud	7. pig	8. tub
9. cat	10. nuts	11. duck	12. rug
13. drum	14. bib	15. hand	16. cup

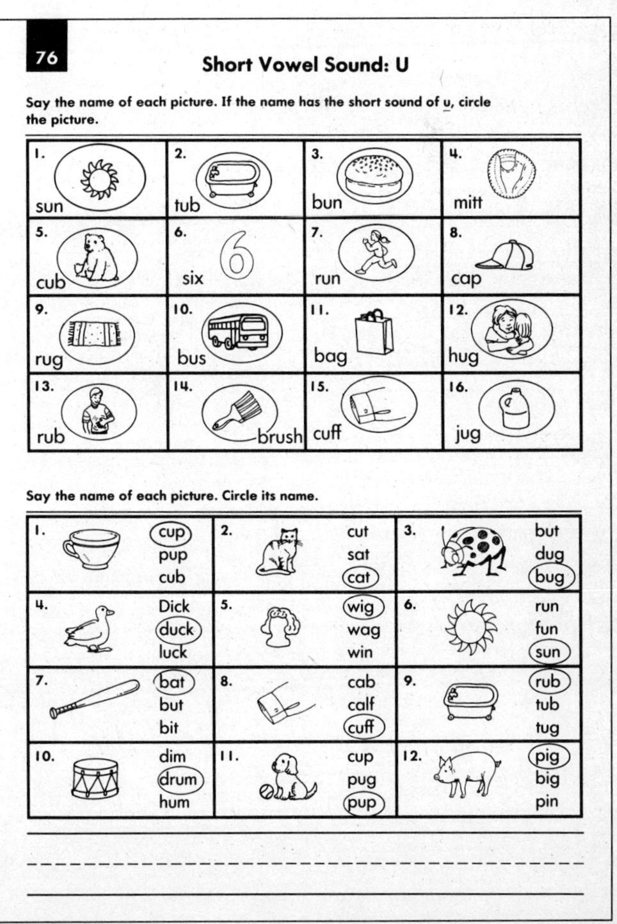
76

Short Vowel Sound: U

Say the name of each picture. If the name has the short sound of u, circle the picture.

1. sun	2. tub	3. bun	4. mitt
5. cub	6. six	7. run	8. cap
9. rug	10. bus	11. bag	12. hug
13. rub	14. brush	15. cuff	16. jug

Say the name of each picture. Circle its name.

1. cup pup cub	2. cut sat cat	3. but dug bug
4. Dick duck luck	5. wig wag win	6. run fun sun
7. bat but bit	8. cab calf cuff	9. rub tub tug
10. dim drum hum	11. cup pug pup	12. pig big pin

Writing Prepare a worksheet containing the incomplete words shown below, or write them on the chalkboard.

Ask the child to complete each word by adding the short vowel *U*.

s__n	*c__p*	*b__d*	*br__sh*
c__ff	*j__g*	*n__t*	*tr__ck*
t__b	*b__g*	*h__t*	*dr__m*

Write or display several short *U* words on the chalkboard. Encourage the child to use these words in short *U* puzzles. Draw the following puzzle formats on the chalkboard, or prepare these formats on a sheet of paper.

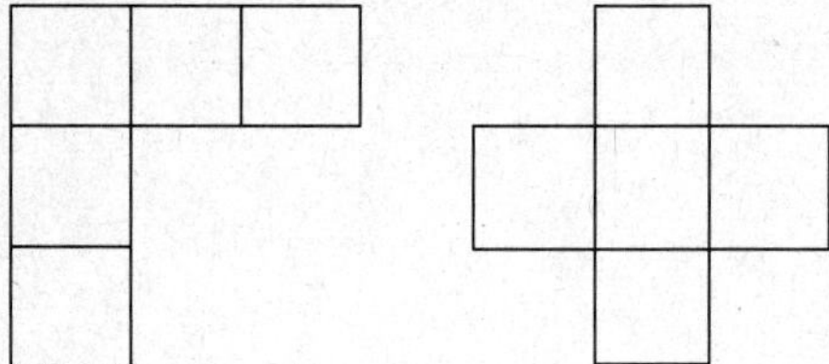

Direct the child to choose two words for each puzzle. Suggest that the child fill in some of the letters for each word but leave some boxes blank. Invite the child to share the puzzles by having other children fill in the blanks.

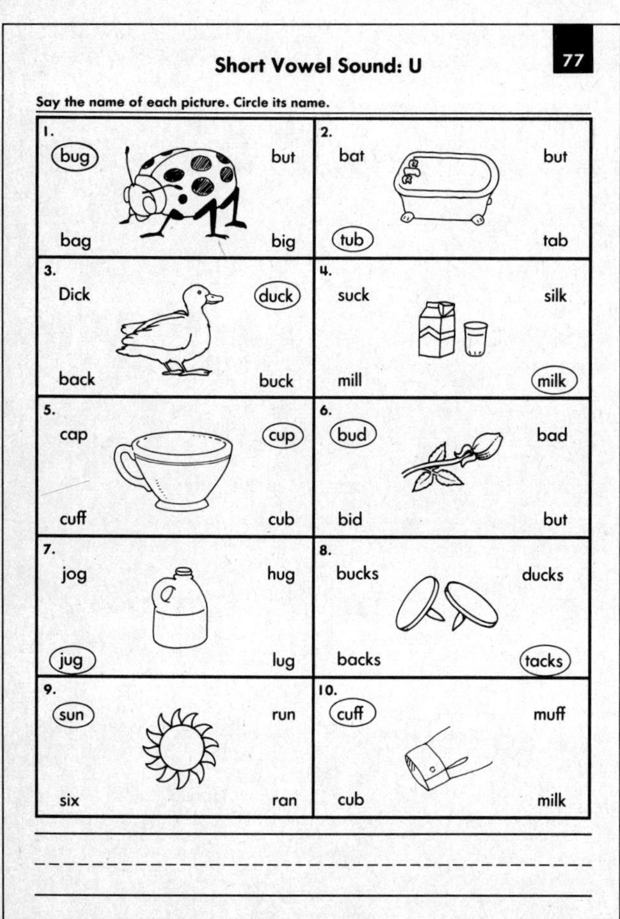

Short Vowel Sound: U 77

Say the name of each picture. Circle its name.

1. (bug) but bag big	2. bat but (tub) tab
3. Dick (duck) back buck	4. suck silk mill (milk)
5. cap (cup) cuff cub	6. (bud) bad bid but
7. jog hug (jug) lug	8. bucks ducks backs (tacks)
9. (sun) run six ran	10. (cuff) muff cub milk

Lesson 35

Short Vowel *U* (pages 78–79)

Objective The child will read short *A*, short *I*, and short *U* words in isolation and in sentences.

Review

Listening To reinforce auditory skills, challenge the children to identify beginning and ending consonants in sample words you recite. Display the words on word cards, or write them on the chalkboard. You may want to use the following words: *bag, lid, cup, hat, gum, tub, fan, pig.*

Teaching Ideas

Mail-a-Letter Game Distribute letter cards for short vowel words to the children. Set three boxes on a table or desk, or draw three boxes on the chalkboard. Print the letter *A* on the first box, *I* on the second, and *U* on the third. Invite each child to read the word on the card, identify the vowel and short vowel sound, and then "mail" the card by placing it in the appropriate box provided or under the drawing provided. You may wish to use the following words: *up, at, did, wig, but, is, ham, gas, fin, and, it, bus, fun.*

Speaking Write the vowels *A, I,* and *U* on separate tagboard circles. On the chalkboard, print each of the following incomplete words.

t__ck *h__t* *b__t*
b__d *h__m* *f__n*
b__g *s__ck* *b__n*

Hold up a vowel card in the blank space between the consonants of the word. Encourage the children to identify the vowel and vowel sound and to say the resulting word aloud. Repeat the activity for the second and third vowel sounds. Continue the process for each word.

Extension

Writing Give the child a sheet of paper with the following sentences on it.

1. *It is fun to run.*
2. *Cut the bun.*
3. *Puff is a cat.*
4. *Ann has the cup.*
5. *Jack is in the bus.*
6. *Run and jump.*

Ask the child to read the sentences aloud and to circle each word that contains the short *U* sound.

Art Encourage the child to look through newspapers and magazines for words with a short *U* sound. Ask the child to cut out the short *U* words and to paste them on a sheet of paper, writing the word below.

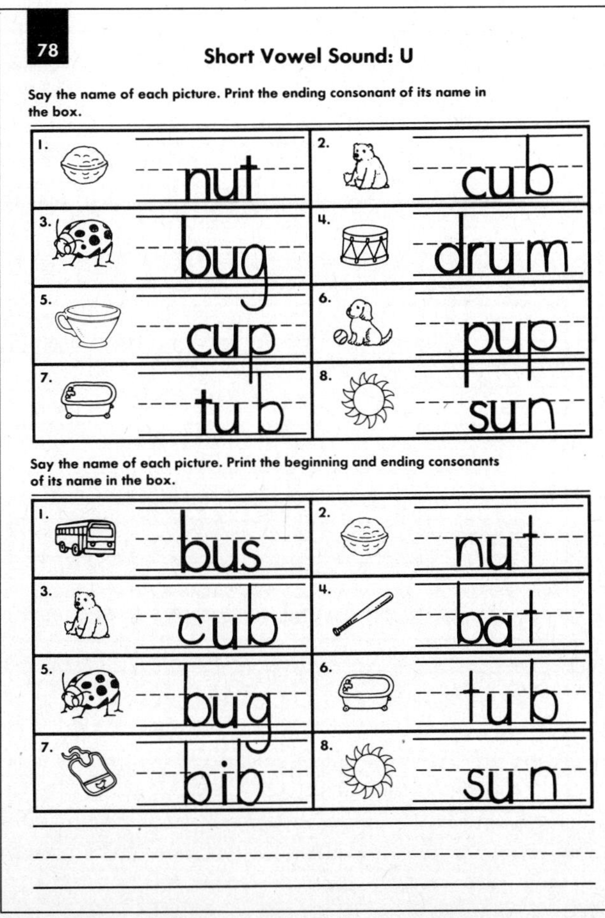

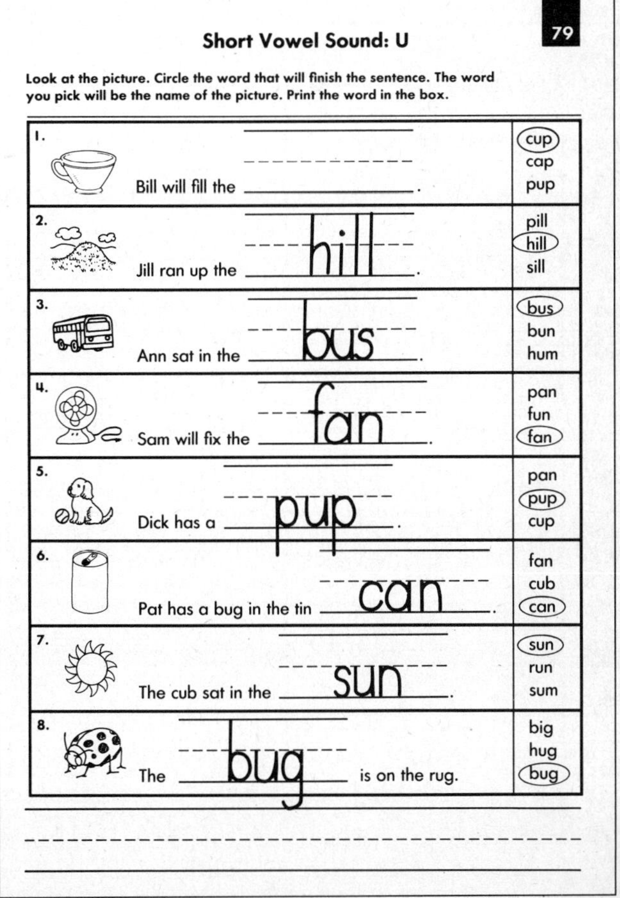

Lesson 36
Short Vowel *U* (pages 80–81)

Objective The child will apply the Short Vowel Rule when reading words with the short vowels *A*, *I*, and *U*.

Short Vowel Rule: If a word or syllable has only one vowel, and it comes at the beginning of the word or between two consonants, the vowel is usually short.

Teaching Ideas

Listening Say each of the following words aloud and ask the children to identify the short vowel sound: *mix, fan, pill, nut, tub, muff, pig, ran, cab, am.*

Speaking Write the following words in two columns on the chalkboard: *up, us, it, and; cup, pig, ran, nut.* Help the children recall the Short Vowel Rule by asking the following questions.

1. *Where do you see the vowels?*
2. *Does each vowel have a long sound or a short sound?*
3. *When does a vowel have a short sound?*

Encourage the children to state the Short Vowel Rule in their own words.

Writing Write the following sentences on the board.

1. The pup had fun.
2. Run in the mud.
3. Pick up the rug.
4. The duck is sick.
5. Crack the nut.
6. It is in the tub.

Invite volunteers, in turn, to read each sentence. Direct the children to circle the short *U* words in each sentence and to explain why the vowel sound is short.

Extension

Reading Encourage the child to identify short *U* words in stories. You may want to have the child select books from the classroom collection.

Art Make a list of familiar short *U* words, or display several picture flashcards for short *U* words. Encourage the child to create a picture composed of two short *U* words. For example, the child might draw a picture of a pup eating a nut. You might have the child write the short *U* words at the bottom of the picture.

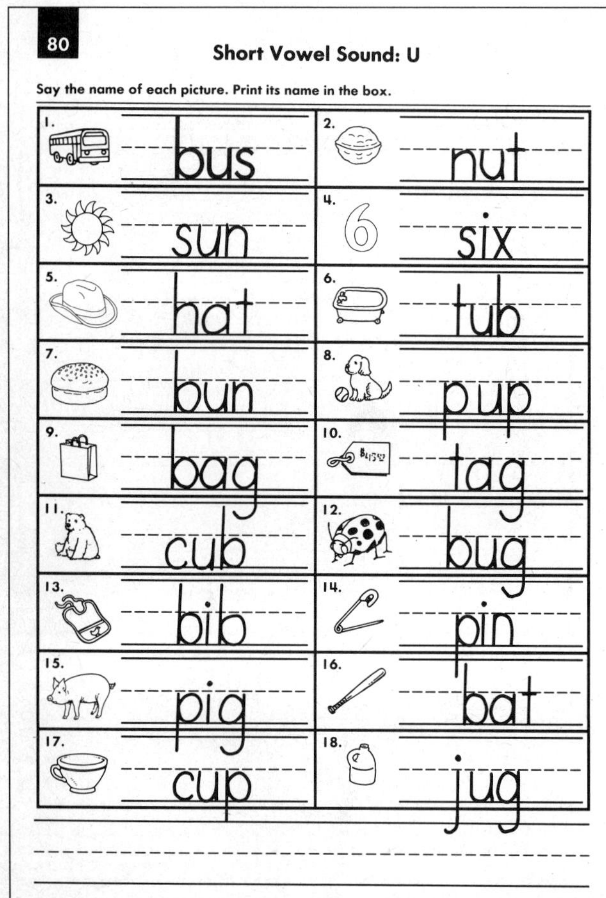
80

Short Vowel Sound: U

Say the name of each picture. Print its name in the box.

1. bus	2. nut
3. sun	4. six
5. hat	6. tub
7. bun	8. pup
9. bag	10. tag
11. cub	12. bug
13. bib	14. pin
15. pig	16. bat
17. cup	18. jug

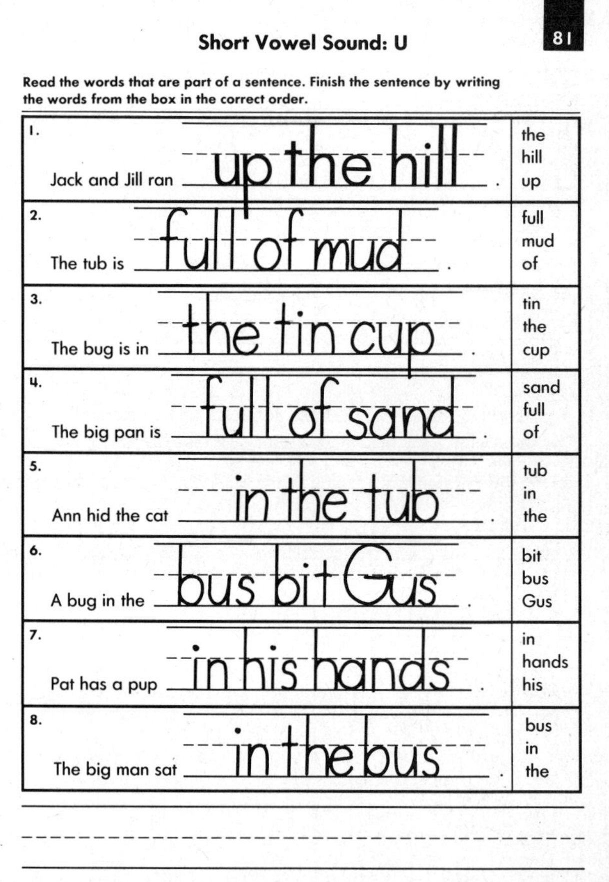
81

Short Vowel Sound: U

Read the words that are part of a sentence. Finish the sentence by writing the words from the box in the correct order.

1. Jack and Jill ran up the hill.	the hill up
2. The tub is full of mud.	full mud of
3. The bug is in the tin cup.	tin the cup
4. The big pan is full of sand.	sand full of
5. Ann hid the cat in the tub.	tub in the
6. A bug in the bus bit Gus.	bit bus Gus
7. Pat has a pup in his hands.	in hands his
8. The big man sat in the bus.	bus in the

Lesson 37
Short Vowel O (pages 82–84)

Objective The child will identify the letter *O* and its short vowel sound in isolation and in words.

Review

Speaking To review the vowel and consonant sounds, challenge the children to spell the following words aloud: *and, it, did, is, dad, cat, cup, up, us, at, sun.* For children who spell words incorrectly, provide the correct spellings and encourage them to repeat the correct spelling of the word.

Teaching Ideas

Listening Present a word card for the word *ox,* or print it on the chalkboard. Say the word for the children and ask them to repeat it. Point out the vowel, explaining to children that the vowel they hear is the sound of the short *O*. Repeat the activity with other short *O* words. You may wish to use the following words: *box, doll, rock, sock, pot, mop, lock.*

Speaking Present pictures or picture flashcards for each of the following short *O* words: *pot, top, box, rock, fox, doll, mop.* Invite volunteers, in turn, to identify the word each picture represents and to say the short *O* sound in each word.

Rhyming Game To develop recognition of the short *O* sound, play the Rhyming Game described in Lesson 34 in this unit. Write the key word *cot* on the chalkboard and ask the children to suggest short *O* words that rhyme. You might use the following key words: *sock, box, lot, mop, Bob.* If you wish to create an extension activity, challenge the children to use each of the words in a sentence.

Writing Write the following short *O* words on the chalkboard: *dock, box, hop, cob, rob, sob, mob, pop.* Encourage the children to circle the letter in each word that makes the short *O* sound.

Write the following words on the chalkboard: *sick, cub, lack, hit, pat, cat.* Challenge the children to erase the vowel in each word and to substitute the vowel *O* in its place. Then have the children say the newly created words aloud.

Extension

Art Encourage the child to create a picture book for a short *O* riddle. Direct the child to fold a large sheet of paper in half. Have the child write the letter *O* on the front page. On the inside, have the child draw a picture clue for a short *O* word, with a blank for each letter of the word beneath the picture. On the back page, have the child write the short *O* word for the picture in the book. Encourage the child to challenge the other children to solve the picture riddle. If the child has time to complete several picture riddles, you might want to staple

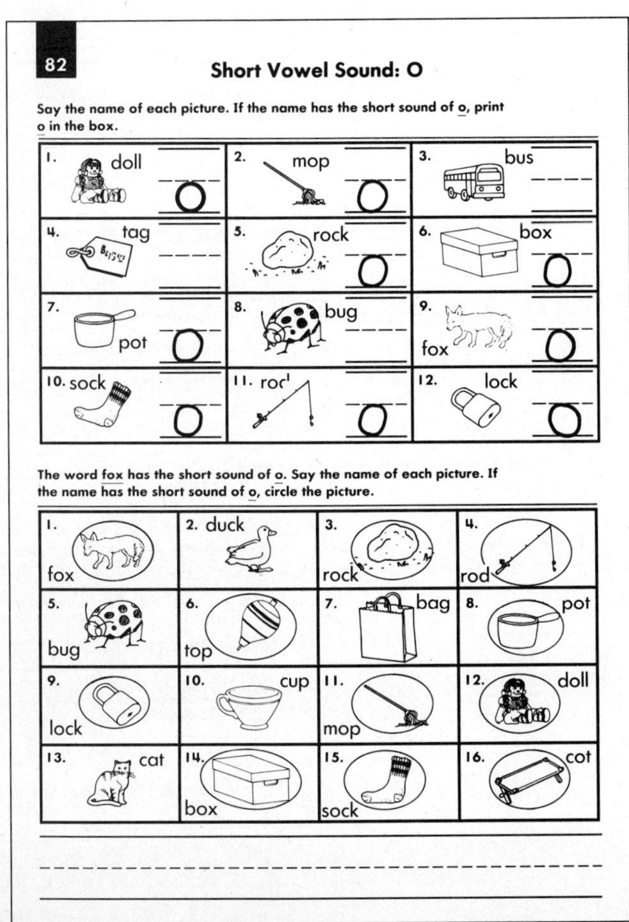

82

Short Vowel Sound: O

Say the name of each picture. If the name has the short sound of o, print o in the box.

1. doll o	2. mop o	3. bus
4. tag	5. rock o	6. box o
7. pot o	8. bug	9. fox o
10. sock o	11. rod o	12. lock o

The word fox has the short sound of o. Say the name of each picture. If the name has the short sound of o, circle the picture.

1. fox	2. duck	3. rock	4. rod
5. bug	6. top	7. bag	8. pot
9. lock	10. cup	11. mop	12. doll
13. cat	14. box	15. sock	16. cot

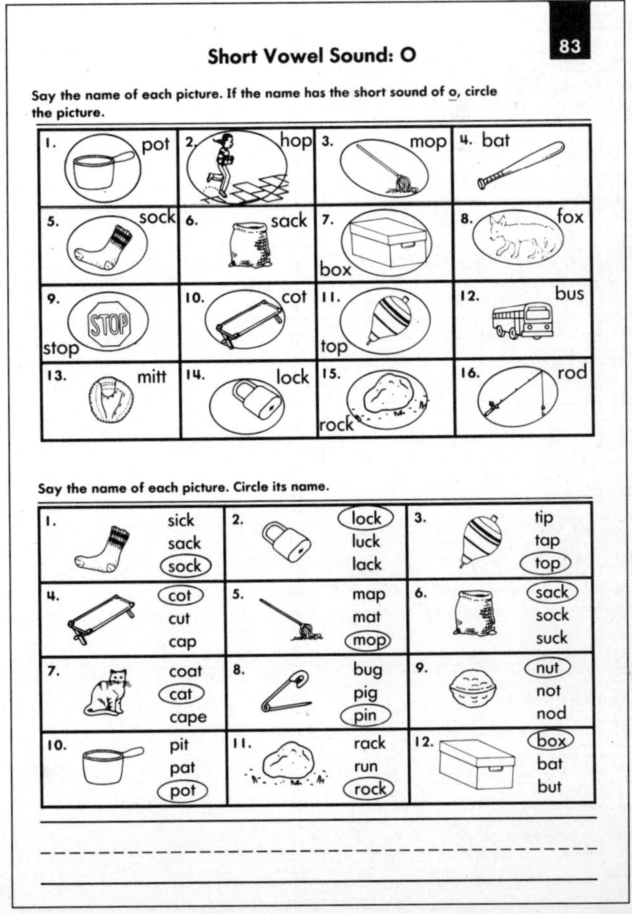

83

Short Vowel Sound: O

Say the name of each picture. If the name has the short sound of o, circle the picture.

1. pot	2. hop	3. mop	4. bat
5. sock	6. sack	7. box	8. fox
9. stop	10. cot	11. top	12. bus
13. mitt	14. lock	15. rock	16. rod

Say the name of each picture. Circle its name.

1. sick sack sock	2. lock luck lack	3. tip tap top
4. cot cut cap	5. map mat mop	6. sack sock suck
7. coat cat cape	8. bug pig pin	9. nut not nod
10. pit pat pot	11. rack run rock	12. box bat but

them together to form a large book. Acknowledge the creativity or design of the drawings.

To vary the activity, encourage the child to create rhyming clues. Print the words *Rhymes with* on the chalkboard and direct the child to copy those words onto the front page of the picture book. On the inside, have the child draw a picture clue for a short *O* word. On the back page, have the child write several short *O* words that rhyme with the name for the picture in the book. Encourage the child to include blank spaces on the inside page for each possible rhyming word. You might want to provide the child with a set of rhyming words, such as the words the children used in the Rhyming Game in this lesson.

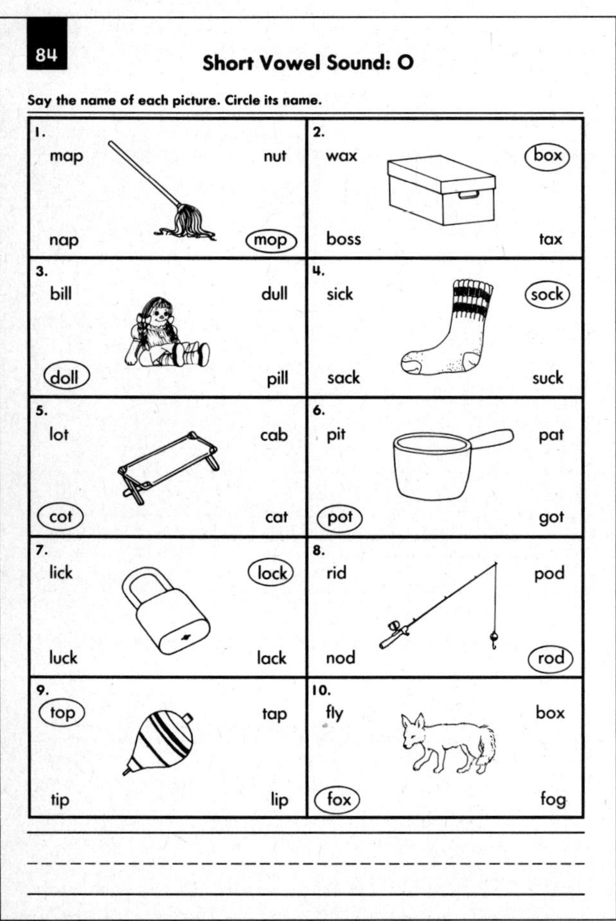
84

Short Vowel Sound: O

Say the name of each picture. Circle its name.

1.		2.	
map	nut	wax	(box)
nap	(mop)	boss	tax
3.		**4.**	
bill	dull	sick	(sock)
(doll)	pill	sack	suck
5.		**6.**	
lot	cab	pit	pat
(cot)	cat	(pot)	got
7.		**8.**	
lick	(lock)	rid	pod
luck	lack	nod	(rod)
9.		**10.**	
(top)	tap	fly	box
tip	lip	(fox)	fog

Lesson 38
Short Vowel *O* (pages 85–86)

Objective The child will read short *O* words in isolation and in sentences.

Review

Speaking To review vowel and consonant sounds, challenge the children to name the vowel and consonant sounds for words naming pictures. Display pictures or picture flashcards for each of the following words: *top, ox, box, ax, bib, cat, mop, tub, pig, map, hill.* Encourage the children to name each of the pictures and to write on the chalkboard the beginning consonant sound (if there is one), the short vowel sound, and the ending consonant sound for each of the pictures named.

Teaching Ideas

Listening Say aloud the following groups of three words, asking the children to identify the short *O* word in each group: *ask/ran/Bob, hip/doll/is, rock/bill/bug, dill/ox/rust, hop/hut/dull.*

Speaking Write the following short *O* words on the chalkboard: *top, cot, box, lock, ox, job, pop, sob, rob, mob.* Point to the words one at a time, encouraging volunteers to read each word and then to use it in a sentence.

To vary this activity, provide sentences that are missing the short *O* word. Challenge the children to supply the missing short *O* word from the words on the chalkboard.

Writing Write the following sentences on the chalkboard.

1. The sun is hot.	*5. Sit on the rock.*
2. Don has a top.	*6. The bun is hot.*
3. Tom got on the bus.	*7. Fix the lock.*
4. Dad got a job.	*8. Mom has the rod.*

Invite volunteers, in turn, to read each sentence and to circle the short *O* words. To check the children's understanding, ask a comprehension question about each sentence.

Extension

Writing Write the following words on the chalkboard: *pot, doll, fox, mom, lock, box, mop, dot.* Give the child a large sheet of paper that has been folded into four squares. Direct the child to write one of the words from the chalkboard in each of the four squares. Encourage the child to illustrate each word. Acknowledge the quality of the writing or the creativity of the drawings.

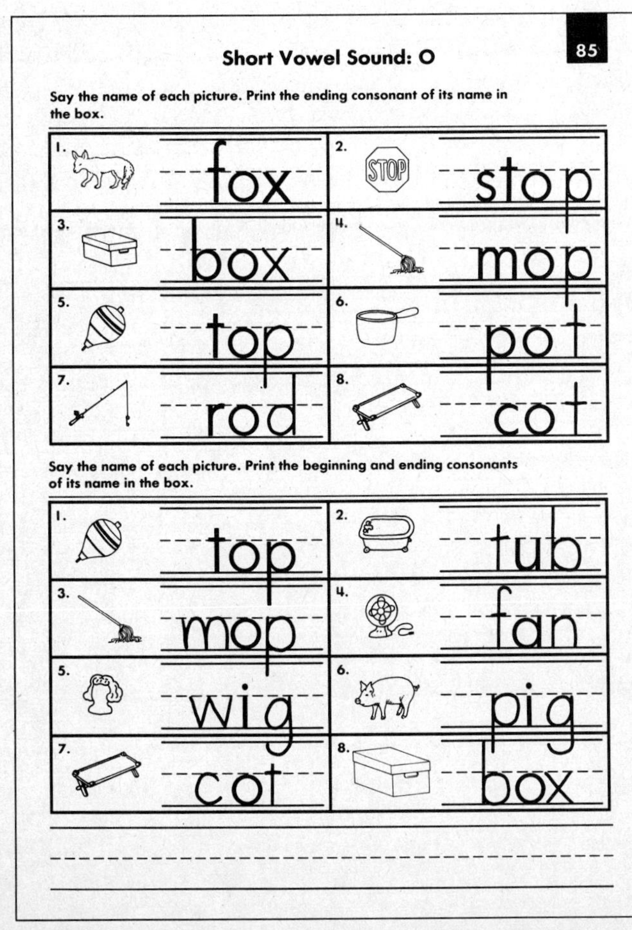
85

Short Vowel Sound: O

Say the name of each picture. Print the ending consonant of its name in the box.

1. fox
2. stop
3. box
4. mop
5. top
6. pot
7. rod
8. cot

Say the name of each picture. Print the beginning and ending consonants of its name in the box.

1. top
2. tub
3. mop
4. fan
5. wig
6. pig
7. cot
8. box

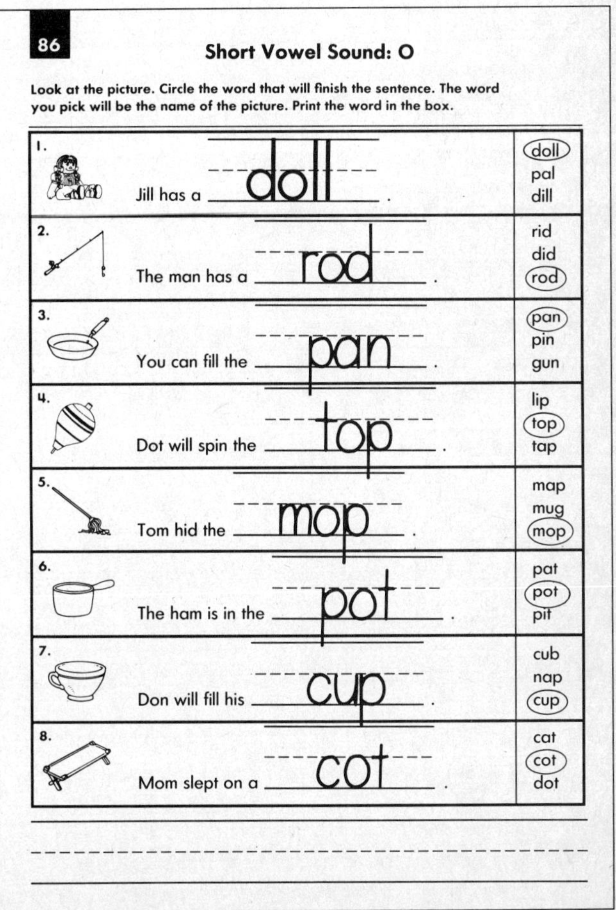
86

Short Vowel Sound: O

Look at the picture. Circle the word that will finish the sentence. The word you pick will be the name of the picture. Print the word in the box.

1. Jill has a doll. (doll, pal, dill)
2. The man has a rod. (rid, did, rod)
3. You can fill the pan. (pan, pin, gun)
4. Dot will spin the top. (lip, top, tap)
5. Tom hid the mop. (map, mug, mop)
6. The ham is in the pot. (pat, pot, pit)
7. Don will fill his cup. (cub, nap, cup)
8. Mom slept on a cot. (cat, cot, dot)

Lesson 39
Short Vowel *O* (pages 87–88)

Objective The child will apply the Short Vowel Rule to read short *O* words in isolation and in sentences.

Short Vowel Rule: If a word or syllable has only one vowel, and it comes at the beginning of the word or between two consonants, the vowel is usually short.

Review

Listening To practice recognition of short vowel sounds, ask the children to identify the vowel sound in each of the following words: *bad, cuff, mix, sick, rug, pill, dip, hop, fox, rust, lump, clock, lamp.* If you wish to provide further practice, encourage the children to name words that rhyme with each word presented.

Teaching Ideas

Writing Write the following words in two columns on the chalkboard: *ox, on, odd; got, doll, mop.* Encourage volunteers to read the words in the first column and to circle the short *O*. Repeat the procedure with the second column. Then reinforce the Short Vowel Rule by asking the following questions about the words on the chalkboard.

1. Where do you see the vowels in these words?
2. What is the sound of each vowel?
3. When does a vowel have a short sound?

Lead the children to state the Short Vowel Rule in their own words.

Write the following incomplete words on the chalkboard.

h__m   __n   b__x   p__p   h__t
b__d   __p   s__b   d__p   p__t

Invite volunteers, in turn, to write the letter *A, I, O,* or *U* in each space to create a word. Encourage the children to tell why the vowel in each word has a short sound.

Extension

Reading Encourage the child to identify short *O* words found in stories. You may want to have the child select books from the classroom collection.

Art Encourage the child to look through old newspapers and magazines for pictures of objects with names that contain the short *I* sound. Direct the child to cut out each picture and paste it onto tagboard or a large sheet of paper. You might want to display the child's poster at the front of the classroom.

87

Short Vowel Sound: O

Say the name of each picture. Print its name in the box.

1. fox	2. box
3. doll	4. mop
5. fan	6. cup
7. sun	8. wig
9. top	10. bug
11. cot	12. man
13. tag	14. pan
15. rod	16. six
17. rug	18. pot

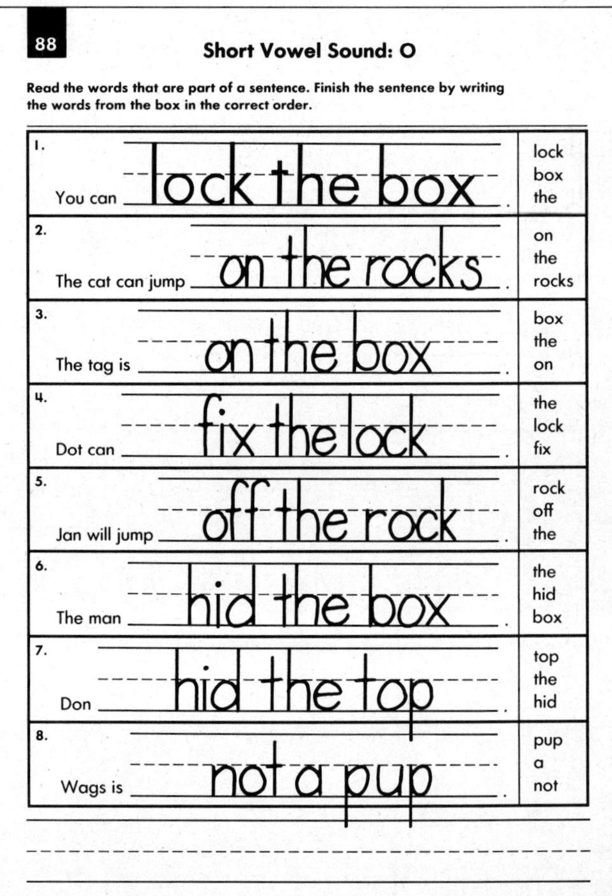

88

Short Vowel Sound: O

Read the words that are part of a sentence. Finish the sentence by writing the words from the box in the correct order.

1. You can lock the box.	lock box the
2. The cat can jump on the rocks.	on the rocks
3. The tag is on the box.	box the on
4. Dot can fix the lock.	the lock fix
5. Jan will jump off the rock.	rock off the
6. The man hid the box.	the hid box
7. Don hid the top.	top the hid
8. Wags is not a pup.	pup a not

Lesson 40

Short Vowel *E* (pages 89–91)

Objective The child will identify the letter *E* and its short vowel sound in isolation and in words.

Teaching Ideas

Listening Present a picture flashcard or photograph of a jet. Say the word *jet* aloud and ask the children to repeat the word. Encourage the children to identify the short *E* sound within the word.

Speaking Display a series of pictures or picture flashcards with names that contain the sound of short *E*. Encourage the children to identify each picture by naming the appropriate short *E* word. You might want to use pictures of the following objects: *pen, bed, net, well, tent, bell, jet, web, desk, sled.* Keep the display for the next activity.

Use the pictures from the previous activity to help the children use short *E* words in sentences. Invite individual volunteers to take pictures or picture flashcards from the front of the classroom. Have them name the pictures and then use the words in sentences. Encourage the children to use the words in the proper context.

Rhyming Game To develop discrimination of the short *E* sound, you may wish to play the Rhyming Game described in Lesson 34 in this unit. Print the following key words in a row on the chalkboard: *bell, bet, ten.* Encourage children who give incorrect answers by pointing out similarities between their answers and actual rhyming words. List the correct responses under the key word *bell.* Continue the activity with each of the key words on the chalkboard.

Writing Write the following short *E* words on the chalkboard: *pet, pen, jet, send, bell, web, vet, fed, set, red, Ned.* Invite volunteers to circle the letter in each word that makes the short *E* sound.

Circle-the-Word Game For this activity, set aside pictures or picture flashcards for the following words: *web, bell, jet, bed, net, ten, hen, desk.* Tape one of the pictures or picture flashcards to the chalkboard and draw a large square around it. Write the correct name for the picture in one corner of the square and incorrect names in each of the other three corners. Encourage a volunteer to identify the picture and to circle its correct name. Continue the activity with the other pictures.

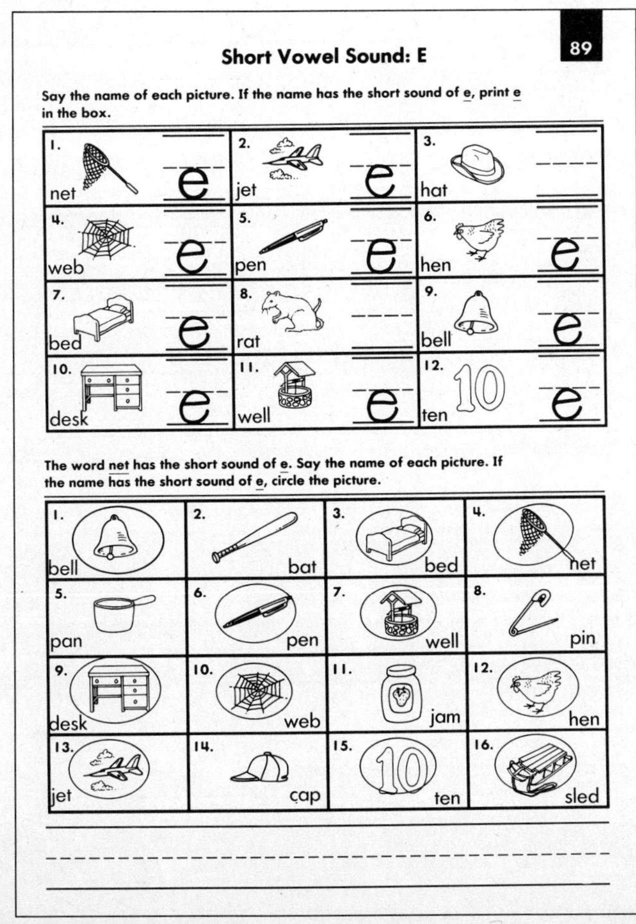
89

Short Vowel Sound: E

Say the name of each picture. If the name has the short sound of e, print e in the box.

1. net e	2. jet e	3. hat
4. web e	5. pen e	6. hen e
7. bed e	8. rat	9. bell e
10. desk e	11. well e	12. ten e

The word net has the short sound of e. Say the name of each picture. If the name has the short sound of e, circle the picture.

1. bell	2. bat	3. bed	4. net
5. pan	6. pen	7. well	8. pin
9. desk	10. web	11. jam	12. hen
13. jet	14. cap	15. ten	16. sled

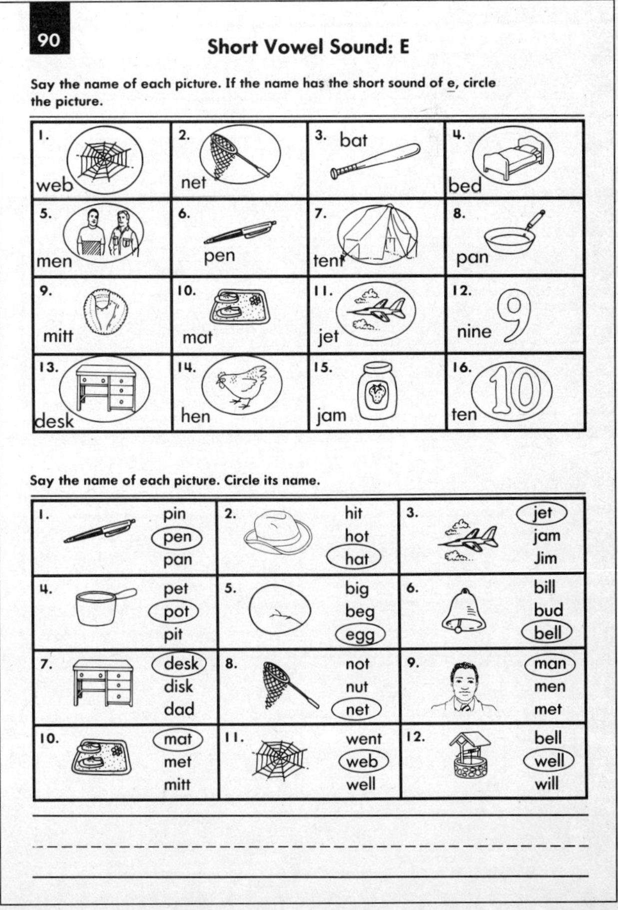
90

Short Vowel Sound: E

Say the name of each picture. If the name has the short sound of e, circle the picture.

1. web	2. net	3. bat	4. bed
5. men	6. pen	7. tent	8. pan
9. mitt	10. mat	11. jet	12. nine
13. desk	14. hen	15. jam	16. ten

Say the name of each picture. Circle its name.

1. pin pen pan	2. hit hot hat	3. jet jam Jim
4. pet pot pit	5. big beg egg	6. bill bud bell
7. desk disk dad	8. not nut net	9. man men met
10. mat met mitt	11. went web well	12. bell well will

Extension

Art Have the child choose two rhyming words from the following columns and draw a picture about them.

vet	*bent*	*wet*	*best*	*red*
met	*tent*	*jet*	*nest*	*sled*
pet	*dent*		*rest*	

You might suggest that the child write the words at the bottom of the drawing.

Writing The child might enjoy writing sentences that contain words with the short vowel *E*. List the following words in random order on the chalkboard: *vent, wet, pest, red, vest, sled, bed, jet, bell, pet, sell, tent, met, nest, rest, dent, best.* Direct the child to write sentences using short *E* words.

To increase the challenge of the activity, encourage the child to write sentences that contain short *E* rhymes. Assure the child that the sentences can be either serious or silly.

Write the following incomplete words on the chalkboard.

*m*__*n* *b*__*ll* *t*__*n* *p*__*t*
*b*__*d* *w*__*t* *f*__*ll* *h*__*m*

Direct the child to write the letter *E* in the blank to complete each word. Encourage the child to read each word aloud.

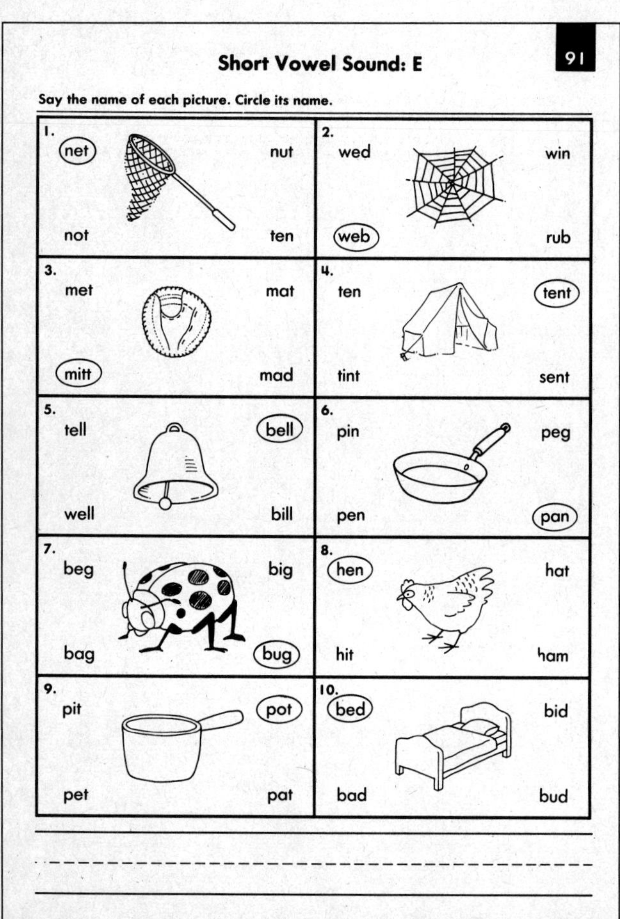

91

Short Vowel Sound: E

Say the name of each picture. Circle its name.

1. net, nut, not, ten
2. wed, win, web, rub
3. met, mat, mitt, mad
4. ten, tent, tint, sent
5. tell, bell, well, bill
6. pin, peg, pen, pan
7. beg, big, bag, bug
8. hen, hat, hit, ham
9. pit, pot, pet, pat
10. bed, bid, bad, bud

Lesson 41

Short Vowel *E* (pages 92–93)

Objective The child will read short *E* words in isolation and in sentences.

Review

Listening To reinforce auditory skills, challenge the children to identify the beginning, middle, and ending consonants in the following words: *camel, butter, never, hotel, dinner, water, final.*

Teaching Ideas

Listening Pronounce each of the following groups of three words, asking the children to identify the short *E* word in each: *red/rid/rod, bill/bell/bull, pick/pack/peck, hem/him/hum.* To add an extension activity, challenge the children to spell the short *E* words.

Speaking Prepare and distribute a sheet of paper with the following sentences on it, or write the sentences on the chalkboard.

1. *Jack is in a bed.*
2. *Let Ann run.*
3. *The mop is wet.*
4. *Ted will run next.*
5. *Get up, Jack.*
6. *The pen is red.*
7. *Jim fed his pet.*
8. *Get ten cups.*

Read the sentences aloud with the children. Invite volunteers to identify the short *E* words in each sentence. Suggest that the children circle the short *E* words in each sentence.

Writing Write the following words on the chalkboard: *lot, pin, tint, pun, bad, not, ball, jot.* Have the children erase the vowel in each word and substitute the vowel *E*. Encourage children to read the resulting words aloud.

Extension

Art Provide the child with a copy of the following story.

Ed and His Pig

Ed has a pig.
It has six spots.
The pig can run in the pen.
The pen has mud.
The pig can dig in the mud.
It has fun in the mess.

Direct the child to read the story silently. Encourage the child to illustrate the story with one or more drawings. You might want to staple the pictures together to create a book.

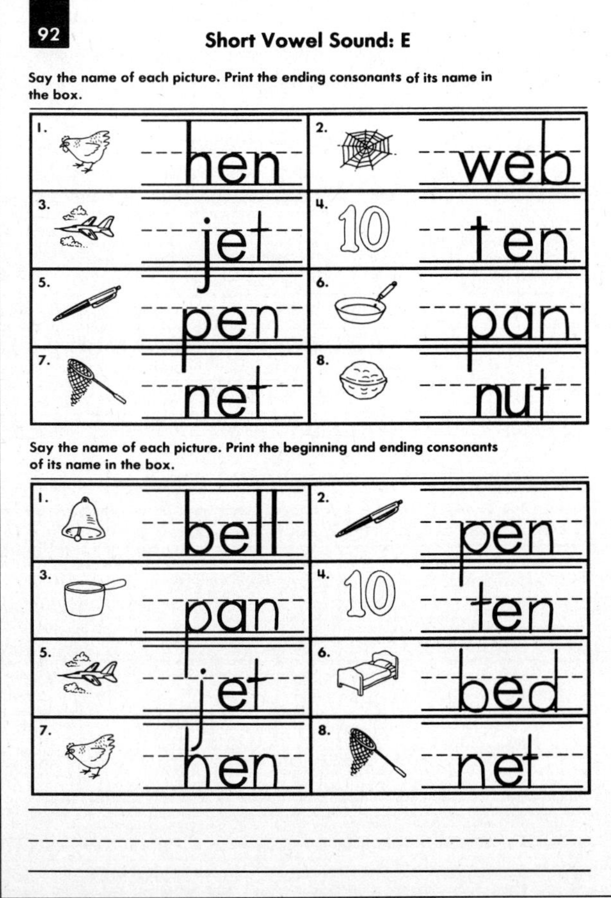

92

Short Vowel Sound: E

Say the name of each picture. Print the ending consonants of its name in the box.

1. hen
2. web
3. jet
4. ten
5. pen
6. pan
7. net
8. nut

Say the name of each picture. Print the beginning and ending consonants of its name in the box.

1. bell
2. pen
3. pan
4. ten
5. jet
6. bed
7. hen
8. net

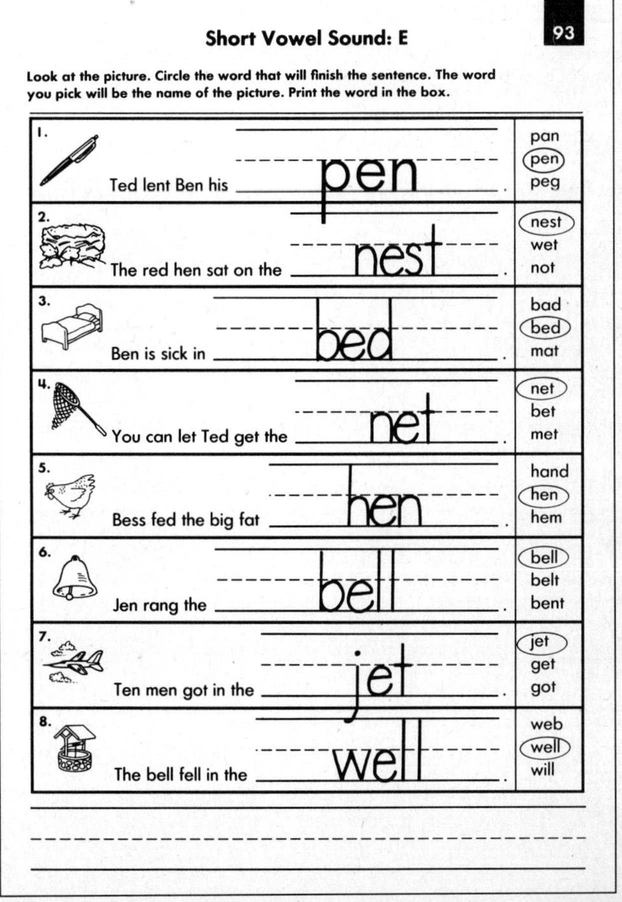

93

Short Vowel Sound: E

Look at the picture. Circle the word that will finish the sentence. The word you pick will be the name of the picture. Print the word in the box.

1. Ted lent Ben his pen. — pan / (pen) / peg
2. The red hen sat on the nest. — (nest) / wet / not
3. Ben is sick in bed. — bad / (bed) / mat
4. You can let Ted get the net. — (net) / bet / met
5. Bess fed the big fat hen. — hand / (hen) / hem
6. Jen rang the bell. — (bell) / belt / bent
7. Ten men got in the jet. — (jet) / get / got
8. The bell fell in the well. — web / (well) / will

Lesson 42
Short Vowel *E* (pages 94–96)

Objective The child will apply the Short Vowel Rule by reading short *E* words in isolation and within sentences.

Short Vowel Rule: If a word or syllable has only one vowel, and it comes at the beginning of the word or between two consonants, the vowel is usually short.

Review

Speaking To review auditory skills, challenge children to say and spell words with short vowel sounds. Display pictures or picture flashcards for the following words: *bed, cat, top, cup, pin, bed, fish, belt, pan, desk, box, jet, wig, sun.* Encourage the children to name the word for each picture and then to spell it. Invite the children to identify the vowel sound in each word they spell.

Teaching Ideas

Writing Write the following words in two columns on the chalkboard: *wet, red, Ed; bed, pet, ten.* Invite volunteers to read the words in the first column and circle each short *E*. Repeat the procedure with the words in the second column. Then reinforce the Short Vowel Rule by asking the following questions about the words on the chalkboard.

1. *Where do you see the vowels in these words?*
2. *What is the sound of each vowel?*
3. *When does a vowel have a short sound?*

Lead the children to state the Short Vowel Rule in their own words.

Write the following sentences on the chalkboard, using blanks to represent missing letters.

1. *Ed will t __ ll Ted.*
2. *Get the w __ t rag.*
3. *The red h __ n will run.*
4. *Ted f __ d ten cats.*
5. *The j __ t was big.*
6. *The bug spun a w __ b.*

Invite volunteers, in turn, to fill in the missing letter *E* in each sentence and then to read the sentence aloud. Then encourage the children to circle all the short *E* words in each sentence and to tell why the vowels have a short sound.

Riddle Game You might play the Riddle Game, described in Lesson 31 in this unit, using the following short *E* words on cards: *bent, wet, ten, belt, send, set, pen, bed.* Invitc volunteers, in turn, to select a card from the stack and to read it silently. Encourage the children to create word riddles for the other children. To provide an example, choose a short *E* word such as *nest* and say the following: *I am thinking of a*

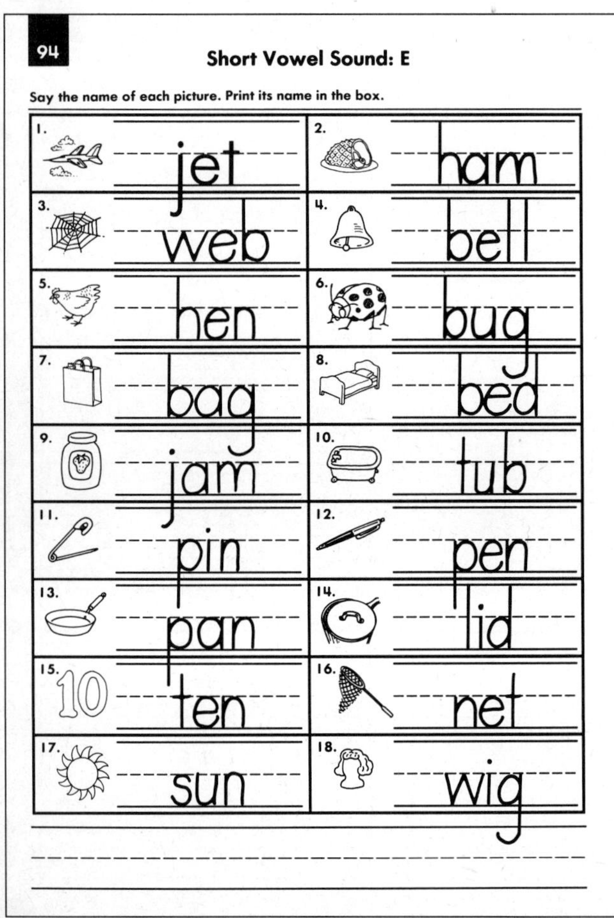
94

Short Vowel Sound: E

Say the name of each picture. Print its name in the box.

1. jet	2. ham
3. web	4. bell
5. hen	6. bug
7. bag	8. bed
9. jam	10. tub
11. pin	12. pen
13. pan	14. lid
15. ten	16. net
17. sun	18. wig

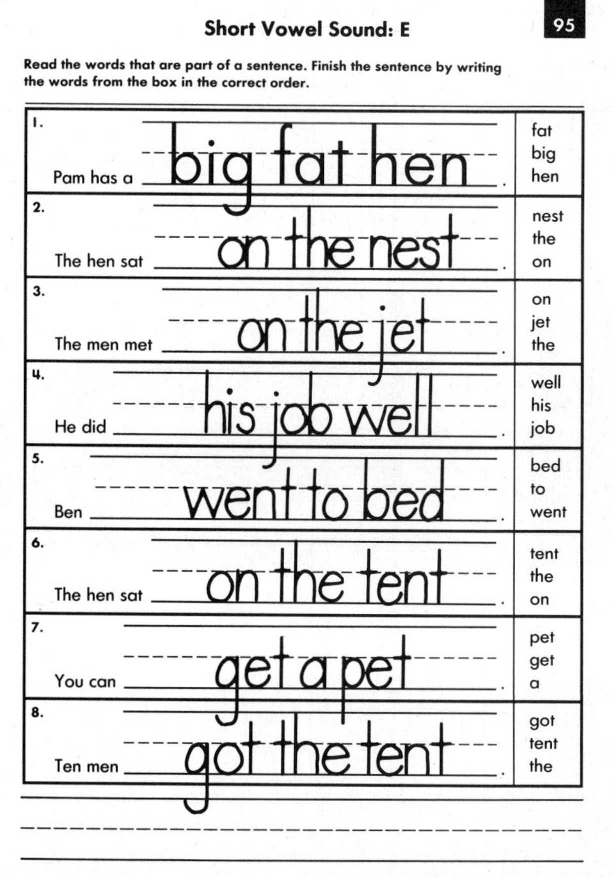
Short Vowel Sound: E

95

Read the words that are part of a sentence. Finish the sentence by writing the words from the box in the correct order.

1. Pam has a big fat hen.	fat big hen
2. The hen sat on the nest.	nest the on
3. The men met on the jet.	on jet the
4. He did his job well.	well his job
5. Ben went to bed.	bed to went
6. The hen sat on the tent.	tent the on
7. You can get a pet.	pet get a
8. Ten men got the tent.	got tent the

home for baby birds. It contains the short E *sound and begins with the letter* N. *What is it?* Encourage the children to guess the answer to each riddle. Invite children who guess correctly to write the short *E* words on the chalkboard.

Extension

Writing Write the following pairs of words on the chalkboard: *red/hen, bent/sled, sell/pet, bell/fell.* Give the child a large sheet of paper that has been folded into four squares. Direct the child to choose one set of words for each square and to print those words in the square. Encourage the child to illustrate each set of words.

Write the following words on the chalkboard: *hat, bell, rid, pan, and, left, is, yet, mill, get, pick, deck, end.* Direct the child to look at the words and to identify the short vowel in each. Encourage the child to write each word on a sheet of paper and to circle the short vowel sound.

Art Ask the child to cut words with short vowel sounds from magazines. Direct the child to group the words by vowel sound. Then ask the child to paste each group of words on a separate sheet of paper.

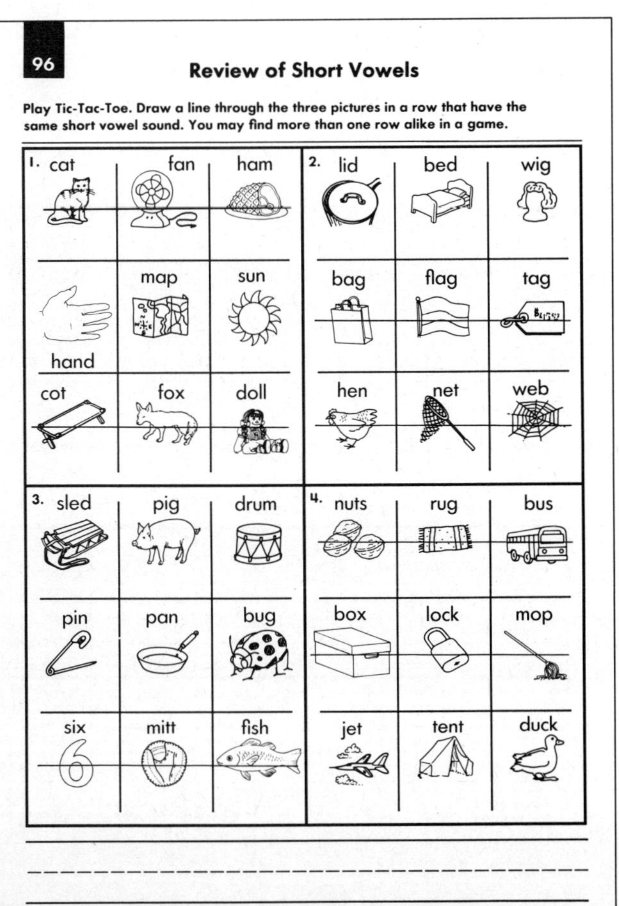

96

Review of Short Vowels

Play Tic-Tac-Toe. Draw a line through the three pictures in a row that have the same short vowel sound. You may find more than one row alike in a game.

1.			2.		
cat	fan	ham	lid	bed	wig
hand	map	sun	bag	flag	tag
cot	fox	doll	hen	net	web
3.			**4.**		
sled	pig	drum	nuts	rug	bus
pin	pan	bug	box	lock	mop
six	mitt	fish	jet	tent	duck

Unit 4 Long Vowels; Suffixes

Lesson 43

Long Vowel *A* (pages 97–100)

Objective The child will identify and read words containing the sound of long *A*.

Long Vowel Rule 1: If one syllable has two vowels, the first vowel is usually long and the second is usually silent.

Teaching Ideas

Listening Display a picture flashcard for the word *cake,* or show the children an actual cake to share. Ask children to name the picture or object and to identify the vowel sound. Explain to the children that the sound they hear is long vowel *A*. To reinforce the children's letter/sound association, print the word *cake* on the chalkboard and circle the letter *A*.

Display pictures or picture flashcards for the following words: *lake, tape, gate, cape, vase.* Invite volunteers to identify the pictures and to repeat the long sound of *A* in each word. Introduce Long Vowel Rule 1 by asking the following questions.

1. *How many vowels do you see in each word?*
2. *What is the first vowel?*
3. *Does the first vowel have a long sound or a short sound?*
4. *What is the second vowel? Does the second vowel make a sound?*

Lead the children to conclude that the first vowel in each word has a long vowel sound and that the second vowel is silent. You might need to explain the meaning of the word *silent*. Encourage the children to state Long Vowel Rule 1 in their own words.

Speaking Develop the children's understanding of the long *A* sound through a series of rhyming words. Write the key word *rake* on the chalkboard and say it aloud. Ask the children to suggest words that rhyme with *rake,* such as the following: *cake, bake, lake, make, sake.* Write the words on the chalkboard as the children say them. Continue the activity using the words *came, gave,* and *ate*. To check the children's comprehension, challenge them to use each of the words in a sentence.

Write the following pairs of words on the chalkboard: *cap/cape, ran/rain, can/cane, pan/pane, at/ate, tap/tape.* Invite volunteers, in turn, to read each pair of words and to explain why the letter *A* has a short sound in the first word but a long sound in the second.

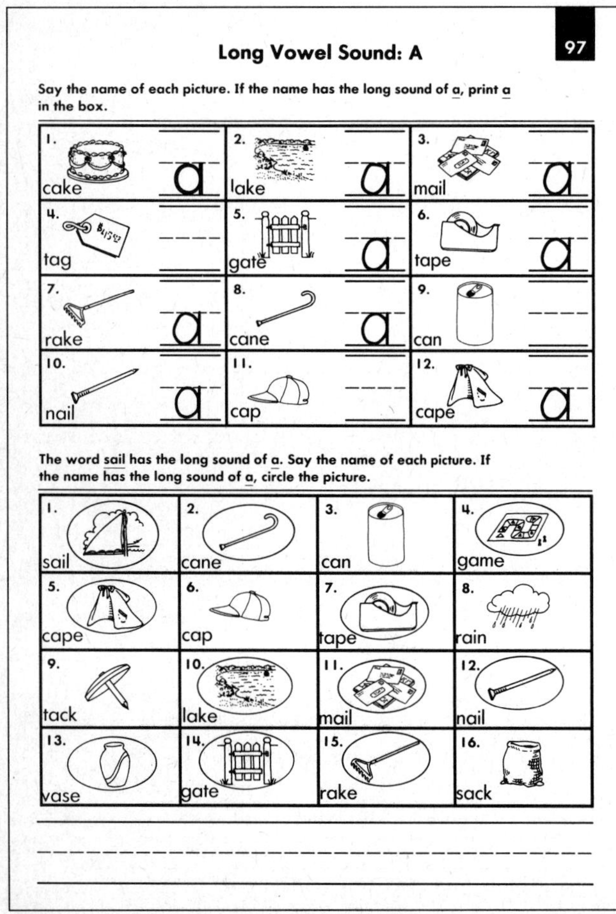

Long Vowel Sound: A 97

Say the name of each picture. If the name has the long sound of a, print a in the box.

1. cake — a	2. lake — a	3. mail — a
4. tag	5. gate — a	6. tape — a
7. rake — a	8. cane — a	9. can
10. nail — a	11. cap	12. cape — a

The word sail has the long sound of a. Say the name of each picture. If the name has the long sound of a, circle the picture.

1. sail	2. cane	3. can	4. game
5. cape	6. cap	7. tape	8. rain
9. tack	10. lake	11. mail	12. nail
13. vase	14. gate	15. rake	16. sack

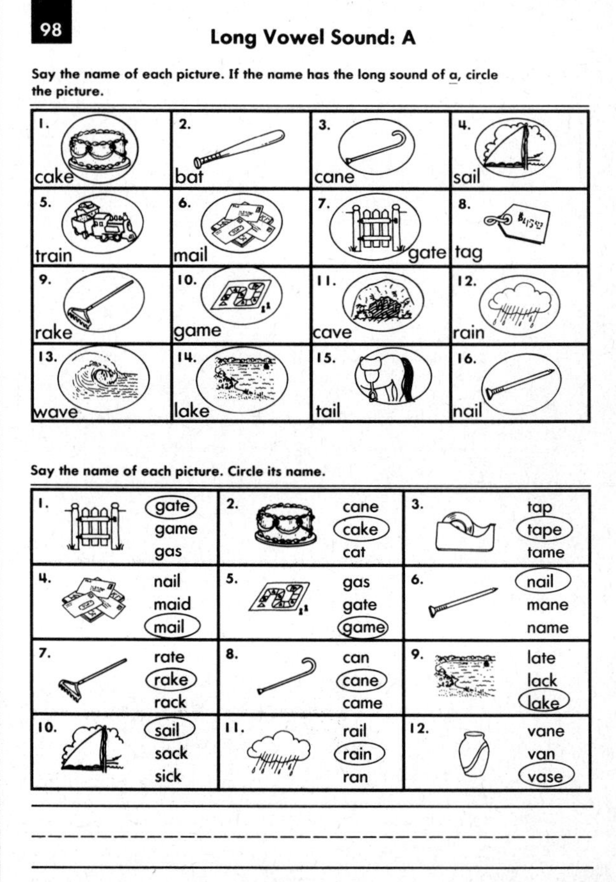

98 **Long Vowel Sound: A**

Say the name of each picture. If the name has the long sound of a, circle the picture.

1. cake	2. bat	3. cane	4. sail
5. train	6. mail	7. gate	8. tag
9. rake	10. game	11. cave	12. rain
13. wave	14. lake	15. tail	16. nail

Say the name of each picture. Circle its name.

1. gate / game / gas	2. cane / cake / cat	3. tap / tape / tame
4. nail / maid / mail	5. gas / gate / game	6. nail / mane / name
7. rate / rake / rack	8. can / cane / came	9. late / lack / lake
10. sail / sack / sick	11. rail / rain / ran	12. vane / van / vase

Extension

Writing Develop the child's awareness of how the silent *e* changes a short vowel sound to a long vowel sound. Write the following short *A* words in a column on a sheet of paper or on the chalkboard: *man, cap, can, pan, at, hat, rat.* Direct the child to add a silent *e* to the end of each word. Point out that the silent *e* changes each word from a short vowel word to a long vowel word. Have the child read aloud the new words that have been created.

Art Write the following sentences on the chalkboard: *Sam ate the cake. Mom has a cape.* Have the child copy the sentences on a sheet of paper. Encourage the child to circle the long *A* word or words in each sentence. Then ask the child to illustrate the sentences. You might want to display the child's work at the front of the classroom.

Reading Encourage the child to identify long *A* words in stories. You may have the child select books from the classroom collection or from the school library.

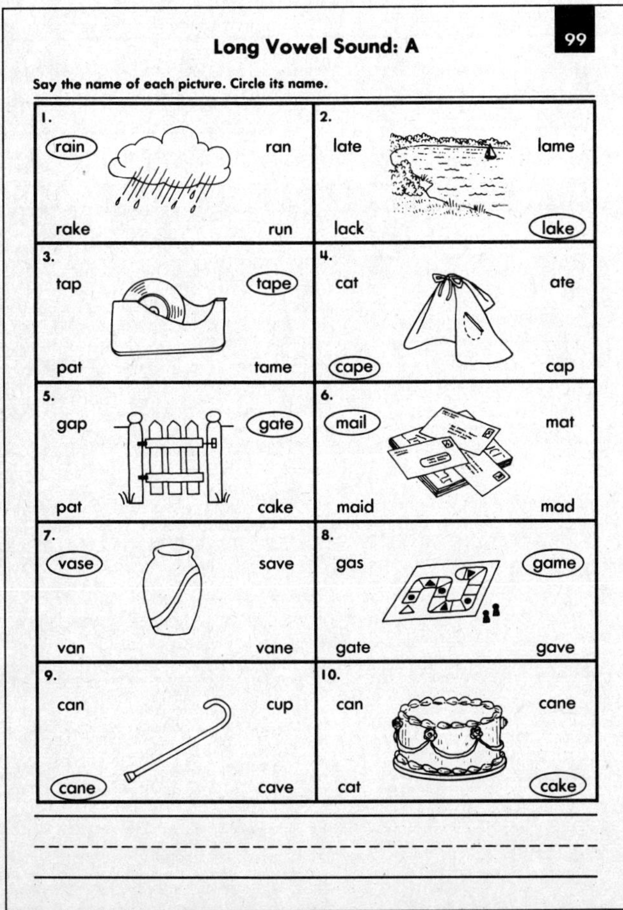

99

Long Vowel Sound: A

Say the name of each picture. Circle its name.

1. rain ran rake run
2. late lame lack lake
3. tap tape pat tame
4. cat ate cape cap
5. gap gate pat cake
6. mail mat maid mad
7. vase save van vane
8. gas game gate gave
9. can cup cane cave
10. can cane cat cake

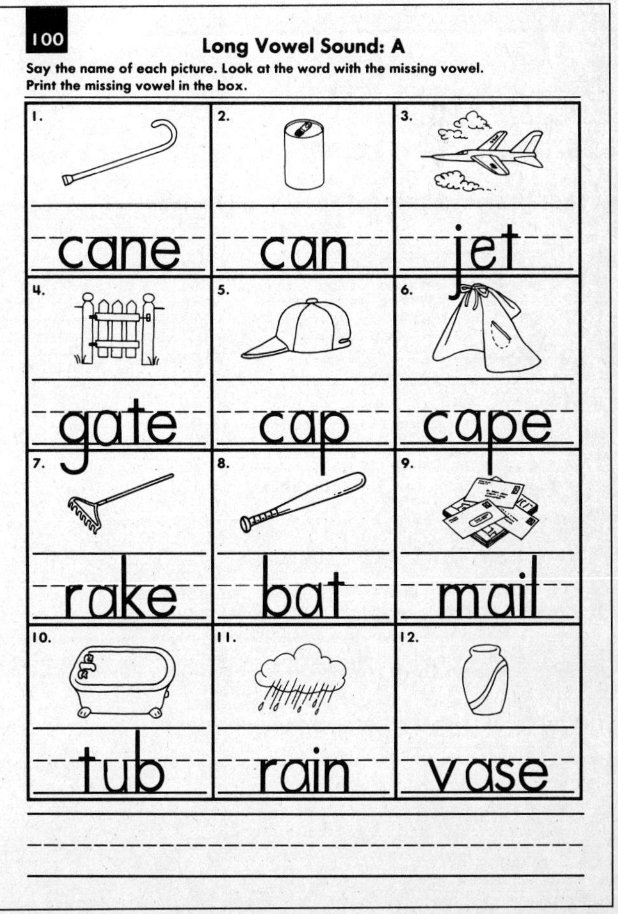

100

Long Vowel Sound: A

Say the name of each picture. Look at the word with the missing vowel. Print the missing vowel in the box.

1. cane
2. can
3. jet
4. gate
5. cap
6. cape
7. rake
8. bat
9. mail
10. tub
11. rain
12. vase

Lesson 44

Long Vowel A (page 101)

Objective The child will read long *A* words in isolation or in sentences.

Teaching Ideas

Listening Pronounce the following words: *base, cat, bat, name, fail, make, lap, mat, at, ate, date.* Invite volunteers to tell whether each word has a long vowel sound or a short vowel sound. To create an extension activity, encourage the children to use each word in a sentence.

Writing Write the following sentences on the chalkboard.

1. Kate can bake a cake.	*5. Kim ate an egg.*
2. The mail came late.	*6. The man has a cane.*
3. His name is Dave.	*7. Dan wades in the lake.*
4. Tex has a sand pail.	*8. Ann made a red cape.*

Ask volunteers, in turn, to circle the long *A* words in each sentence and to tell why the letter *A* has a long sound in those words.

Long Vowel Sound: A 101

Look at the picture. Circle the word that will finish the sentence. The word you pick will be the name of the picture. Print the word in the box.

	Sentence	Answer	Choices
1.	Dad gave Abe a ____.	game	(game) gave gas
2.	You can bake a ____.	cake	cat (cake) cane
3.	The box came in the ____.	mail	maid (mail) nail
4.	The dog will wag its ____.	tail	(tail) take tag
5.	Jill got wet in the ____.	rain	ran (rain) rake
6.	Sam hid in the ____.	cave	came cake (cave)
7.	Kate has a red ____.	cape	(cape) cake can
8.	Dad paid the man to ____.	rake	rack (rake) rain

Extension

Art Write the following pairs of words on the chalkboard: *cat/cave, ran/rain, sat/gate.* Encourage the child to read each pair of words aloud and to choose one to illustrate.

Lesson 45

Long Vowel A (pages 102–103)

Objective The child will read long *A* words in isolation and in sentences.

Review

Giant-Step Game To practice recognition of long *A* and short *A* words, play the Giant-Step Game. Tape parallel lines on the floor, two feet apart, for a total distance of twelve feet. Designate the first line as the starting line and the last line as the goal line. While you stand at the goal line, invite the children to stand at the starting line. Say one of the following words and ask each child to identify the vowel sound as the sound of short *A* or long *A: cat, Dave, pan, sale, lack, Kate, sand, Dan, fan, cane*. Permit children who identify the sound correctly to step to the first line. Continue the game by reinforcing each correct response with advancement toward the goal. Play the game until each child has reached the goal.

Teaching Ideas

Speaking Write the following words on the chalkboard: *cake, gate, tape, rain, nail, rake, sail, lake*. Create riddles and challenge the children to answer them by choosing one of the long *A* words on the chalkboard. For example, for the word *cake* you might repeat the following riddle: *I am thinking of a long* A *word for a treat we eat on birthdays. What is it?* To provide an extension activity, ask the children to spell the words they guess correctly.

Dueling-Rhymes Game Divide the class into two teams. Tell the children to listen to each long *A* word you say and then have the children offer rhyming words. Explain that the teams will earn a point for each rhyming word they suggest. Point out that the team with the most points will win the game. Begin the first round by pronouncing the word *cake*. Encourage volunteers from each team to suggest words that rhyme with *cake*. Call on the children one at a time, alternating between teams. Permit the team that wins the first round to begin the second round. Continue the game with the following words: *game, mail, rate,* and *gain*.

Extension

Writing Write the following long *A* words on the chalkboard or at the top of a sheet of paper: *pail, bake, lake, game*. Then write the following incomplete sentences.

1. *Jim had a sand* ________ .
2. *I will* ________ *a cake.*
3. *Play the* ________ .
4. *Sam swims in the* ________ .

Encourage the child to choose one long *A* word to complete each sentence.

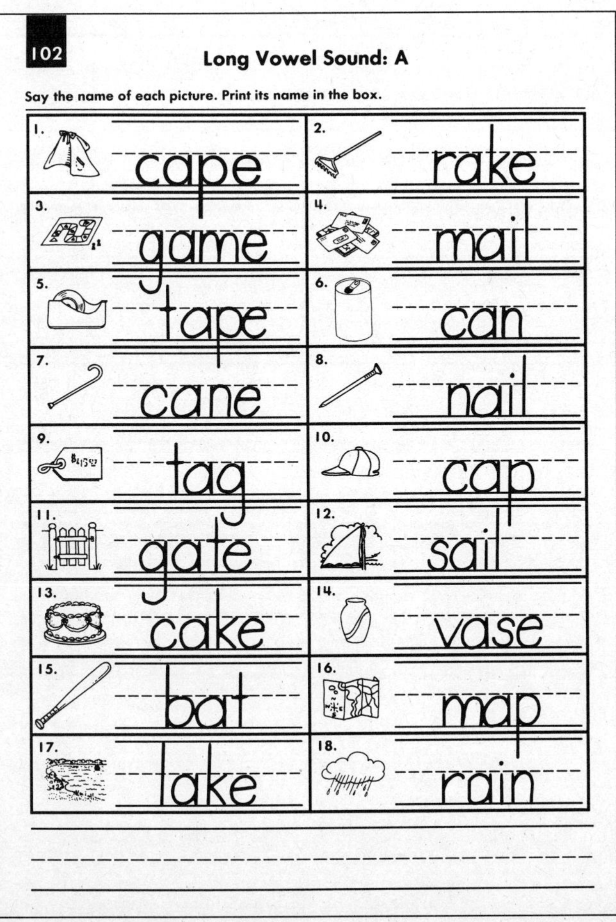

102 **Long Vowel Sound: A**

Say the name of each picture. Print its name in the box.

1. cape	2. rake
3. game	4. mail
5. tape	6. can
7. cane	8. nail
9. tag	10. cap
11. gate	12. sail
13. cake	14. vase
15. bat	16. map
17. lake	18. rain

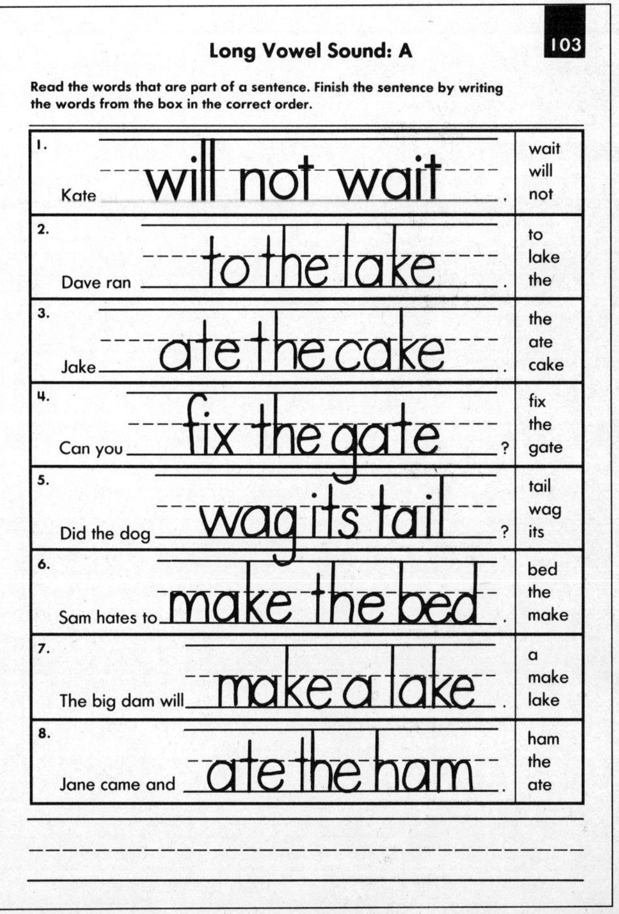

Long Vowel Sound: A 103

Read the words that are part of a sentence. Finish the sentence by writing the words from the box in the correct order.

1. Kate will not wait.	wait will not
2. Dave ran to the lake.	to lake the
3. Jake ate the cake.	the ate cake
4. Can you fix the gate?	fix the gate
5. Did the dog wag its tail?	tail wag its
6. Sam hates to make the bed.	bed the make
7. The big dam will make a lake.	a make lake
8. Jane came and ate the ham.	ham the ate

Lesson 46

Long Vowel *I* (pages 104–106)

Objective The child will identify the sound of long *I* and read long *I* words.

Long Vowel Rule 1: If one syllable has two vowels, the first vowel is usually long and the second is usually silent.

Review

Name Game You can play the Name Game to review the short vowels and the long *A* sounds. Tell the children that you will say two names and ask them to decide which name uses the vowel sound that you specify. For example: *Which name contains the short* A *sound: Andy or Angel?* Invite volunteers to answer. If possible, use the names of children in your class. You also can use the following pairs: *(E) Ted or Gene, (I) Kim or Mike, (O) Tom or Tony, (U) Beulah or Bud, (A) Dave or Dan.* You might stress the key vowel sounds as you pronounce each name.

If you wish to create an extension activity, have the children think of rhyming words for names using the targeted sounds. Then challenge the children to think of a rhyme using the two words. For example, *Ted/bed* might produce *Ted went to bed.* Some other short names with possible rhymes are the following.

Dan/man/pan/tan	*Kim/slim/trim/him*
Dot/hot/pot/lot	*Sid/bid/did/rid*

Teaching Ideas

Listening Show the children a picture of a glass filled with ice, or ask them what they can use to make a drink cold. When a volunteer answers *ice*, tell the children to listen for the beginning sound as you repeat the word. Explain that the sound they hear at the beginning of *ice* is the long *I* sound. Have the children repeat the word, listening for the beginning sound. To reinforce the lesson, you may want to write the word on the chalkboard and circle the *i*.

Use picture flashcards or make simple sketches on the chalkboard of the following items: *bike, tire, fire, tie, five, nine.* Say each word and have the children listen for the sound of long *I*. Write each word beneath the pictures and have a volunteer circle the long *I* as they repeat the word.

Speaking Use cards with the following words: *time, pie, side, nine, pipe, tie, hike.* Call on children to read each word aloud and to point out the long *I* sound. You also may want to have them explain how each word follows Long Vowel Rule 1.

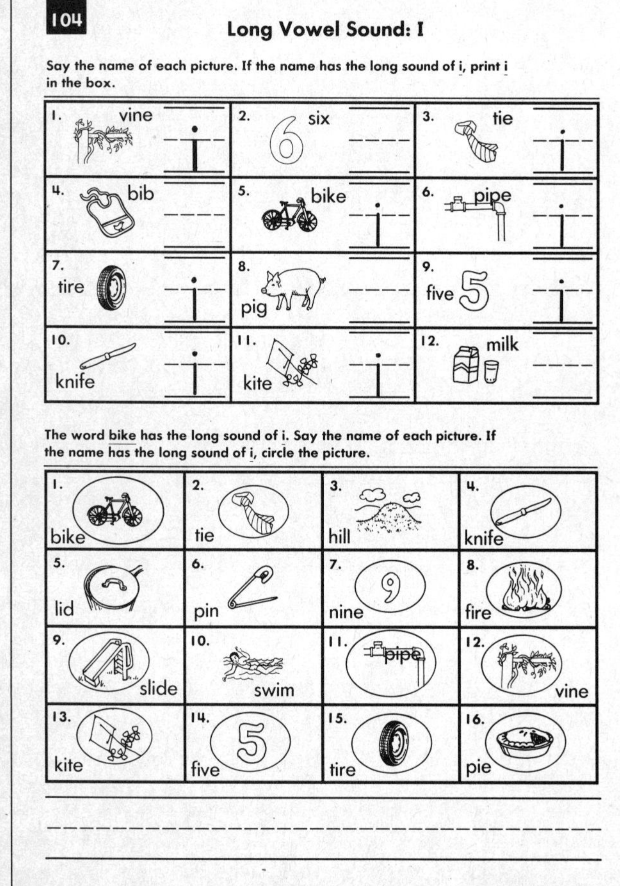

104

Long Vowel Sound: I

Say the name of each picture. If the name has the long sound of i, print i in the box.

1. vine — i	2. six	3. tie — i
4. bib	5. bike — i	6. pipe — i
7. tire — i	8. pig	9. five — i
10. knife — i	11. kite — i	12. milk

The word bike has the long sound of i. Say the name of each picture. If the name has the long sound of i, circle the picture.

1. bike	2. tie	3. hill	4. knife
5. lid	6. pin	7. nine	8. fire
9. slide	10. swim	11. pipe	12. vine
13. kite	14. five	15. tire	16. pie

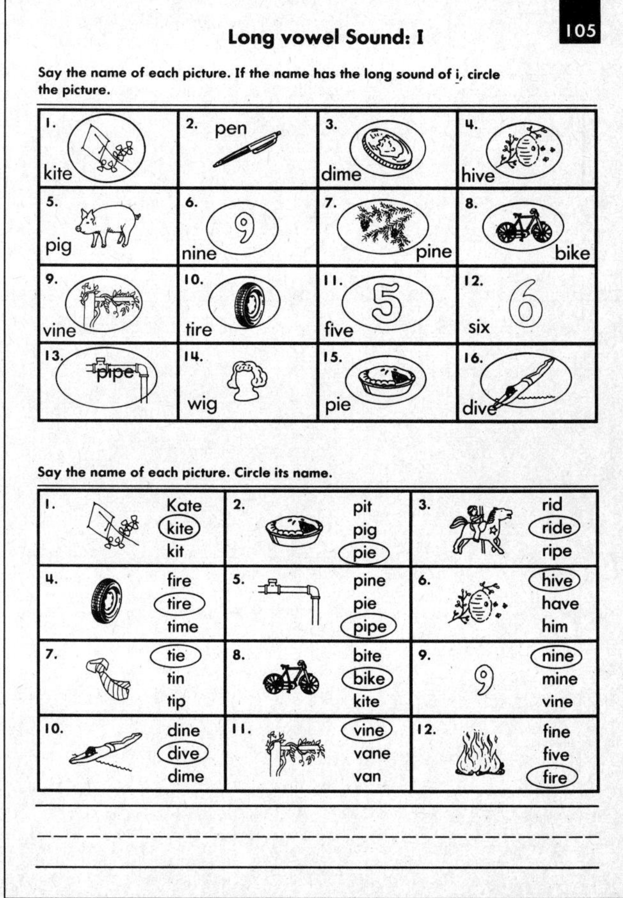

105

Long vowel Sound: I

Say the name of each picture. If the name has the long sound of i, circle the picture.

1. kite	2. pen	3. dime	4. hive
5. pig	6. nine	7. pine	8. bike
9. vine	10. tire	11. five	12. six
13. pipe	14. wig	15. pie	16. dive

Say the name of each picture. Circle its name.

1. Kate, kite, kit	2. pit, pig, pie	3. rid, ride, ripe
4. fire, tire, time	5. pine, pie, pipe	6. hive, have, him
7. tie, tin, tip	8. bite, bike, kite	9. nine, mine, vine
10. dine, dive, dime	11. vine, vane, van	12. fine, five, fire

You may develop recognition of the long *I* sound by using a series of rhyming words. Write the following list of words on the chalkboard, underlining the key word at the top of each column.

<u>ride</u>	*<u>nine</u>*	*<u>bike</u>*	*<u>fire</u>*	*<u>dive</u>*
hide	*fine*	*like*	*tire*	*five*
side	*line*	*pike*	*wire*	*hive*
wide	*mine*	*hike*	*hire*	*live*

You may want to read aloud each column with the children. Then point to a random word and ask a child to read the word and use it in a sentence. Encourage the children to think of sentences that include a rhyme. For example: *I took a ride and the road was wide.*

Writing You can teach the long *I* sound by developing the children's awareness of how the silent *E* changes the short vowel sound to a long vowel sound. For each set of words following, write the short vowel word on the chalkboard: *rip/ripe, fin/fine, win/wine, hid/hide, bit/bite, pin/pine.* Say the word and have the children repeat it. Then call on a volunteer to write a silent *e* at the end of the word and read the new word aloud.

Family Involvement Activity Duplicate the Family Letter on page 106 of this Teacher's Edition. Send the letter home with the children.

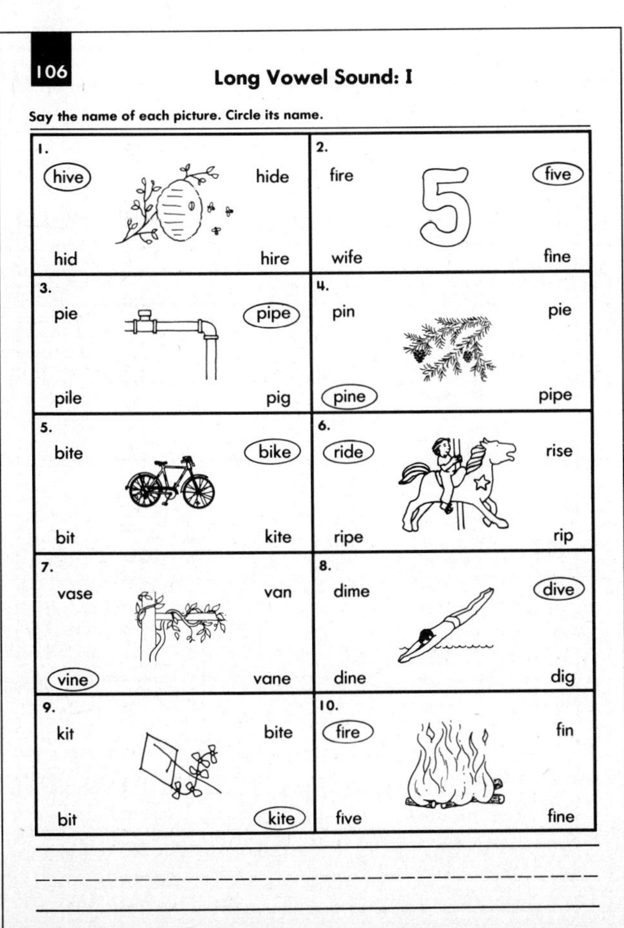

106

Long Vowel Sound: I

Say the name of each picture. Circle its name.

1.		2.	
(hive)	hide	fire	(five)
hid	hire	wife	fine
3.		**4.**	
pie	(pipe)	pin	pie
pile	pig	(pine)	pipe
5.		**6.**	
bite	(bike)	(ride)	rise
bit	kite	ripe	rip
7.		**8.**	
vase	van	dime	(dive)
(vine)	vane	dine	dig
9.		**10.**	
kit	bite	(fire)	fin
bit	(kite)	five	fine

Lesson 47

Long Vowel *I* (pages 107–108)

Objective The child will read long *I* words in isolation and within sentences.

Teaching Ideas

Writing Use picture flashcards or draw the following items and numbers on the chalkboard: *cap, tie, nine, five, six, cup, ten.* Above each picture, write its name, leaving a blank for the vowel. Have a volunteer tell the name of each item and write the missing vowel in the blank. Call on another child to tell why the vowel is long or short.

Speaking Remind the children that the letter *I* is used to spell the word that refers to oneself. To reinforce the lesson you can call on individual children to tell something about themselves by completing sentences such as *I like* _______ . You may want to point out that they can hear the long *I* sound in the first two words of the sentence. Encourage the children to create a sentence that includes another long *I* word. For example, a child might say, *I like ice cream.*

Reading Write the following sentences on the chalkboard.

1. *I like to ride a bike.*
2. *Tom went on a hike.*
3. *Bill has a fine time.*
4. *Can you hide the top?*
5. *Dad gave Mike a dime.*
6. *I will wipe the cup.*

Call on different children to read each sentence. Then have these children come forward and circle the long *I* words, explaining why the vowel is long in each word.

Extension

Art Provide the child with a "shopping list" of words that use long *I*. The list might include: *bike, tire, tie, knife, pie, ice cream, five.* Have the child read the list to you. Invite the child to find a picture of each item on the shopping list in an advertising flyer, a newspaper, or a magazine. (You can bring in such materials for children to use in the classroom or have them look through materials at home.) Have the child cut out each item, glue it on a sheet of paper, and print the name of the item below it. If the child enjoys drawing, you might suggest the child draw each item and write the word beneath it.

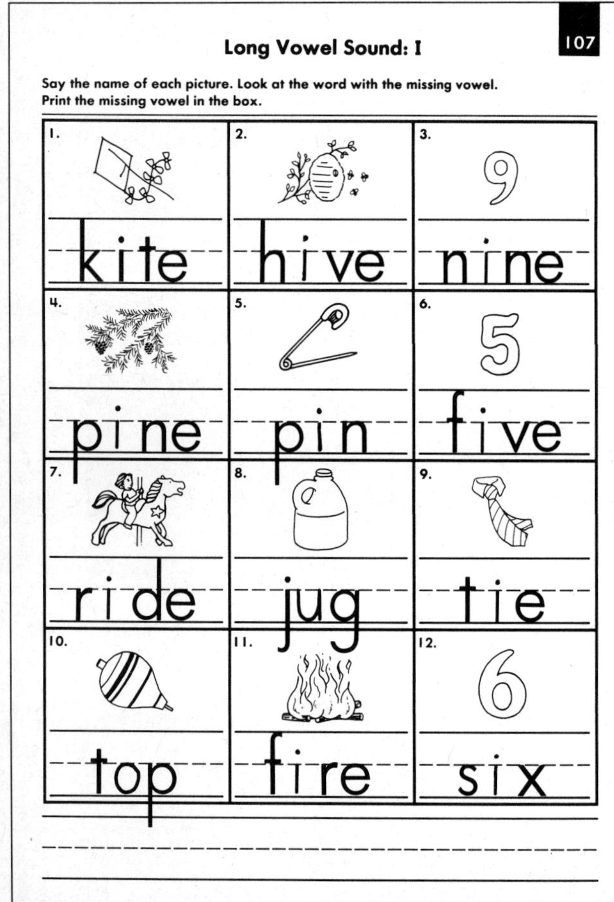

107

Long Vowel Sound: I

Say the name of each picture. Look at the word with the missing vowel. Print the missing vowel in the box.

1. kite	2. hive	3. nine
4. pine	5. pin	6. five
7. ride	8. jug	9. tie
10. top	11. fire	12. six

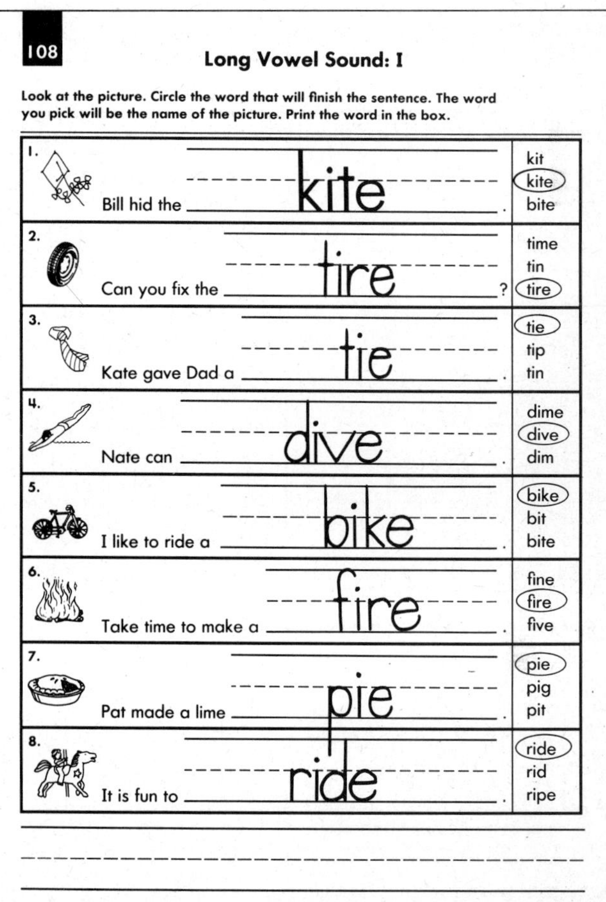

108

Long Vowel Sound: I

Look at the picture. Circle the word that will finish the sentence. The word you pick will be the name of the picture. Print the word in the box.

1.	Bill hid the kite.	kit / (kite) / bite
2.	Can you fix the tire?	time / tin / (tire)
3.	Kate gave Dad a tie.	(tie) / tip / tin
4.	Nate can dive.	dime / (dive) / dim
5.	I like to ride a bike.	(bike) / bit / bite
6.	Take time to make a fire.	fine / (fire) / five
7.	Pat made a lime pie.	(pie) / pig / pit
8.	It is fun to ride.	(ride) / rid / ripe

Lesson 48

Long Vowel *I* (pages 109–110)

Objective The child will apply Long Vowel Rule 1 to spell long *I* words and will complete comprehension sentences.

Teaching Ideas

Writing To review Long Vowel Rule 1, write the following numerals on the chalkboard: *5, 10, 6, 9.* Call on volunteers, in turn, to write the name of each numeral on the chalkboard. Tell the child to say each word silently before spelling it on the chalkboard. You can remind the children that words that have a long vowel sound may have a silent *e* at the end of the word. If the children need more practice, you can use picture flashcards or draw on the chalkboard stick figures of the following words: *bike, tie, kite, pie.*

Vowel Game To play the Vowel Game, make word cards with the following sets of words: *mad/maid, kit/kite, can/cane, win/wine, dim/dime.* Ask ten children to come forward. Pass out the word cards at random and challenge the children to find a partner who has a word that begins with the same consonant letter. When all the children are paired up, have each pair step forward and show their word cards. Encourage each pair to read the words they are holding, having them identify the long or short vowel sound. If the children need more practice, repeat the game with the following word pairs: *pan/pain, hid/hide, pin/pine, at/ate, rid/ride.*

Reading Write the following sentences on the chalkboard.

1. *I came on time.*
2. *Bill gave Mike a dime.*
3. *Take a big bite.*
4. *Hide the cake.*
5. *Make a wide line.*
6. *Tell him to dive.*
7. *Bob ran to the fire.*

For each sentence, have all the children read the sentence silently and then read it aloud together. You may ask content questions such as: *Who came on time? What did Bill give Mike?* You might want to challenge the children to think up similar questions to ask their classmates. Remind the children to answer each question with a complete sentence.

Reteaching

Reading and Writing Create word cards with sets of words such as the following.

pies/bake/five *the/time/take* *hide/bike/the*
tire/fix/the *make/lines/nine*

Challenge the child to arrange the words in each set to form a command. You might have the child read each sentence aloud and write the sentence on a sheet of paper.

109

Long Vowel Sound: I

Say the name of each picture. Print its name in the box.

1. bike	2. pipe
3. dive	4. 5 five
5. tie	6. hive
7. kite	8. pin
9. lid	10. pie
11. ride	12. pig
13. 9 nine	14. pine
15. tire	16. fire
17. 6 six	18. wig

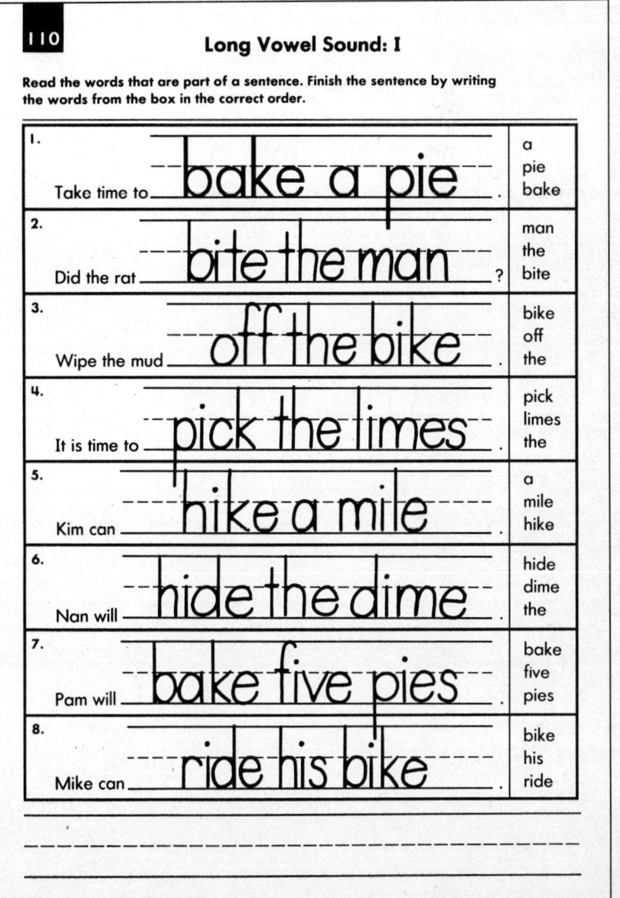

110

Long Vowel Sound: I

Read the words that are part of a sentence. Finish the sentence by writing the words from the box in the correct order.

1. Take time to bake a pie.	a pie bake
2. Did the rat bite the man?	man the bite
3. Wipe the mud off the bike.	bike off the
4. It is time to pick the limes.	pick limes the
5. Kim can hike a mile.	a mile hike
6. Nan will hide the dime.	hide dime the
7. Pam will bake five pies.	bake five pies
8. Mike can ride his bike.	bike his ride

Lesson 49
Long Vowel *U* (pages 111–113)

Objective The child will identify the long *U* sound and read long *U* words.

Long Vowel Rule 1: If one syllable has two vowels, the first vowel is usually long and the second is usually silent.

Teaching Ideas

Writing Introduce the long *U* sound by having children review the short *U* sound in the following activity. After pronouncing each of the following words, invite the children to spell and write each word on the chalkboard: *sun, bus, tub, jug, us, cup, up*. Challenge the children to tell why the vowel is short in each word.

Listening You can use the word *tune* to introduce the long *U* sound. You may wish to have the children share the names of their favorite tunes. Then have the children repeat the word *tune* after you, identifying the long *U* sound. You may want to write the word on the chalkboard and point to the *U* as it is pronounced.

Riddle Game You can use the Riddle Game to help children identify the long *U* sound. Write the following words on the chalkboard: *tube, fruit, tune, suit, Luke, mule*. You may want to read each word as you write it or call on volunteers to do so. Tell the children you are going to ask them some riddles about words with the long *U* sound. Explain that the answer to each riddle will be one of the words on the chalkboard. As the children give correct responses, you might encourage them to come forward and write the words again on the chalkboard. You can use riddles such as the following.

1. *I am very good to eat. What am I? (fruit)*
2. *You can hear me in a song. What am I? (tune)*
3. *A man wears me to go to work. (suit)*
4. *I am a boy's name. (Luke)*
5. *I am a strong farm animal. (mule)*
6. *You squeeze toothpaste out of me. (tube)*

You may want to challenge the children to create long *U* word riddles on their own.

Long-*U*-Kids Game Tell the children that *Luke, Sue, June,* and *Duke* are the "Long-*U* Kids." They all have the long *U* sound in their names and they always like to choose things that also have the long *U* sound. Call on volunteers to tell which of the following things each "Long-*U* Kid" would choose, using questions such as the following.

1. *Would Luke choose a jacket or a suit?*
2. *Would Sue choose a mouse or a mule for a pet?*
3. *Would Duke choose to eat meat or to eat fruit?*
4. *Would June choose something that was pretty or something that was cute?*

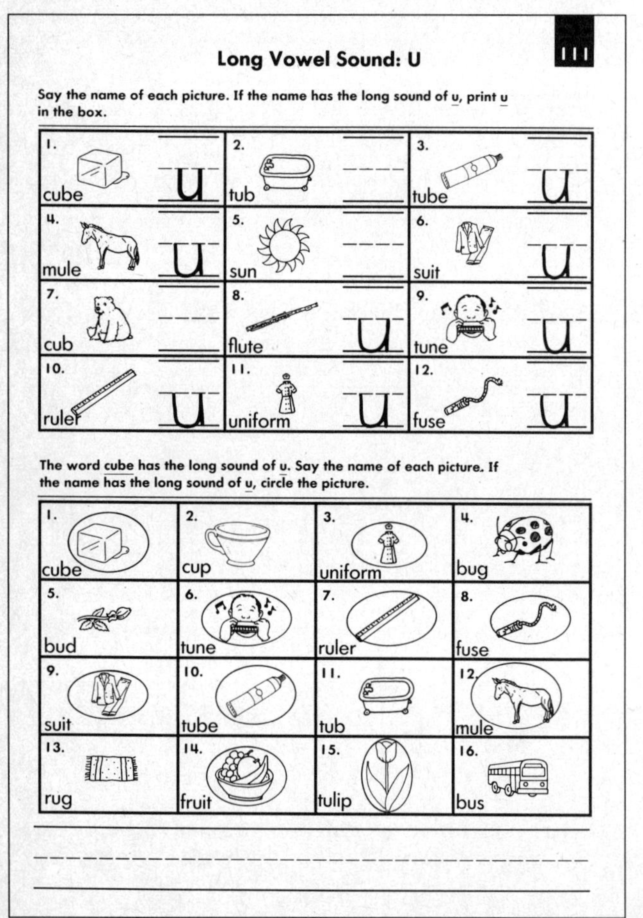
111

Long Vowel Sound: U

Say the name of each picture. If the name has the long sound of u, print u in the box.

1. cube u	2. tub	3. tube u
4. mule u	5. sun	6. suit u
7. cub	8. flute u	9. tune u
10. ruler u	11. uniform u	12. fuse u

The word cube has the long sound of u. Say the name of each picture. If the name has the long sound of u, circle the picture.

1. cube	2. cup	3. uniform	4. bug
5. bud	6. tune	7. ruler	8. fuse
9. suit	10. tube	11. tub	12. mule
13. rug	14. fruit	15. tulip	16. bus

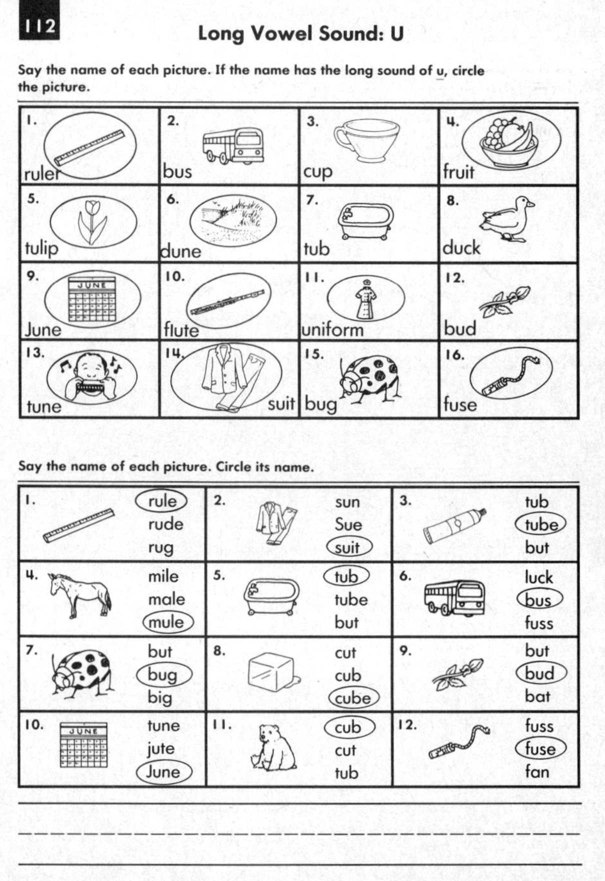
112

Long Vowel Sound: U

Say the name of each picture. If the name has the long sound of u, circle the picture.

1. ruler	2. bus	3. cup	4. fruit
5. tulip	6. dune	7. tub	8. duck
9. June	10. flute	11. uniform	12. bud
13. tune	14. suit	15. bug	16. fuse

Say the name of each picture. Circle its name.

1. rule rude rug	2. sun Sue suit	3. tub tube but
4. mile male mule	5. tub tube but	6. luck bus fuss
7. but bug big	8. cut cub cube	9. but bud bat
10. tune jute June	11. cub cut tub	12. fuss fuse fan

Reading Write the following words on the chalkboard.

tube suit Luke cure June use mule
cube cute flute pure tune fuse rule

Call on a volunteer to read the words, first horizontally, then vertically. Ask the children if the words in the rows or the words in the columns rhyme. Then ask if they all have the long *U* sound. You may want to have the children review how each word follows Long Vowel Rule 1.

For additional practice, you may write the following word pairs on the chalkboard: *tub/tube, cub/cube, cut/cute, hug/huge, us/use*. Invite children to read each word pair and tell in which words they hear the long *U* sound and in which words they hear the short *U* sound. Encourage the children to state the vowel rules in their own words. If you find that a word is unfamiliar to the children, you might use it in a sentence to establish a context clue, or you may want to invite other children to explain the word or think of a sample sentence.

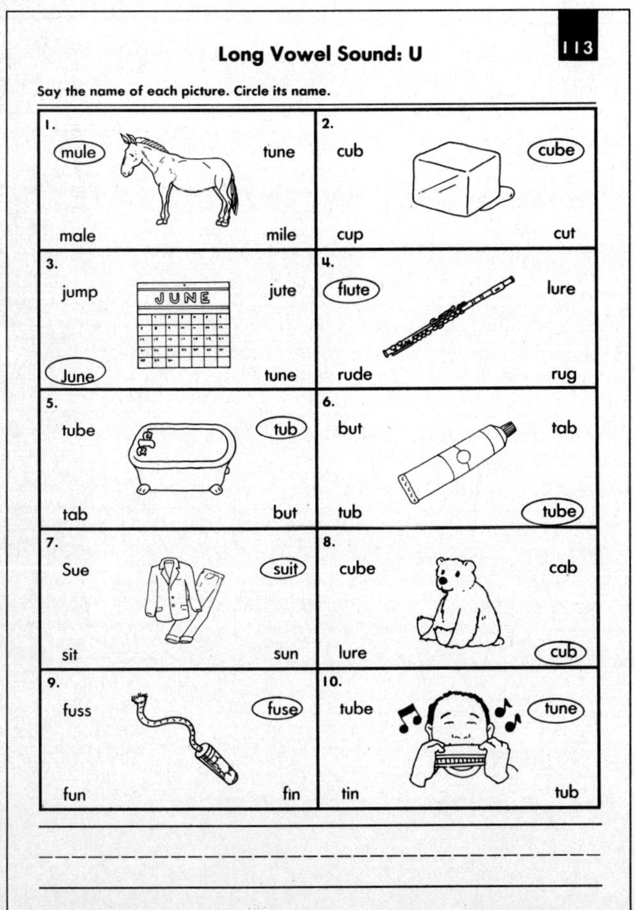

113

Long Vowel Sound: U

Say the name of each picture. Circle its name.

1.	(mule) tune male mile
2.	cub (cube) cup cut
3.	jump jute (June) tune
4.	(flute) lure rude rug
5.	tube (tub) tab but
6.	but tab tub (tube)
7.	Sue (suit) sit sun
8.	cube cab lure (cub)
9.	fuss (fuse) fun fin
10.	tube (tune) tin tub

Lesson 50

Long Vowel *U* (pages 114–115)

Objective The child will read long *U* words in isolation and demonstrate comprehension by inserting the words correctly into sentences.

Teaching Ideas

Writing Print the following incomplete words on the chalkboard.

J _ ne	*t _ ne*	*h _ m*	*c _ te*
c _ be	*S _ e*	*L _ ke*	*t _ b*
f _ n	*m _ le*	*s _ it*	*r _ ler*

For each word, invite a child to come forward, to print the missing *U* , and then to read and spell the word. Challenge the child to use the word in a sentence. Encourage the child to use another short or long vowel *U* word in the sentence.

Open-Shut Game Explain that you are going to read a list of words that have a vowel *U* sound such as the following: *tube, drum, tuba, fruit, thumb, hunt, hush, human, unicorn, cucumber, bunny, supper.* Explain to the children that after you read each word, they are to respond by holding up a fist if thc word has the short vowel *U* sound, or an open hand if the word has a long vowel *U* sound. To reinforce reading skills, distribute word cards of easy words with the vowel *U*. Invite a volunteer to read the word on a card and have the other children respond with an open hand or a fist, according to the previously described system.

Reading Print the following sentences on the chalkboard.

1. *Tell us the rule.*
2. *Sue can sing a tune.*
3. *The pup is cute.*
4. *Will you fix the tube?*
5. *That baby can use a cup.*

Call on a child to read each sentence. Invite a volunteer to circle the long *U* words and to explain why the *U* is long.

Extension

Writing The following simple research activity can enhance the child's awareness of words containing the long *U* sound. Giving assistance if necessary, have the child compile a list of the first names of the children in the class. Provide a few samples of names with the long *U* sound that the child has encountered in previous lessons (Luke, Sue, June). Then challenge the child to study the completed list and circle any names that have the long *U* sound.

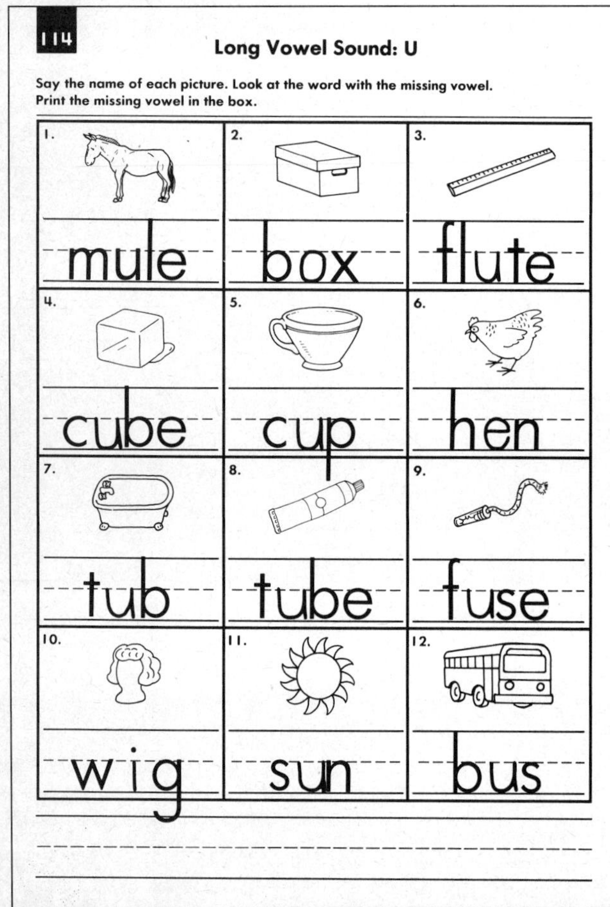

114

Long Vowel Sound: U

Say the name of each picture. Look at the word with the missing vowel. Print the missing vowel in the box.

1. mule	2. box	3. flute
4. cube	5. cup	6. hen
7. tub	8. tube	9. fuse
10. wig	11. sun	12. bus

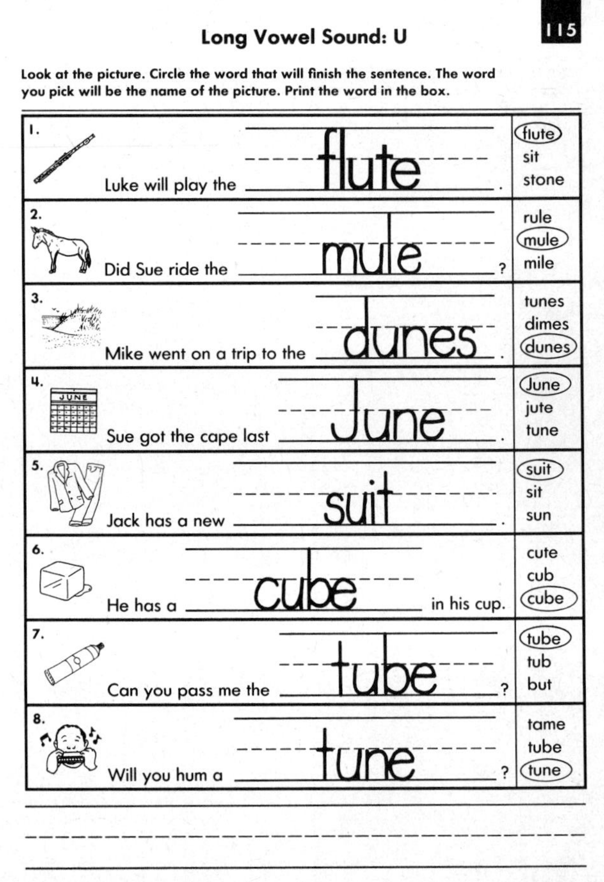

115

Long Vowel Sound: U

Look at the picture. Circle the word that will finish the sentence. The word you pick will be the name of the picture. Print the word in the box.

1. Luke will play the flute. (flute) sit stone
2. Did Sue ride the mule? rule (mule) mile
3. Mike went on a trip to the dunes. tunes dimes (dunes)
4. Sue got the cape last June. (June) jute tune
5. Jack has a new suit. (suit) sit sun
6. He has a cube in his cup. cute cub (cube)
7. Can you pass me the tube? (tube) tub but
8. Will you hum a tune? tame tube (tune)

Lesson 51

Long Vowel *U* (pages 116–117)

Objective The child will identify the long *U* sound and read long *U* words in isolation and within sentences.

Review

Vowel-House Game Invite the children to play the Vowel-House Game. Sketch two houses side by side on the chalkboard. Label one *Short Vowel House* and the other *Long Vowel House*. Then distribute cards that show names containing all the short vowel sounds and the long vowel sounds of *A*, *I*, and *U*. You might consider using the following names: *Ann, Andy, Jane, Jack, Dave, Ed, Meg, Fred, Mike, Jill, Tim, Jim, Tom, Jon, Lon, Bob, Sue, Luke, June*. Explain that each name on the cards has a home in one of the two houses. Call on each child in turn to read the name on the card and tell if the vowel is short or long. Have the child place the card on the chalkboard ledge under the correct house.

Teaching Ideas

Writing Write the following words on the chalkboard: *tub, us, pin, cub, at, hop, cut, Tim, tap*. Point to one of the words and call on a volunteer to come forward and read the word. Instruct the child to write an *E* at the end of the word and read the new word aloud.

Reading Write the following sentences on the chalkboard.

1. *Sue will hunt for the bunny.*
2. *That cute pup can run.*
3. *June can ride the mule.*
4. *The paste is in the tube.*
5. *Luke has a nice suit.*
6. *Dad wants an ice cube.*
7. *Tom may use the bike.*
8. *Lulu can hum a tune.*

Invite volunteers to read the sentences aloud. Build comprehension skills by asking questions similar to the following.

1. *Which sentence tells something that Dad wants?*
2. *Can you tell me what he wants?*
3. *Which sentence tells who can hum a tune?*
4. *Can you tell me who can hum?*
5. *Which sentence tells what Sue can do?*

Encourage the children to respond in complete sentences. (Save the sentences to use in the Reteaching activity that follows.)

Reteaching

Art and Writing Write the previous sentences on tagboard strips. Have a child who needs further practice read several of the sentences to you. Then give the child a piece of paper with a ruled line on the bottom. Have the child copy one of the sentences on this line and draw a picture showing what the sentence is about.

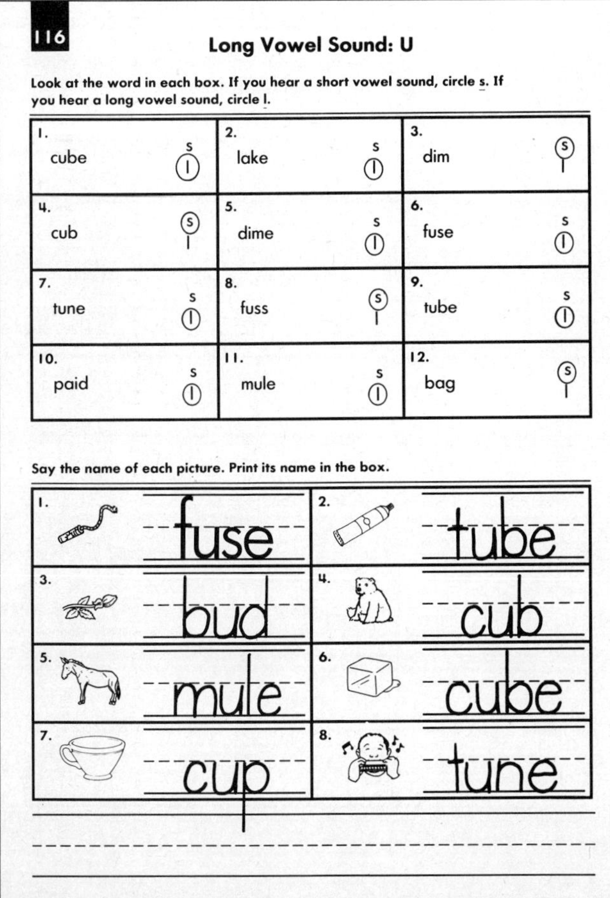

116

Long Vowel Sound: U

Look at the word in each box. If you hear a short vowel sound, circle s. If you hear a long vowel sound, circle l.

1. cube s (l)	2. lake s (l)	3. dim (s) l
4. cub (s) l	5. dime s (l)	6. fuse s (l)
7. tune s (l)	8. fuss (s) l	9. tube s (l)
10. paid s (l)	11. mule s (l)	12. bag (s) l

Say the name of each picture. Print its name in the box.

1. fuse	2. tube
3. bud	4. cub
5. mule	6. cube
7. cup	8. tune

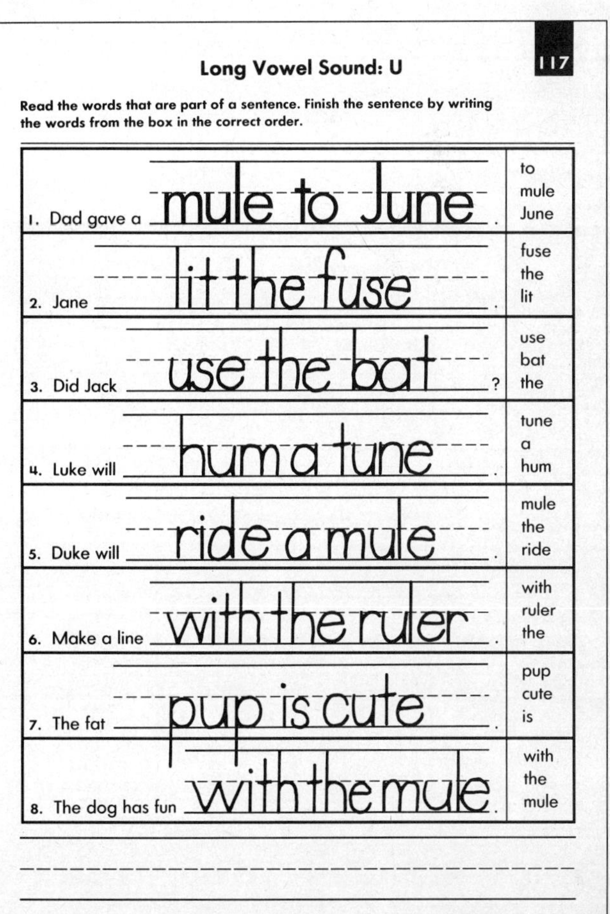

Long Vowel Sound: U

117

Read the words that are part of a sentence. Finish the sentence by writing the words from the box in the correct order.

1. Dad gave a mule to June.	to mule June
2. Jane lit the fuse.	fuse the lit
3. Did Jack use the bat?	use bat the
4. Luke will hum a tune.	tune a hum
5. Duke will ride a mule.	mule the ride
6. Make a line with the ruler.	with ruler the
7. The fat pup is cute.	pup cute is
8. The dog has fun with the mule.	with the mule

Lesson 52

Long Vowel *O* (pages 118–120)

Objective The child will identify the sound of long *O* and read long *O* words.

Long Vowel Rule 1: If one syllable has two vowels, the first vowel is usually long and the second is usually silent.

Review

Change-the-Word Game To practice visual and auditory discrimination, play Change the Word. Print the following words on the chalkboard: *June, big, net, bike, top*. Tell the children that each word can be made into a rhyming word by changing the first letter. Then ask questions such as the following for each word: *If we change the* J *in June to* T, *what new word will we get?* To challenge children's auditory discrimination, use the consonant sound rather than the consonant name. Invite a child who gives a correct response to come forward and write the new word on the board beneath its rhyming word.

Teaching Ideas

Listening Encourage children to listen for the sound of the vowel *O* in words you say. Direct the children to raise their hands when they hear the long *O* sound at the beginning of a word: *ocean, oar, okay, oven, orange, oats.*

Reading You can help develop the children's ability to recognize the long *O* sound by printing the following words on the chalkboard: *soap, bone, boat, rose, rope, hoe, toe.* As you point to each word, call on a volunteer to read the word aloud. Then ask the child to name the two vowels in the word so that you can underline them. Reinforce Long Vowel Rule 1 by asking whether the first vowel or the second vowel makes the long *O* sound. Encourage the children to say the Long Vowel Rule 1 in their own words.

For additional practice with the long *O* sound, write the following words in a row on the chalkboard: *bone, nose, goat, toad.* Point to each word, pronounce it, and encourage the children to think of long *O* rhyming words. (The following are possible responses: *bone: cone/tone/phone; nose: hose/rose/toes; goat: boat/coat/float; toad: road/load/code.*) If the children have difficulty, you might offer them clues such as the following.

> *I can think of a word that rhymes with bone that is the name of something you put ice cream in. Who can tell me what that word is?*

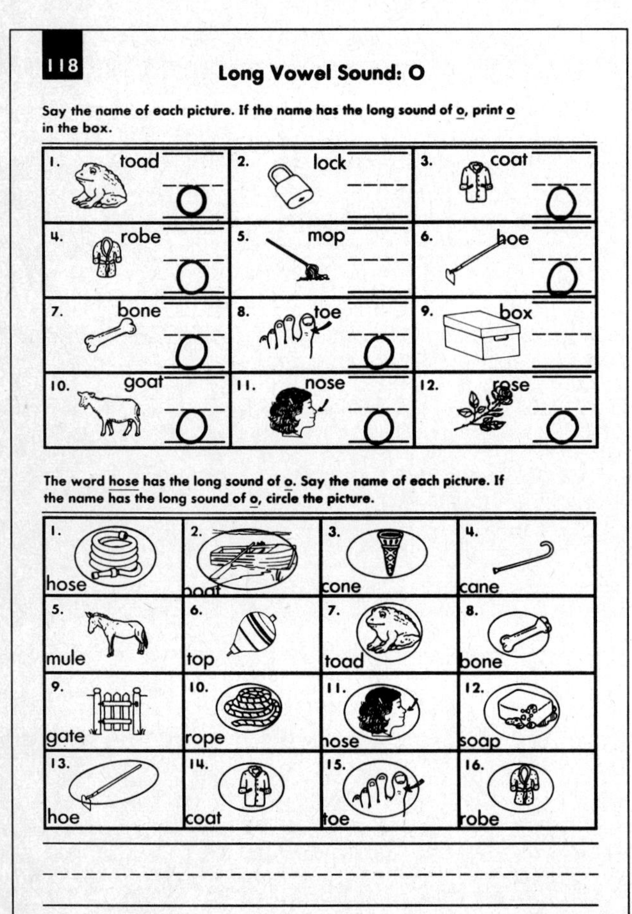

118

Long Vowel Sound: O

Say the name of each picture. If the name has the long sound of o, print o in the box.

1. toad o	2. lock	3. coat o
4. robe o	5. mop	6. hoe o
7. bone o	8. toe o	9. box
10. goat o	11. nose o	12. rose o

The word hose has the long sound of o. Say the name of each picture. If the name has the long sound of o, circle the picture.

1. hose	2. boat	3. cone	4. cane
5. mule	6. top	7. toad	8. bone
9. gate	10. rope	11. nose	12. soap
13. hoe	14. coat	15. toe	16. robe

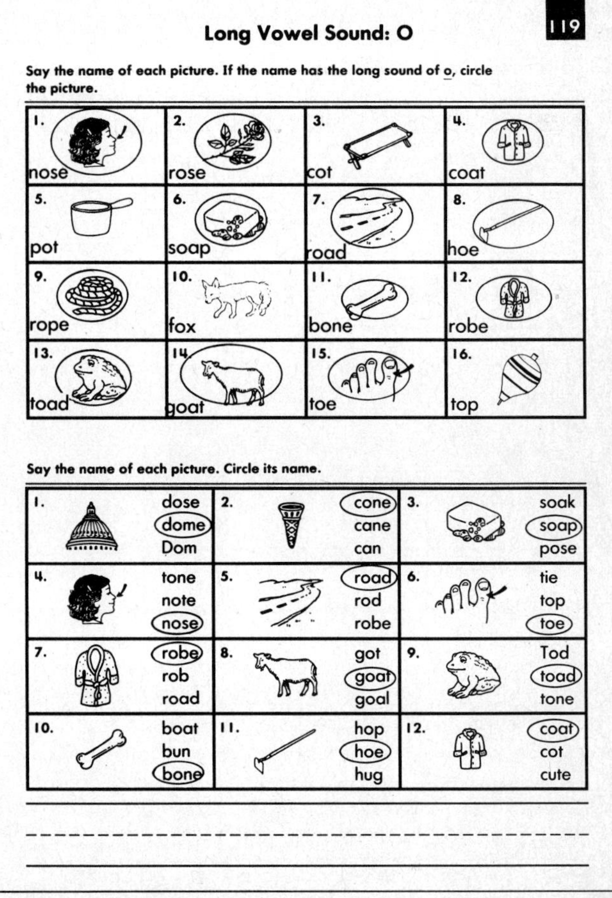

119

Long Vowel Sound: O

Say the name of each picture. If the name has the long sound of o, circle the picture.

1. nose	2. rose	3. cot	4. coat
5. pot	6. soap	7. road	8. hoe
9. rope	10. fox	11. bone	12. robe
13. toad	14. goat	15. toe	16. top

Say the name of each picture. Circle its name.

1. dose / dome / Dom	2. cone / cane / can	3. soak / soap / pose
4. tone / note / nose	5. road / rod / robe	6. tie / top / toe
7. robe / rob / road	8. got / goat / goal	9. Tod / toad / tone
10. boat / bun / bone	11. hop / hoe / hug	12. coat / cot / cute

To reinforce the concept, repeat each rhyming word and write it on the chalkboard.

Writing Print the following incomplete words on the chalkboard: *t __ ad, c __ at, t __ es, t __ ast, n __ se, g __ at.* Call on a child to complete each word with the letter *O*. Ask the child to read the word.

Vary this activity by having the children guess the missing letters in the words. Use picture flashcards as clues. Display the corresponding picture flashcard on the chalkboard ledge, directly beneath each word . Invite a volunteer to pronounce the name of the picture and then to fill in the missing letter (*O*) in the word above. Take the opportunity to compliment children whose printed letters are well formed.

Sorting Game Write the following headings in a row on the chalkboard: *Animals, Good to Eat, Parts of My Body, From the Garden.* Distribute the following word cards: *toad, rose, toes, hose, toast, goat, roast, hoe, nose.* Then invite volunteers, in turn, to read the word on a card and to write it under an appropriate heading. Note: More than one answer may be correct. Because the activity has a critical thinking objective, encourage children to express the reason for placing a word in a given category.

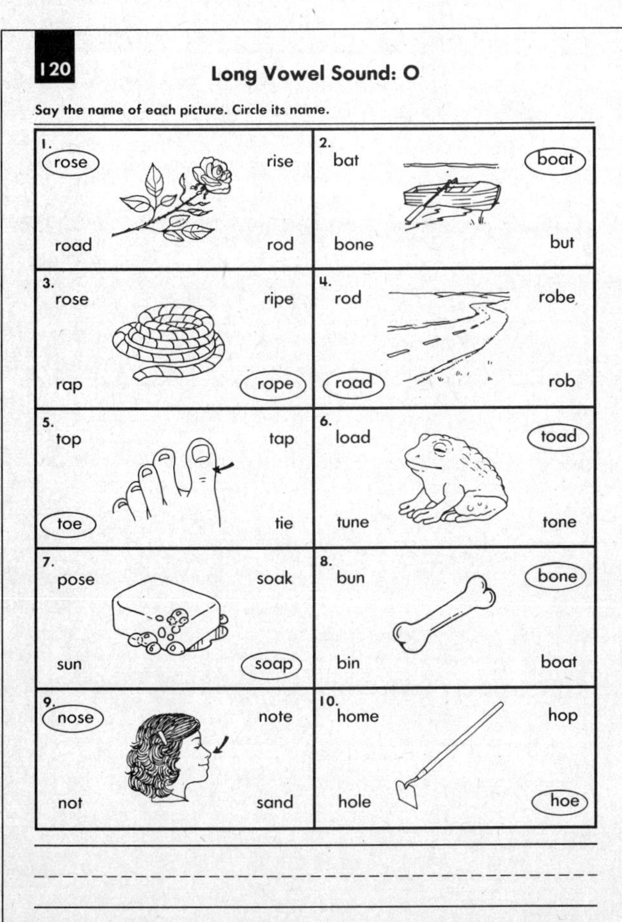

Lesson 53

Long Vowel *O* (pages 121–122)

Objective The child will read long *O* words in isolation and within sentences.

Review

Speaking Develop visual and auditory skills while you review Long Vowel Rule 1. Hold up word cards containing the following words: *hid, pan, hop, kit, can, at, mad, rat, not, tub.* Invite volunteers to read each word. Then have the children change each to a long vowel word by adding silent *e.*

Teaching Ideas

Reading Write the following word pairs on the chalkboard: *hop/hope, Todd/toad, rob/robe, got/goat, cot/coat, Rod/road.* Invite a volunteer to read each pair of words. Ask the child to explain why the letter *O* has a short sound in one word and a long sound in the other word of each pair.

If you feel the class will benefit from an additional reading activity, write the following sentences on the chalkboard.

1. *Mom gave Rose a note.*
2. *Joe rode his bike home.*
3. *Dad will sail the boat.*
4. *The goat ran to the road.*
5. *Sue came home late.*

Ask the children to read each sentence silently. Then invite volunteers to each read a sentence aloud and to circle the long *O* words.

Reteaching

Reading and Writing Make a sentence strip for sentence 2, in the prior Reading activity, omitting the name. Then write the names *Rose* and *Joe* on word cards. Place one of the word cards on the sentence strip and ask the child to read the sentence. Then change the name, and have the child read the sentence again. To give the child further practice, have the child copy the sentences on a sheet of paper. You might suggest the child place his or her own name in the sentence as well. Stimulate the child's imagination by pointing out that the three sentences sound like a story of friends who were bicycle riding together. Invite the child to draw a picture to go with the story.

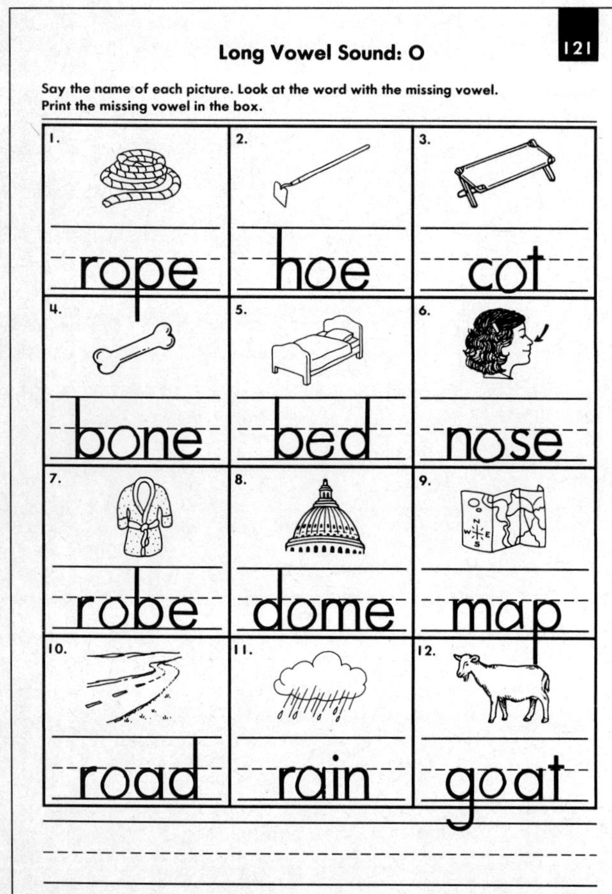

Lesson 54

Long Vowel *O* (pages 123–124)

Objective The child will read long *O* words in isolation and within sentences.

Teaching Ideas

Riddle Game You might play the Riddle Game described in Lesson 49 in this unit. Explain that you are going to ask some riddles and that all the answers will be long *O* words. Then ask riddles for the following words: *coat, cone, bone, boat, road, nose, toe.* You might pose a riddle such as the following: *What long* O *word is the name of something you wear to keep warm?* To reinforce a sense of achievement and writing skill, have the child who solves the riddle print the correct answer on the chalkboard.

If you have picture flashcards, you might vary the game by putting the cards for the words on the chalkboard ledge. Invite the children to each select a picture and think of a riddle question such as the example given above. Ask volunteers to share riddles. Challenge the other children in the class to guess the answers and print the words above the picture flashcards.

Reading Print the following sentences on sentence strips.

1. *Tell the joke to Bob.*
2. *Rose likes to jump rope.*
3. *Joe has a hole in his coat.*
4. *The pail is in the road.*
5. *Take the note to Joan.*
6. *I hope Joe will go.*

Distribute the sentence strips and have the children read them. Then ask the children to each place their sentence strips in the pocket chart and to read them aloud. Ask content questions such as the following to check for comprehension: *What does Rose like? Where is the pail?* You might use this activity to help children develop their abilities to formulate questions by inviting the children to ask classmates a content question based on the sentence just read.

Extension

What's-in-What? Game This game will give the child practice composing and reading a sentence using long *O* words. Prepare the following sentence strip, leaving blank spaces as indicated: *The* _______ *is in the* _______. Give the child the strip along with sets of rhyming word cards such as *road/toad* or *goat/boat.* Challenge the child to use the rhyming words to make different sentences. Mention that some of the sentences, such as *The goat is in the coat,* will be "silly sentences." Have the child read each sentence aloud. Then ask the child to write one of the sentences on a sheet of paper and to illustrate it.

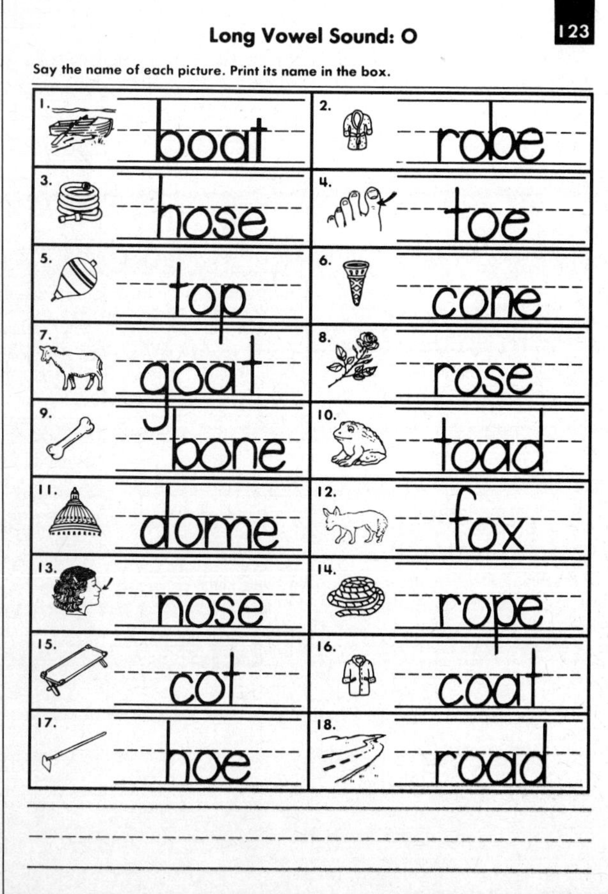

123

Long Vowel Sound: O

Say the name of each picture. Print its name in the box.

1. boat	2. robe
3. hose	4. toe
5. top	6. cone
7. goat	8. rose
9. bone	10. toad
11. dome	12. fox
13. nose	14. rope
15. cot	16. coat
17. hoe	18. road

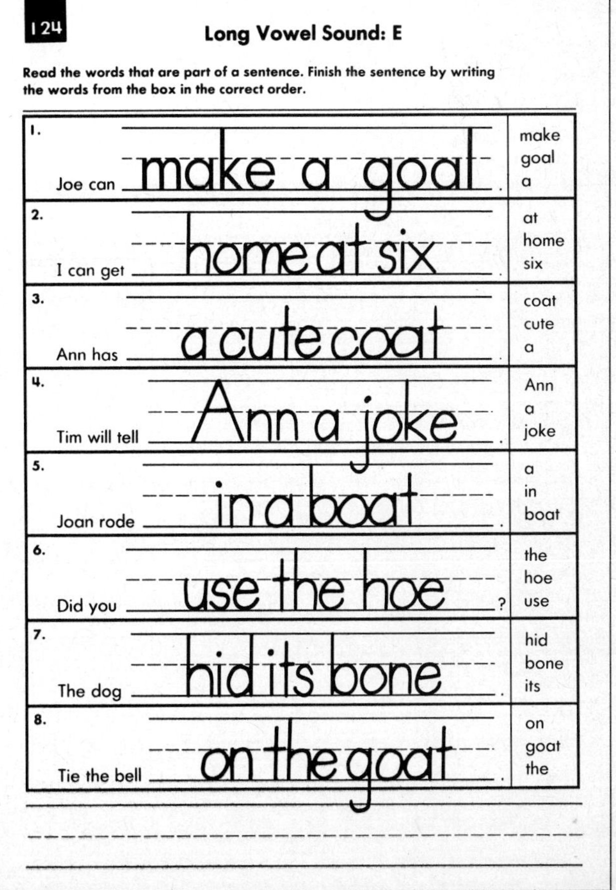

124

Long Vowel Sound: E

Read the words that are part of a sentence. Finish the sentence by writing the words from the box in the correct order.

1. Joe can make a goal	make goal a
2. I can get home at six	at home six
3. Ann has a cute coat	coat cute a
4. Tim will tell Ann a joke	Ann a joke
5. Joan rode in a boat	a in boat
6. Did you use the hoe?	the hoe use
7. The dog hid its bone	hid bone its
8. Tie the bell on the goat	on goat the

Lesson 55
Long Vowel *E* (pages 125–127)

Objective The child will identify the sound of long *E* and read long *E* words.

Long Vowel Rule 1: If one syllable has two vowels, the first vowel is usually long and the second is usually silent.

Teaching Ideas

Listening You might introduce the long sound of vowel *E* by reviewing the short *E* sound. Use word cards or write the following words on the chalkboard: *pet, sell, ten, beg, well, net.* For each word, invite a volunteer to identify the vowel sound. Acknowledge, especially, the children who can tell why the vowel sound is short.

Then use the word *seal* to introduce the long vowel *E* sound. You might show a picture of a seal or print the word on the chalkboard. Pronounce the word and then identify the long *E* sound heard. Have the children repeat the word after you. Invite several children in turn to say the word and to identify the long *E* sound.

You may wish to reinforce the lesson by saying other long *E* words. Use a phonics chart, picture flashcards, or pronounce the following words, one by one: *eat, deep, meat, sleep, meal, feet, heel.* Ask the children to repeat the word after you. Then ask a volunteer to compare the sound of *E* in each word to the long *E* sound in *seal.* You may wish to further reinforce the concept by printing each word on the chalkboard. Then call on a child to come forward and underline the two vowels in the word, explaining how they follow Long Vowel Rule 1.

Vowel Game To offer additional practice differentiating between words with long and short vowel sounds, you might play the Vowel Game described in Lesson 48 in this unit, using the following word pairs: *met/meet, bet/beat, set/seat, red/read, fed/feed, bed/bead.*

Sorting Game Play a variation of the Sorting Game described in Lesson 52 in this unit. Write the following headings on the chalkboard: *Living Things, Good to Eat,* and *Parts of My Body.* Distribute the following word cards and have the children follow the procedure as previously described: *meat, feet, heel, seal, peas, beets, ear, teeth, bee, beans.*

Speaking and Reading Take advantage of the many rhyming words that use the long *E* sound to encourage recognition of the sound. Write the following groups of rhyming words on the chalkboard.

seat	*bead*	*seal*	*peek*	*see*
heat	*read*	*meal*	*week*	*bee*
neat	*lead*	*heal*	*seek*	*Lee*
feet	*feed*	*peel*		
meet	*need*			
beet	*weed*			

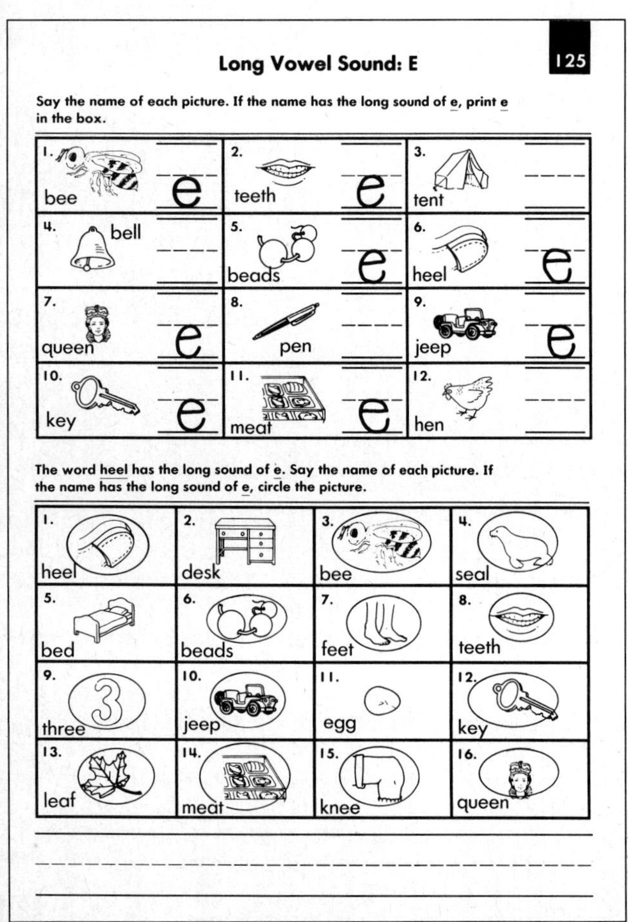
125 Long Vowel Sound: E

Say the name of each picture. If the name has the long sound of e, print e in the box.

1. bee — e	2. teeth — e	3. tent
4. bell	5. beads — e	6. heel — e
7. queen — e	8. pen	9. jeep — e
10. key — e	11. meat — e	12. hen

The word heel has the long sound of e. Say the name of each picture. If the name has the long sound of e, circle the picture.

1. heel	2. desk	3. bee	4. seal
5. bed	6. beads	7. feet	8. teeth
9. three	10. jeep	11. egg	12. key
13. leaf	14. meat	15. knee	16. queen

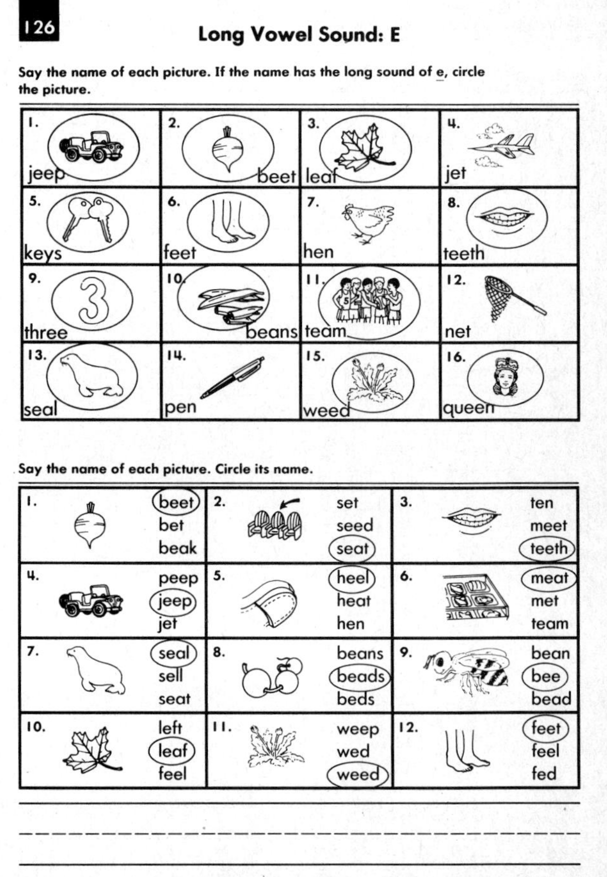
126 Long Vowel Sound: E

Say the name of each picture. If the name has the long sound of e, circle the picture.

1. jeep	2. beet	3. leaf	4. jet
5. keys	6. feet	7. hen	8. teeth
9. three	10. beans	11. team	12. net
13. seal	14. pen	15. weed	16. queen

Say the name of each picture. Circle its name.

1. beet, bet, beak	2. set, seed, seat	3. ten, meet, teeth
4. peep, jeep, jet	5. heel, heat, hen	6. meat, met, team
7. seal, sell, seat	8. beans, beads, beds	9. bean, bee, bead
10. left, leaf, feel	11. weep, wed, weed	12. feet, feel, fed

Ask a child to read across each row. Then have a child read down each column. Ask whether the rhyming words are in the rows or in the columns.

Discuss how most long *E* words do not have a silent *E*. Point out that the two vowels in these words usually come one right after the other. Explain that some words, like *see*, have two *E*'s together; others, like *meat*, spell the sound with *ea*. To emphasize the point, write the two categories of spellings for the long *E* on the chalkboard and have the children tell which category fits the word card they are holding.

Extension

Reading and Art Have the child divide a sheet of paper in half, labeling one section with *ee* and the other section with *ea*. Ask the child to write a word in each section that has the long sound of *E* formed by the letters in the label. (Words for *ee* might include *beet, feet, jeep,* and *bee;* words for *ea* might include *beads, leaf, seal,* and *meat.*) You might have the child illustrate each of the words in the remaining space.

Lesson 56

Long Vowel *E* (pages 128–129)

Objective The child will read long *E* words in isolation and within sentences and will spell picture names.

Teaching Ideas

Writing Write the following incomplete words on the chalkboard.

l _ af *j _ t* *p _ a* *b _ et*
s _ at *f _ et* *_ at* *t _ a*
j _ ep *h _ n* *s _ e* *b _ d*

Invite a volunteer to complete each word by writing an *E* and then to read the word. Challenge the child to use the word in a sentence and to tell why the *E* is either long or short.

Place picture flashcards on the chalkboard ledge, or sketch the following items on the chalkboard: *jeep, bee, beads, bed, bag, belt, dog, tree, leaf.* Distribute word cards for each of the items to the children. Encourage the children to match their cards with the picture and to read the word. To reinforce the lesson, have the children write the words above the pictures.

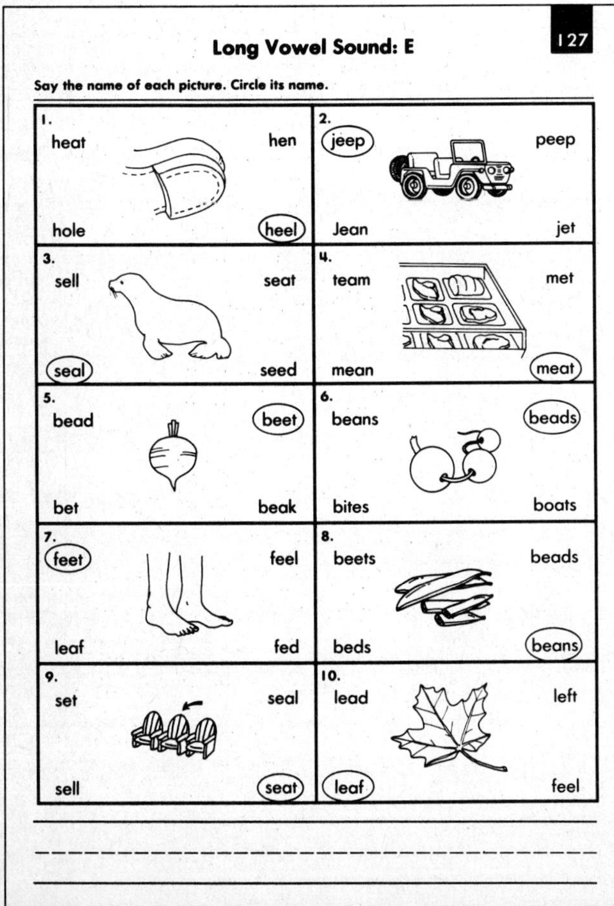
127

Long Vowel Sound: E

Say the name of each picture. Circle its name.

1. heat, hen, hole, (heel)
2. (jeep), peep, Jean, jet
3. sell, seat, (seal), seed
4. team, met, mean, (meat)
5. bead, (beet), bet, beak
6. beans, (beads), bites, boats
7. (feet), feel, leaf, fed
8. beets, beads, beds, (beans)
9. set, seal, sell, (seat)
10. lead, left, (leaf), feel

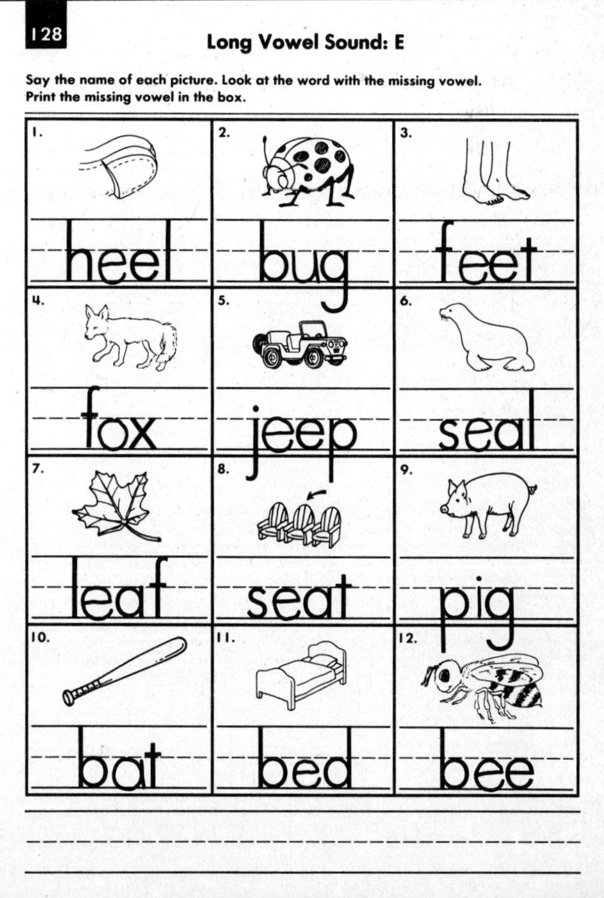
128

Long Vowel Sound: E

Say the name of each picture. Look at the word with the missing vowel. Print the missing vowel in the box.

1. heel
2. bug
3. feet
4. fox
5. jeep
6. seal
7. leaf
8. seat
9. pig
10. bat
11. bed
12. bee

Reading Write the following sentences on the chalkboard.

1. *See the seal in the deep lake.*
2. *Keep the beans in the bag.*
3. *Lee likes to eat meat.*
4. *Jean has a big box of beads.*
5. *We will meet at the lake.*

Ask the children to read each sentence silently. Invite volunteers to each read a sentence aloud and then to circle the words that contain the long *E* sound. To build comprehension skills, ask questions such as the following: *What does Lee like to eat? Where can you see the seal? Who has beads?* Encourage the children to respond in complete sentences. Vary the activity by challenging each child who reads a sentence to think of a content question about the sentence.

Reteaching

Reading Make sentence strips using the above sentences for a child who needs more practice. Have the child read the sentences aloud to you. After each sentence, have the child point out the words with the long *E* sound.

Lesson 57

Long Vowel *E* (pages 130–131)

Objective The child will read long *E* words in isolation and within sentences.

Teaching Ideas

Speaking Write the following words on small squares of construction paper or tagboard: *tea, seal, peep, bean, feel, beet, weed, jeep, meal, neat, beat.* (The cards may be prepared prior to the lesson or made by the children as part of the lesson.) Place the cards facedown on a desk or table. Invite the children to choose a card and read aloud the word on the card. Ask the children to identify the vowel sound they hear. Then, challenge the children to use the long *E* words in sentences.

To expand the activity, you may wish to have the children think of more words with the long *E* sound. Remind the children that *ee* and *ea* can have the sound of long *E*. Provide help with spelling as needed.

Write the following sentences on strips of paper.

1. *I can feel heat from the sun.*
2. *We had tea at the meal.*
3. *We will meet next week.*
4. *Jack eats peas and beans.*
5. *Tammy had her feet on the seat.*
6. *The bee is on the leaf of the flower.*

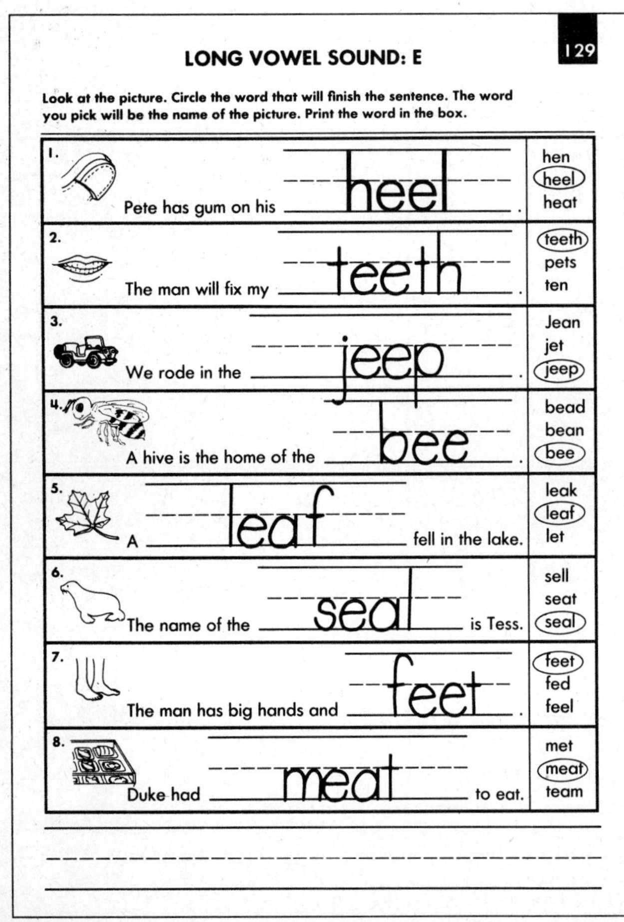

129

LONG VOWEL SOUND: E

Look at the picture. Circle the word that will finish the sentence. The word you pick will be the name of the picture. Print the word in the box.

1.	Pete has gum on his heel.	hen, (heel), heat
2.	The man will fix my teeth.	(teeth), pets, ten
3.	We rode in the jeep.	Jean, jet, (jeep)
4.	A hive is the home of the bee.	bead, bean, (bee)
5.	A leaf fell in the lake.	leak, (leaf), let
6.	The name of the seal is Tess.	sell, seat, (seal)
7.	The man has big hands and feet.	(feet), fed, feel
8.	Duke had meat to eat.	met, (meat), team

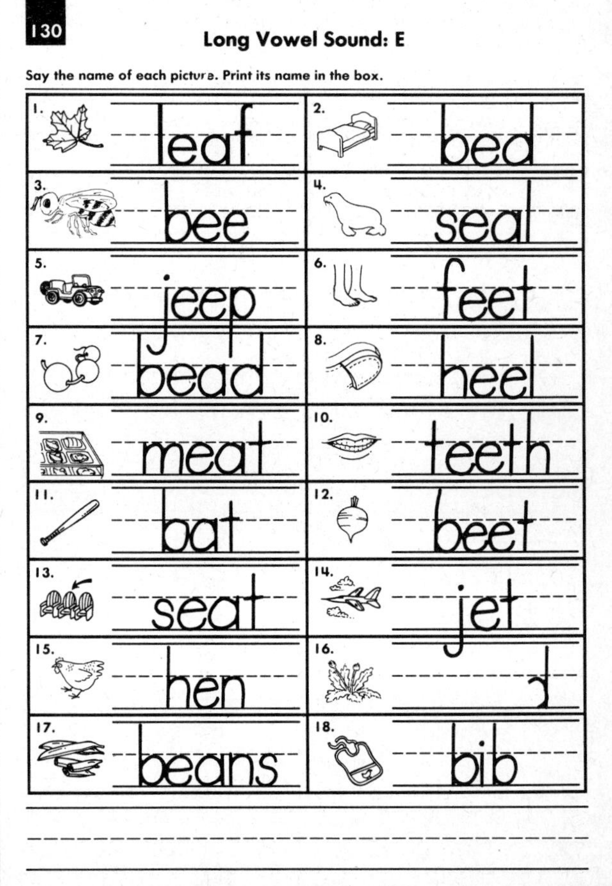

130

Long Vowel Sound: E

Say the name of each picture. Print its name in the box.

1.	leaf	2.	bed
3.	bee	4.	seal
5.	jeep	6.	feet
7.	bead	8.	heel
9.	meat	10.	teeth
11.	bat	12.	beet
13.	seat	14.	jet
15.	hen	16.	
17.	beans	18.	bib

Invite volunteers to each read a sentence aloud. Encourage the children to answer the following content questions with words from the sentences.

1. *What can I feel from the sun?*
2. *What did we have at the meal?*
3. *What will we do next week?*
4. *What does Jack eat?*
5. *Where did Tammy have her feet?*
6. *Where is the bee?*

Continue the activity by asking the children to copy the sentences onto the chalkboard and circle the words in each sentence that have the long *E* vowel sound.

Writing Challenge the children to create their own sentences and content questions. If you wish, encourage the children to trade papers and answer each other's questions.

Extension

Writing Write the following incomplete words on the chalkboard.

l _____ *f*	*s* _____ *t*
b _____	*j* _____ *p*
tr _____	*s* _____ *d*
f _____ *t*	*s* _____
h _____ *l*	*w* _____ *d*

Have the child complete each word by adding *ea* or *ee*. Point out that in some cases, either combination would be correct.

Lesson 58

Review of Vowels (pages 132–134)

Objective The child will use the Short and Long Vowel Rules to read words containing short and long vowels.

Long Vowel Rule 2: If a word or a syllable has one vowel, and it comes at the end of the word or syllable, that vowel is usually long.

Review

Silent-*E* Game Provide each child with a small square of tagboard or construction paper. Ask the children to print the small letter *e* on their squares. Then, place the following word cards facedown on a desk or table: *rob, dim, hop, can, rod, cut, rip, mad, tub, rid, tap, us, hat, kit, pin, hid, not, at.* Invite volunteers to choose a card and read the work aloud. Ask the children to identify the vowel sound heard in the word. Challenge the volunteers to place a silent e card at the end of a word card and read the new word. Point out that the silent e card now changes the vowel sound in the word.

Encourage the children to identify the new vowel sound. Repeat the procedure until all the word cards have been used.

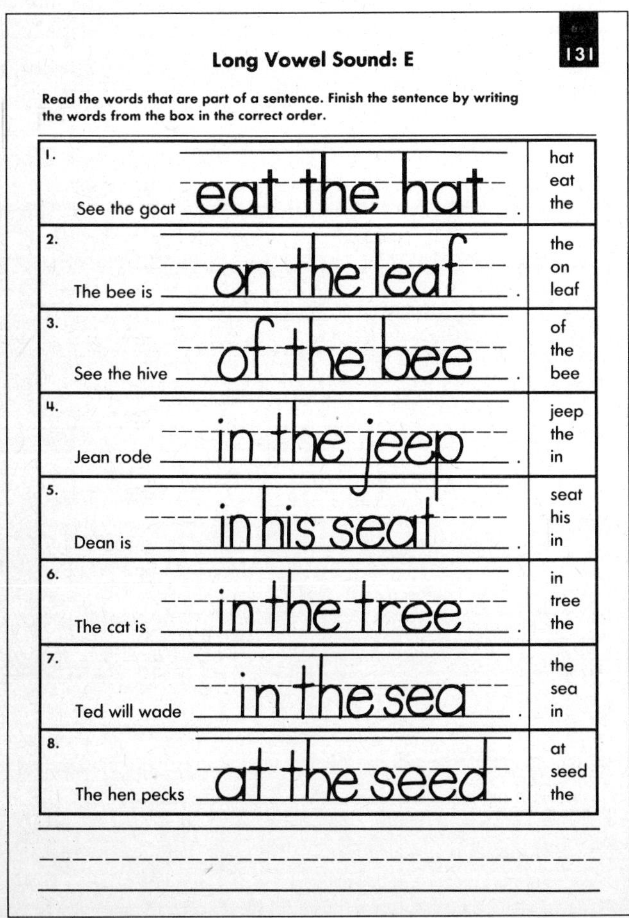

131

Long Vowel Sound: E

Read the words that are part of a sentence. Finish the sentence by writing the words from the box in the correct order.

1. See the goat eat the hat.	hat eat the
2. The bee is on the leaf.	the on leaf
3. See the hive of the bee.	of the bee
4. Jean rode in the jeep.	jeep the in
5. Dean is in his seat.	seat his in
6. The cat is in the tree.	in tree the
7. Ted will wade in the sea.	the sea in
8. The hen pecks at the seed.	at seed the

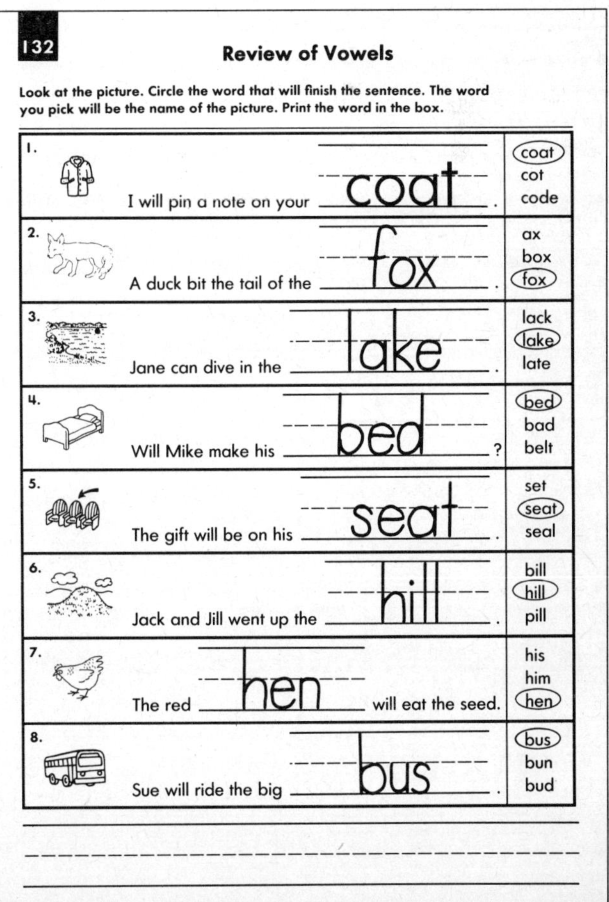

132

Review of Vowels

Look at the picture. Circle the word that will finish the sentence. The word you pick will be the name of the picture. Print the word in the box.

1. I will pin a note on your coat.	(coat) cot code
2. A duck bit the tail of the fox.	ax box (fox)
3. Jane can dive in the lake.	lack (lake) late
4. Will Mike make his bed?	(bed) bad belt
5. The gift will be on his seat.	set (seat) seal
6. Jack and Jill went up the hill.	bill (hill) pill
7. The red hen will eat the seed.	his him (hen)
8. Sue will ride the big bus.	(bus) bun bud

Teaching Ideas

Listening Encourage the children to listen for the vowel sound in each of the following words as you say them aloud: *be, no, we, go, so, he*. Have the children repeat the words as you say them again. Challenge the children to name the vowel sound heard in each word.

Reading Write the words from the previous activity on the chalkboard. Point out to the children that the vowel in each word is located at the end of the word. Review with the children Long Vowel Rule 2. Invite the children to read each word again, name the vowel sound, and explain in their own words how Long Vowel Rule 2 applies to the word.

Speaking Print the following words in two columns on the chalkboard: *is, it, us, on, egg; be, we, no, go, me*. Encourage the children to read the words in the first column and explain why the words have a short vowel sound. Then ask the children to read the words in the second column and explain why they have a long vowel sound. Point out that the vowels in the first column are followed by a consonant, making them short vowels, while the vowels in the second column are at the end of the word, making them long vowels.

Write the following words on the chalkboard: *ax, ox, bug, rake, pie, mule, hose, lid, tent, bee*. Challenge the children to read each word and tell whether the word has a long or short vowel sound. Encourage the children to explain, in their own words, why the vowel has the long or short sound.

Vowel-Chain Game Write the following sentences on the chalkboard.

1. *He will stay at the lake cottage.*
2. *I came home late.*
3. *He ran faster than I ran.*
4. *Pam gave us a ride.*
5. *No, I cannot play the game today.*
6. *Mom gave me an apple.*

Invite a volunteer to read the first sentence aloud. Have the volunteer choose a classmate to circle the short vowel words in that sentence. Ask the second child to choose another classmate to underline the long vowel words. Encourage the children to choose those classmates who have not yet had a turn, so that as many children as possible may participate. Continue the game with each of the remaining sentences.

Extension

Mail-a-Letter Game Invite the child to play Mail a Letter using short and long vowel words. Distribute letter cards for long and short vowel words to the child. Draw a box on the chalkboard for each long and short vowel and label each box. Invite the child to read the word on a card, identify the vowel and its sound, and then "mail" the card by placing it under the appropriate drawing.

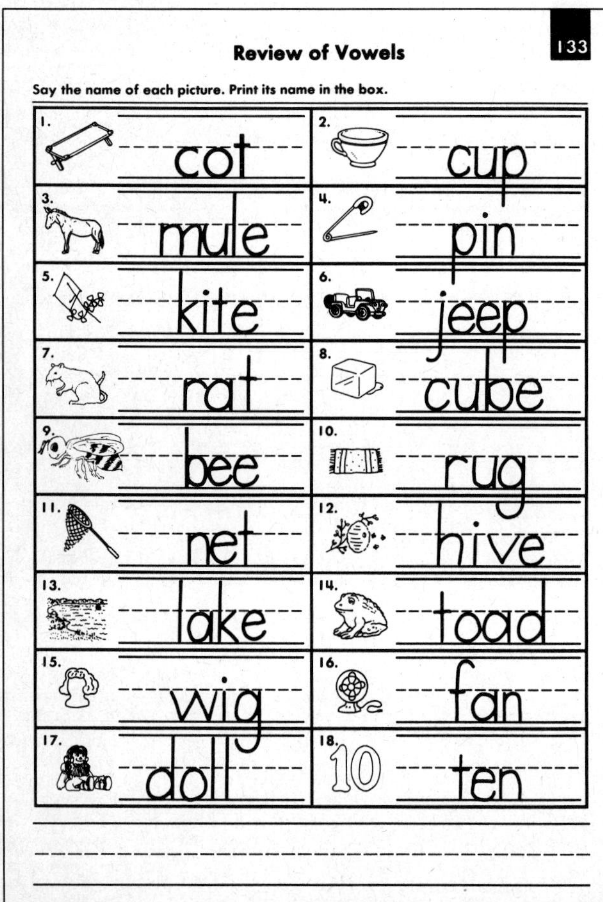

Review of Vowels 133

Say the name of each picture. Print its name in the box.

1. cot	2. cup
3. mule	4. pin
5. kite	6. jeep
7. rat	8. cube
9. bee	10. rug
11. net	12. hive
13. lake	14. toad
15. wig	16. fan
17. doll	18. ten

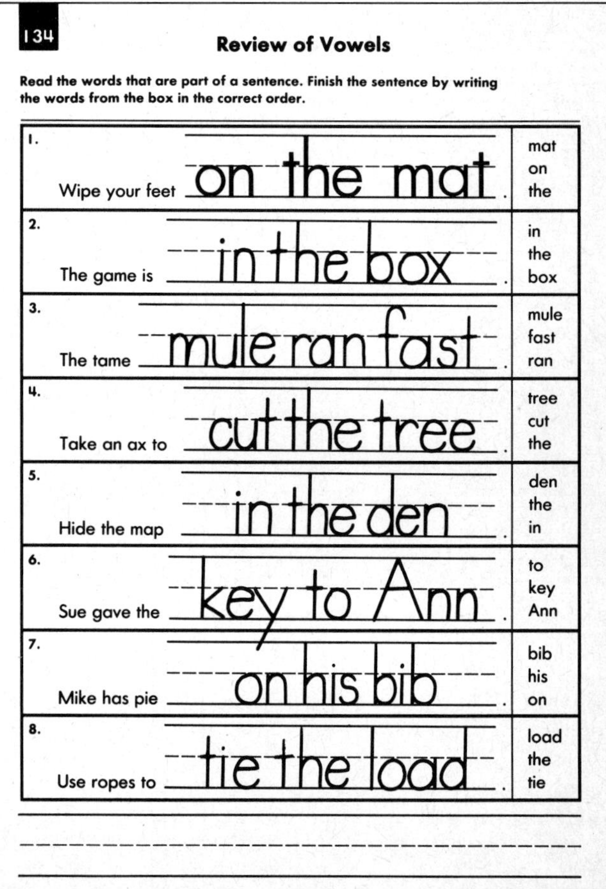

134 **Review of Vowels**

Read the words that are part of a sentence. Finish the sentence by writing the words from the box in the correct order.

1. Wipe your feet on the mat.	mat on the
2. The game is in the box.	in the box
3. The tame mule ran fast.	mule fast ran
4. Take an ax to cut the tree.	tree cut the
5. Hide the map in the den.	den the in
6. Sue gave the key to Ann.	to key Ann
7. Mike has pie on his bib.	bib his on
8. Use ropes to tie the load.	load the tie

Lesson 59
Endings S and *ED* (pages 135–136)

Objective The child will read base words with the endings *s* and *ed* (sounded as *ed*) in isolation and within sentences.

Teaching Ideas

Writing Show the children a picture of a single object (for example, a nut). Invite a volunteer to write the picture's name on the chalkboard. Then show a picture flashcard containing several of the same object. Ask another volunteer to copy the word and to add an *s* ending. Challenge the children to tell the meanings of the two words.

Speaking Write the following words on the chalkboard: *pig/pigs, bike/bikes, boat/boats, cat/cats, lip/lips, cube/cubes.* Ask for volunteers to read each pair of words and to identify the base words that refer to more than one thing.

Write the following words on the chalkboard and have a volunteer read them aloud: *paint, seat, end, melt, rest, dust, land, need.* Write *ed* next to the word *paint* and ask the children to listen for the sound of the ending as you say the word. Invite volunteers to come to the chalkboard and add *ed* to the other words. Ask each volunteer to say the word aloud, then encourage the rest of the children to repeat the word. You may wish to extend the activity by having the children use each new word in a sentence.

Line-Up Game Select a variety of word cards containing words with either the *s* or the *ed* endings and distribute one card, facedown, to each child. Designate an *s* line at the front of the room with tape and an *ed* line at the back of the room. Call on each child to turn over the card, read the word, and stand on the line that matches the ending of the word.

Extension

Speaking Give the child word cards containing base words only. Prepare a separate card that has an *s* on it. Have the child read aloud one of the base words. Then have the child hold the *s* card next to the word, reading the new word aloud. You may want to challenge the child further by repeating the activity with verb word cards and an *ed* card.

135

Word Ending: S

Say the name of each picture. Circle its name.

1. tack (tacks)
2. nail (nails)
3. nine (nines)
4. (cone) cones
5. (goat) goats
6. (cat) cats
7. rod (rods)
8. sock (socks)
9. rose (roses)
10. pig (pigs)
11. (cake) cakes
12. (mule) mules

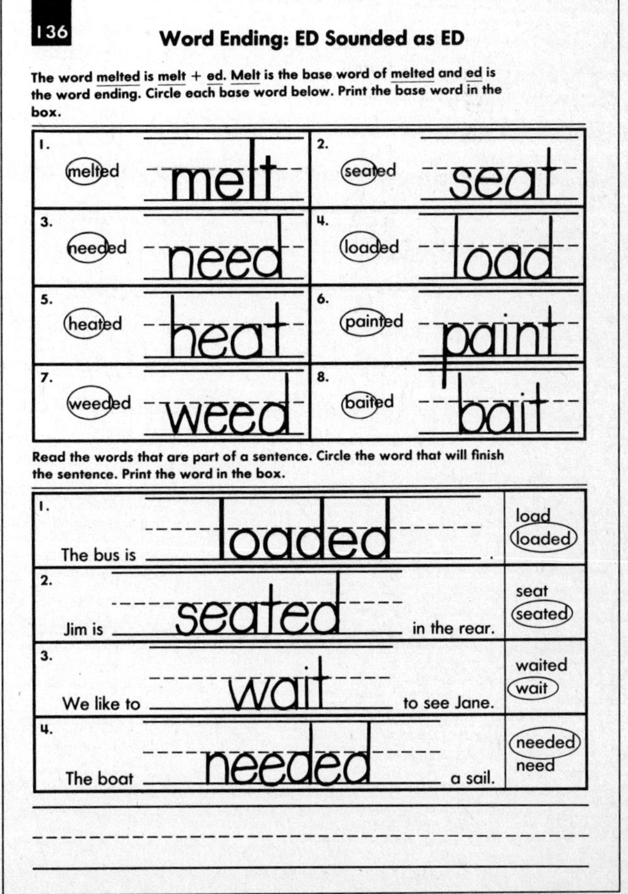

136

Word Ending: ED Sounded as ED

The word melted is melt + ed. Melt is the base word of melted and ed is the word ending. Circle each base word below. Print the base word in the box.

1. melted — melt
2. seated — seat
3. needed — need
4. loaded — load
5. heated — heat
6. painted — paint
7. weeded — weed
8. baited — bait

Read the words that are part of a sentence. Circle the word that will finish the sentence. Print the word in the box.

1. The bus is loaded. — load / (loaded)
2. Jim is seated in the rear. — seat / (seated)
3. We like to wait to see Jane. — waited / (wait)
4. The boat needed a sail. — (needed) / need

Lesson 60

Ending *ED* (pages 137–138)

Objective The child will read base words with the *ed* ending, sounded as *d* or *t*.

Review

Listening You may wish to review the *ed* ending sounded as *ed*, by writing the following pairs of words on the chalkboard.

land/landed	*melt/melted*
need/needed	*end/ended*
paint/painted	*load/loaded*

Invite the children to say each pair of words after you, listening for the sound that *ed* has. Remind the children that when the ending *ed* follows *D* or *T* in a base word, it usually has the *ed* sound.

Teaching Ideas

Listening Write the following words on the chalkboard: *jump, kiss, lock, rock, help, kick, huff, toss.* Have the children read each word aloud. Add the ending *ed* to each word. Then ask the children to listen for the sound of *ed* as you read the new words aloud. Encourage the children to identify the sound of the *ed* ending. Point out that the words end with a *t* sound when the *ed* ending is added. Encourage the children to read the new words aloud and then use each word in a sentence.

Explain to the children that the *ed* ending can make another sound. Write the following words on the chalkboard: *rain, play, mail, fill, yell, peel, bill, moan.* Ask the children to read the words aloud. Next, add the *ed* ending to each word. Encourage the children to listen for the sound of *ed* as you read the words aloud. Ask the children to identify the sound *ed* has in these words. Invite the children to read the new words aloud and use each in a sentence.

Extension

Listening Provide the child with three letter cards, each of which has been printed with one of the following: *ed*, *T*, or *D*. Say the following words aloud.

sailed	*picked*	*filled*	*neared*	*mixed*
landed	*melted*	*painted*	*jumped*	*tossed*
played	*mailed*	*ended*	*painted*	

Invite the child to listen for the sound of the *ed* ending in each word. Challenge the child to hold up the appropriate card for the sound *ed* has in each word. You may wish to continue the activity by adding more words with the *ed* ending.

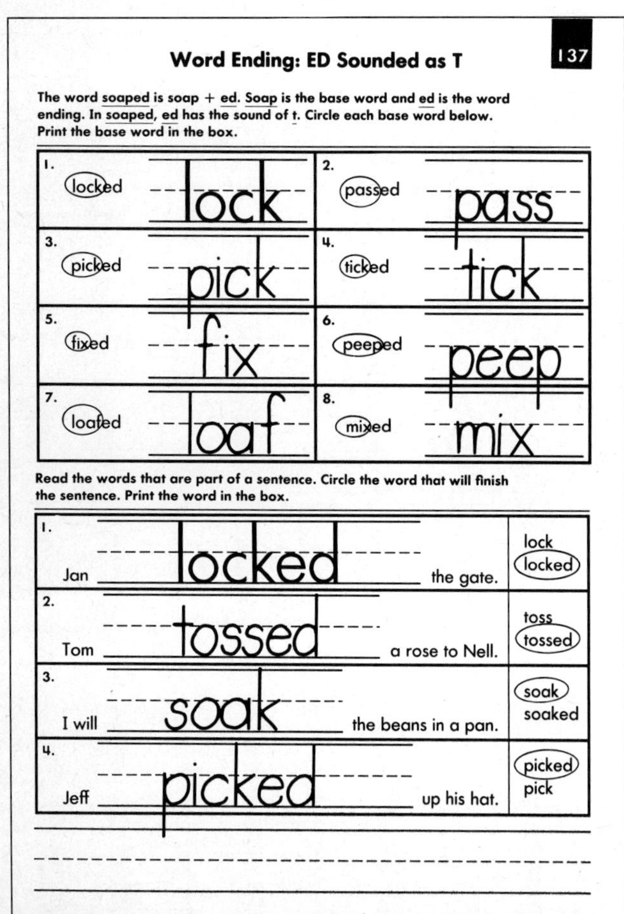

137

Word Ending: ED Sounded as T

The word soaped is soap + ed. Soap is the base word and ed is the word ending. In soaped, ed has the sound of t. Circle each base word below. Print the base word in the box.

1. locked	lock	2. passed	pass
3. picked	pick	4. ticked	tick
5. fixed	fix	6. peeped	peep
7. loafed	loaf	8. mixed	mix

Read the words that are part of a sentence. Circle the word that will finish the sentence. Print the word in the box.

1. Jan locked the gate.	lock / locked
2. Tom tossed a rose to Nell.	toss / tossed
3. I will soak the beans in a pan.	soak / soaked
4. Jeff picked up his hat.	picked / pick

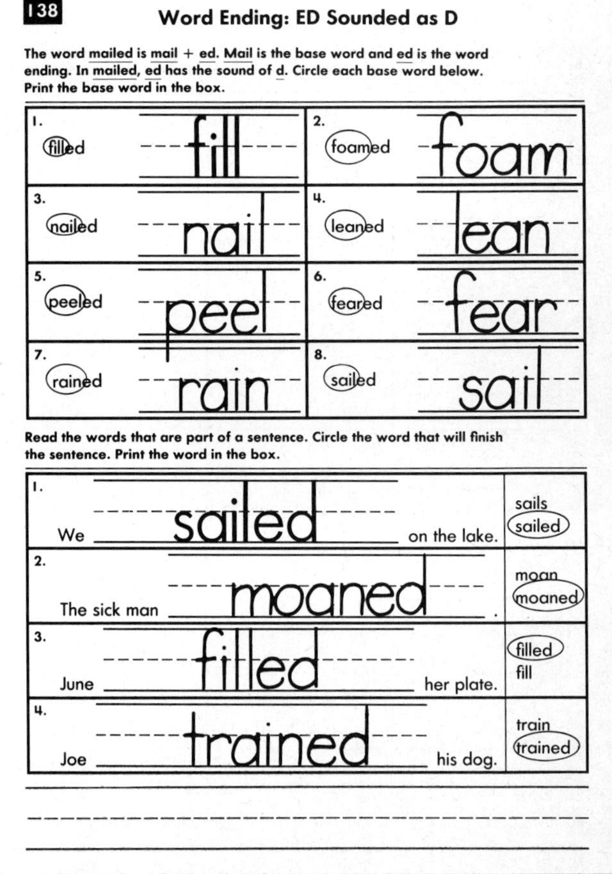

138

Word Ending: ED Sounded as D

The word mailed is mail + ed. Mail is the base word and ed is the word ending. In mailed, ed has the sound of d. Circle each base word below. Print the base word in the box.

1. filled	fill	2. foamed	foam
3. nailed	nail	4. leaned	lean
5. peeled	peel	6. feared	fear
7. rained	rain	8. sailed	sail

Read the words that are part of a sentence. Circle the word that will finish the sentence. Print the word in the box.

1. We sailed on the lake.	sails / sailed
2. The sick man moaned.	moan / moaned
3. June filled her plate.	filled / fill
4. Joe trained his dog.	train / trained

Lesson 61
Ending *ING* (page 139)

Objective The child will read base words with the *ing* ending.

Review

Writing To review the sounds of the *ed* ending, write the following words on the chalkboard and ask the children to read them aloud: *bumped, jumped, tasted, ended, asked, sailed, rained, joked, peeled, passed, needed, dusted.* Invite volunteers to underline the ending in each word, identifying the sound of the *ed*. Challenge the children to write a sentence on the chalkboard for each word. Encourage the children to read the sentences aloud.

Teaching Ideas

Writing Write the following words on the chalkboard: *jump, dust, pick, eat, feed, help, paint, sink.* Have the children read each word aloud. Explain that each word can be changed by adding the *ing* ending. Invite volunteers to write the *ing* ending after each word. You might provide a different color of chalk for the endings. Challenge the children to read the new words aloud and to use each word in a sentence.

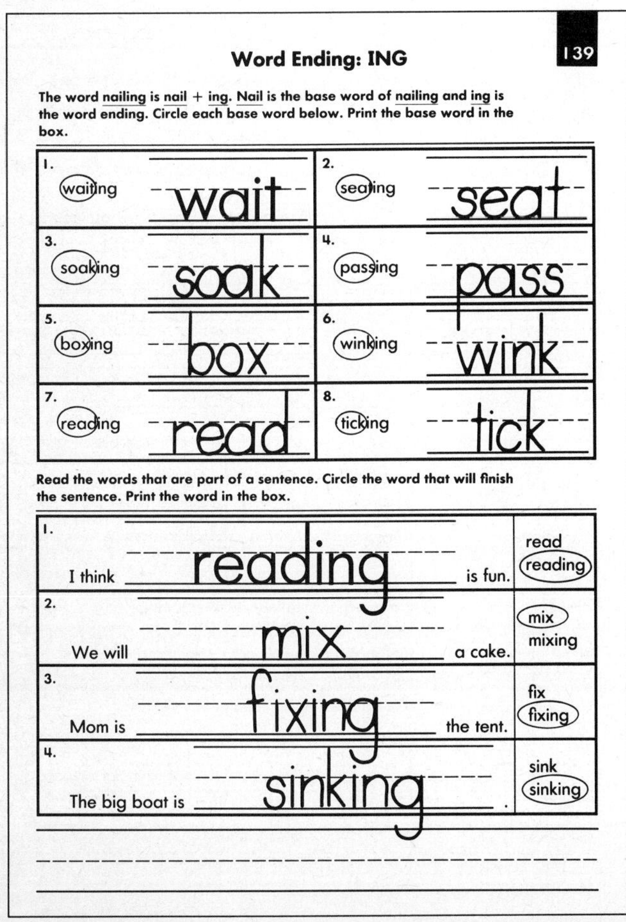

Word Ending: ING 139

The word nailing is nail + ing. Nail is the base word of nailing and ing is the word ending. Circle each base word below. Print the base word in the box.

1. waiting	wait	2. seating	seat
3. soaking	soak	4. passing	pass
5. boxing	box	6. winking	wink
7. reading	read	8. ticking	tick

Read the words that are part of a sentence. Circle the word that will finish the sentence. Print the word in the box.

1. I think reading is fun.	read / reading
2. We will mix a cake.	mix / mixing
3. Mom is fixing the tent.	fix / fixing
4. The big boat is sinking.	sink / sinking

Speaking Write the following words on the chalkboard: *playing, rains, reading, sailed, telling, boats, rocking, passing, waxing, pays, mixing, bumped.* Invite the children to say the words aloud. Ask volunteers to identify each base word and to circle and identify each ending. Challenge the children to use each of the words in a sentence.

Writing Write the following sentences on the chalkboard, and point out that there is one word in each sentence that is missing an ending.

1. *Read is fun.*
2. *Dad fix the bus.*
3. *The boat is float on the river.*
4. *I pass into grade one.*
5. *Dan fix a meat loaf for dinner.*
6. *She wait for us.*

Invite volunteers to identify the word in each sentence that requires an ending. Have the volunteer add the ending to the appropriate word. Reinforce a correct response by having the child reread the sentence with the correction.

Reteaching

Writing Provide the child with a small square of tagboard or construction paper. Ask the child to print the *ing* ending on the square. Write the following words on the chalkboard and invite the child to read aloud each word: *read, play, dust, feed, help, float, feed, soak, seat, wink.* Ask the child to place the *ing* square at the end of each word and read the new word. Challenge the child to write sentences using the new words.

Unit 5 Consonant Blends; Vowel Y

Lesson 62

R Blends (pages 140–143)

Objective The child will decode *r* blend words and use them in sentences.

A consonant blend is two or three consonants sounded together in which the sound of each letter can be heard.

Review

Listening To review auditory discrimination, say the following words, and encourage the children to repeat the sound they hear at the beginning of each word: *train, brick, pretzel, grapes, cry, frown.* Challenge the children to identify the letters that represent the sound heard at the beginning of each word. You may then wish to have the children use each word in a sentence.

Teaching Idea

Listening Say the following words, and encourage the children to listen for the beginning sound in each: *tree, truck, train, trip.* Point out that each word has two beginning sounds that are blended together. Have the children repeat each of the words as you say them again. Encourage the children to identify the beginning blend in each word. Point out that each beginning blend contains the letters *T* and *R.* Explain to the children that when two consonants are blended together, the sound is called a *consonant blend.*

Speaking Next, write on the chalkboard the words from the previous activity. Encourage the children to read the words aloud. Invite volunteers to circle the beginning blends in each of the words. Ask the children to identify the sound made by the *tr* blend.

Print the following words on the chalkboard: *crib, dress, grape, green, pretzel, prize, brick, brush.* Ask the children to say the words aloud, listening for the beginning blend in each. Circle the beginning blend in each word. Explain to the children that the circled letters in each word are blends. Encourage the children to identify the one letter that is common to all of the blends. Explain that because each blend has an *R,* these blends are called *r* blends.

Write the following sentences on the chalkboard.

1. *The man tried to trick Fred.*
2. *The gray brick is cracked.*
3. *Your bread will win a prize.*
4. *The train runs on a track.*
5. *Jane's dress is green and gray.*

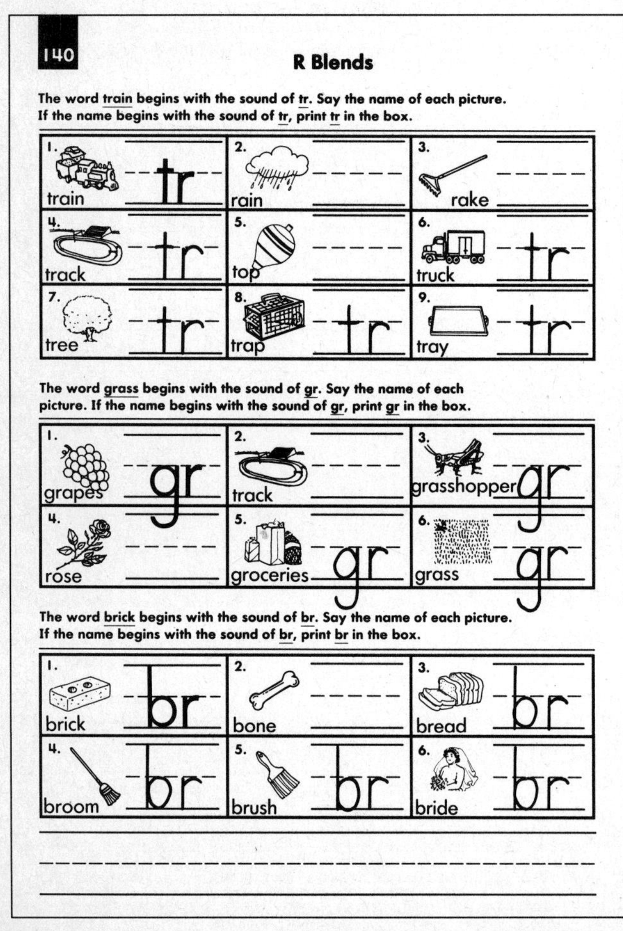
140

R Blends

The word train begins with the sound of tr. Say the name of each picture. If the name begins with the sound of tr, print tr in the box.

1. train tr	2. rain	3. rake
4. track tr	5. top	6. truck tr
7. tree tr	8. trap tr	9. tray tr

The word grass begins with the sound of gr. Say the name of each picture. If the name begins with the sound of gr, print gr in the box.

1. grapes gr	2. track	3. grasshopper gr
4. rose	5. groceries gr	6. grass gr

The word brick begins with the sound of br. Say the name of each picture. If the name begins with the sound of br, print br in the box.

1. brick br	2. bone	3. bread br
4. broom br	5. brush br	6. bride br

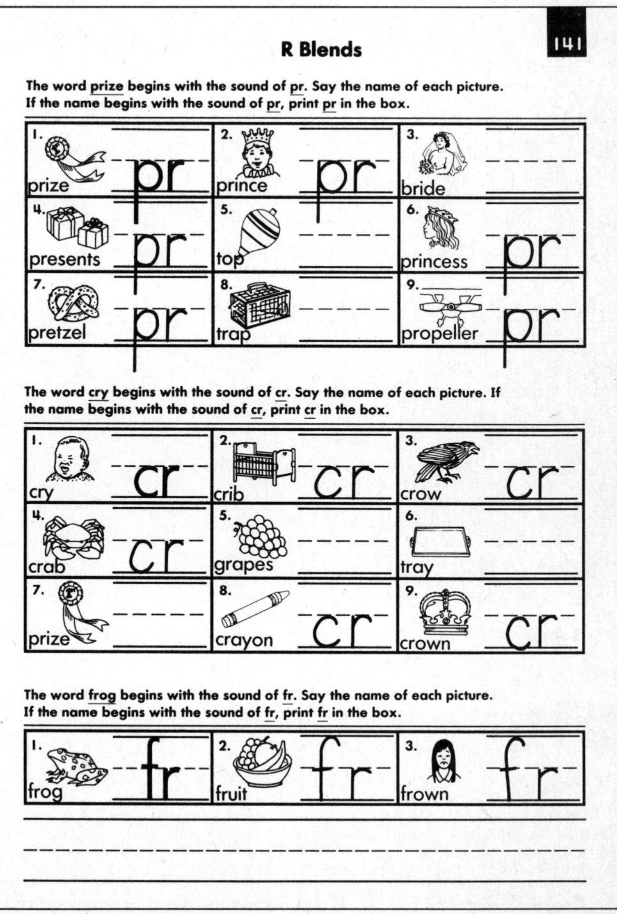
R Blends

141

The word prize begins with the sound of pr. Say the name of each picture. If the name begins with the sound of pr, print pr in the box.

1. prize pr	2. prince pr	3. bride
4. presents pr	5. top	6. princess pr
7. pretzel pr	8. trap	9. propeller pr

The word cry begins with the sound of cr. Say the name of each picture. If the name begins with the sound of cr, print cr in the box.

1. cry cr	2. crib cr	3. crow cr
4. crab cr	5. grapes	6. tray
7. prize	8. crayon cr	9. crown cr

The word frog begins with the sound of fr. Say the name of each picture. If the name begins with the sound of fr, print fr in the box.

1. frog fr	2. fruit fr	3. frown fr

Invite the children to read each sentence aloud. Encourage the children to circle the words that have an *r* blend. (You may wish to provide different colored chalk to circle the words with an *r* blend.) Ask the children to identify the beginning blend in each circled word.

Writing Arrange pictures of the following objects on the chalkboard ledge: *bread, broom, crown, dress, fruit, grapes, trailer.* (These pictures may be prepared prior to the lesson or by the children as part of the lesson.) Ask the children to say the name of each picture. Challenge the children to write on the chalkboard above each picture the *r* blend heard in the name of the picture.

Print the following words on the chalkboard.

drop	*trick*	*grade*	*treat*
crock	*brick*	*green*	*brave*
greet	*crib*	*drink*	*dress*

Invite the children to read the words aloud. Encourage volunteers to underline the *r* blend in each word and to write each word in a sentence.

Extension

Art Provide the child with a piece of newsprint or white construction paper. Write the following words on the chalkboard: *drum, crib, dress, brick, grass, frog, crow, tray.* Ask the child to fold the paper into four squares and to write one word from the chalkboard at the top of each square. Encourage the child to use markers, crayons, or paints to illustrate each word.

To expand the activity, provide a second sheet of paper and challenge the child to illustrate the remaining words.

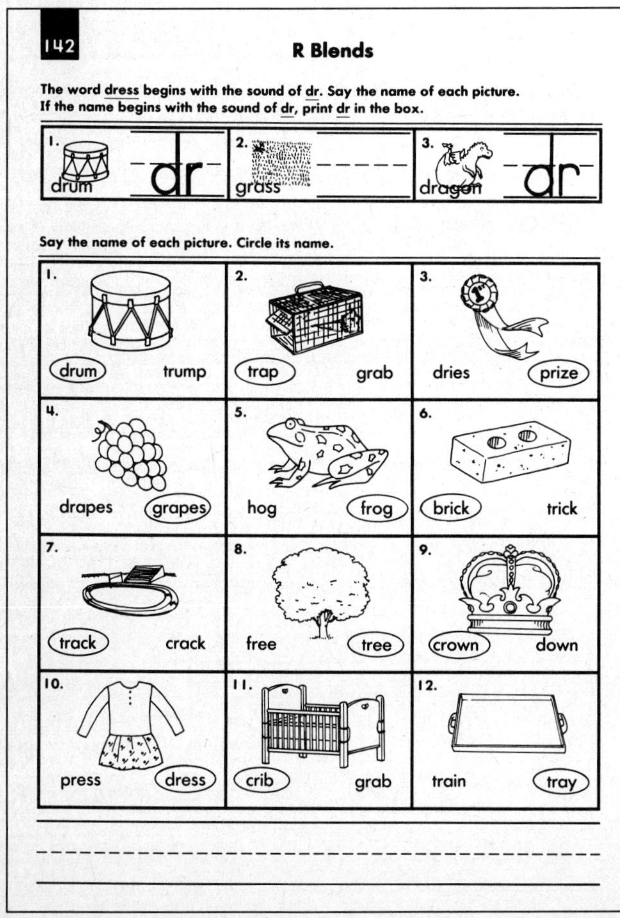
142

R Blends

The word dress begins with the sound of dr. Say the name of each picture. If the name begins with the sound of dr, print dr in the box.

1. drum — dr	2. grass —	3. dragon — dr

Say the name of each picture. Circle its name.

1. (drum) trump	2. (trap) grab	3. dries (prize)
4. drapes (grapes)	5. hog (frog)	6. (brick) trick
7. (track) crack	8. free (tree)	9. (crown) down
10. press (dress)	11. (crib) grab	12. train (tray)

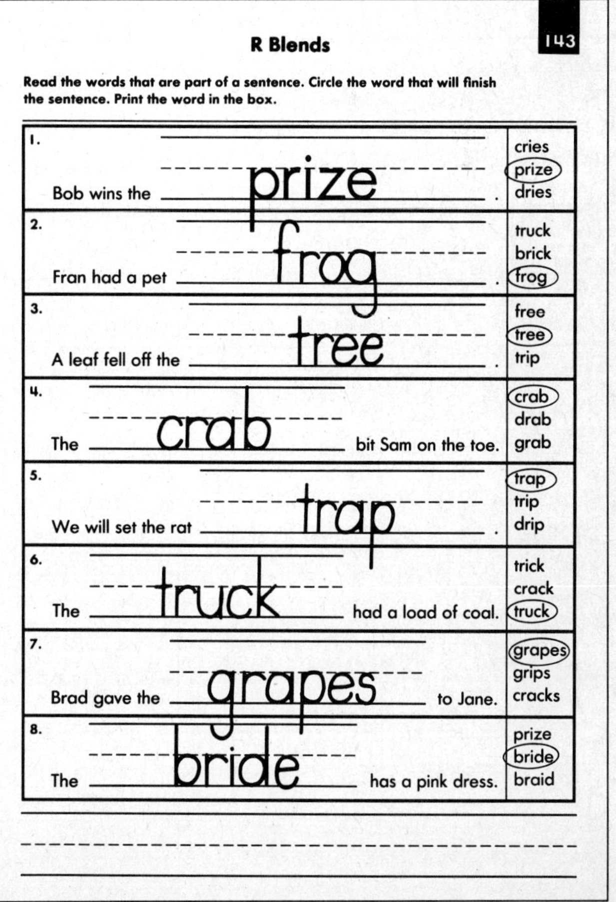
143

R Blends

Read the words that are part of a sentence. Circle the word that will finish the sentence. Print the word in the box.

1.	Bob wins the prize .	cries (prize) dries
2.	Fran had a pet frog .	truck brick (frog)
3.	A leaf fell off the tree .	free (tree) trip
4.	The crab bit Sam on the toe.	(crab) drab grab
5.	We will set the rat trap .	(trap) trip drip
6.	The truck had a load of coal.	trick crack (truck)
7.	Brad gave the grapes to Jane.	(grapes) grips cracks
8.	The bride has a pink dress.	prize (bride) braid

Lesson 63

L Blends (pages 144–147)

Objective The child will identify *l* blends and read words containing *l* blends.

Review

Listening To review the *r* blends, encourage the children to listen for the beginning sound in the following groups of words.

bride/broke/brave	*price/press/print*
free/from/frame	*cry/creep/crack*
grade/grand/green	*drive/drop/drink*
tree/train/truck	*fry/fret/frail*

Ask the children to identify the beginning blend in each group of words. Reinforce a correct response by inviting a volunteer to write the blend on the chalkboard.

Teaching Ideas

Listening Direct the children to listen for the beginning blends in words you say. Pronounce the following words: *blouse, blanket, blue, block.* Encourage the children to identify the beginning sound in each word. Point out that the beginning sound in each word is the blend of the letters *B* and *L*.

Speaking Write the following words on the chalkboard: *flat, blow, plant, climb, plane, flag, glow, glad, clay, flash, cloud.* Ask the children to read the words aloud and identify the beginning sound in each. Point out that each of the words begins with an *l* blend. You may wish to remind the children that a blend is two consonants sounded together in which the sound of each letter can be heard. Invite volunteers to trace the *l* blend in each word. Invite the children to use each in a sentence.

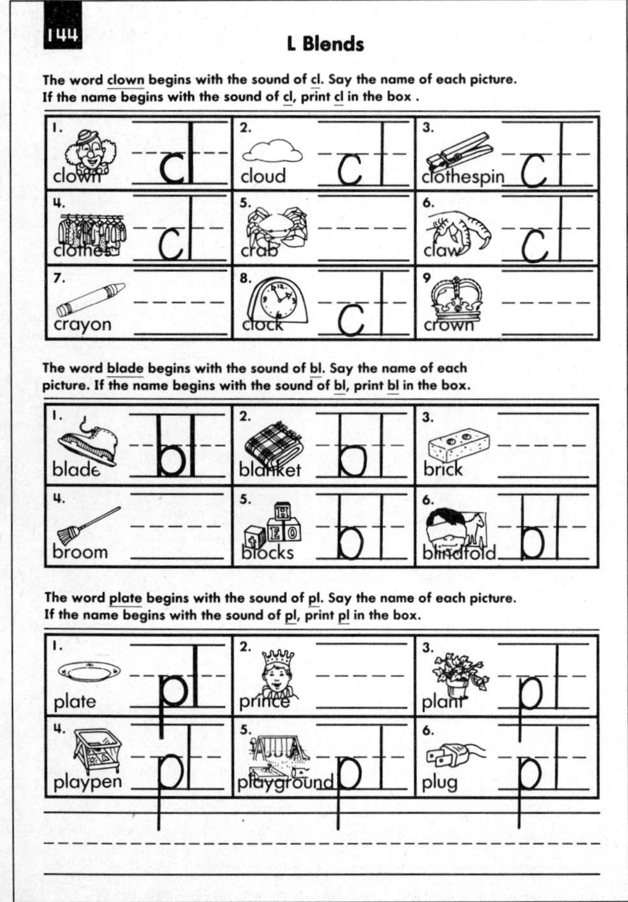

144

L Blends

The word clown begins with the sound of cl. Say the name of each picture. If the name begins with the sound of cl, print cl in the box .

1. clown 2. cloud 3. clothespin 4. clothes 5. crab 6. claw 7. crayon 8. clock 9. crown

The word blade begins with the sound of bl. Say the name of each picture. If the name begins with the sound of bl, print bl in the box.

1. blade 2. blanket 3. brick 4. broom 5. blocks 6. blindfold

The word plate begins with the sound of pl. Say the name of each picture. If the name begins with the sound of pl, print pl in the box.

1. plate 2. prince 3. plant 4. playpen 5. playground 6. plug

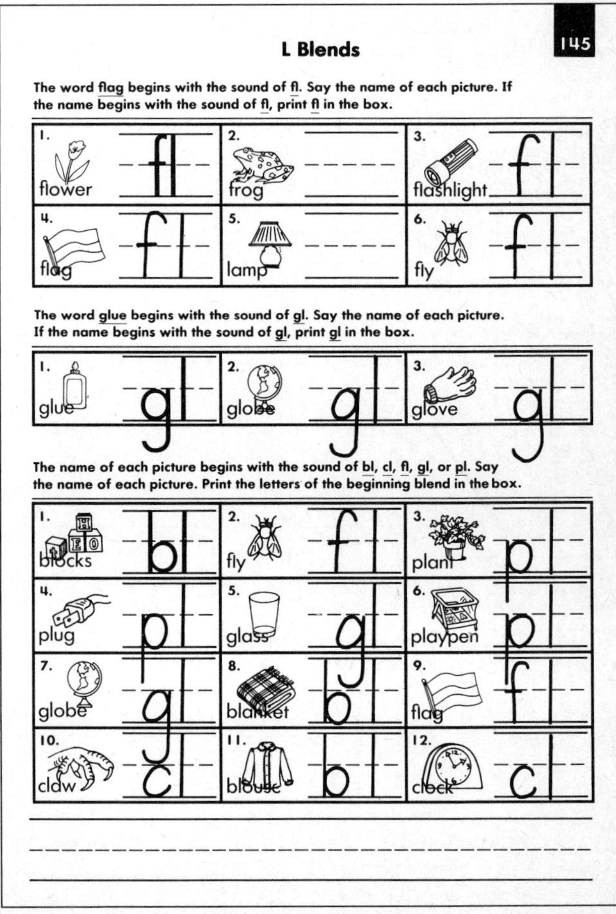

145

L Blends

The word flag begins with the sound of fl. Say the name of each picture. If the name begins with the sound of fl, print fl in the box.

1. flower 2. frog 3. flashlight 4. flag 5. lamp 6. fly

The word glue begins with the sound of gl. Say the name of each picture. If the name begins with the sound of gl, print gl in the box.

1. glue 2. globe 3. glove

The name of each picture begins with the sound of bl, cl, fl, gl, or pl. Say the name of each picture. Print the letters of the beginning blend in the box.

1. blocks 2. fly 3. plant 4. plug 5. glass 6. playpen 7. globe 8. blanket 9. flag 10. claw 11. blouse 12. clock

Writing Direct the children to work in pairs. Ask each pair to create sentences using as many words that begin with *l* blends as possible. For example: *The blue plane glowed as it climbed through the clouds.* You may want to provide a list of *l* blend words on the chalkboard to help the children get started. Have the children record their sentences on a sheet of paper and underline each *l* blend word in the sentences. Invite the pairs of children to share their sentences with the rest of the class.

Extension

Writing Write the following words in a row on the chalkboard: *flat, clown, blue, glad, plate.* Ask the child to read each word and trace the *l* blend. Encourage the child to think of another word that begins with each of the *l* blends: *fl, cl, bl, gl, pl.* Ask the child to write the word under the appropriate *l* blend word on the chalkboard. Encourage the child to read each pair of words. If you wish, have the child use the words in one or more sentences.

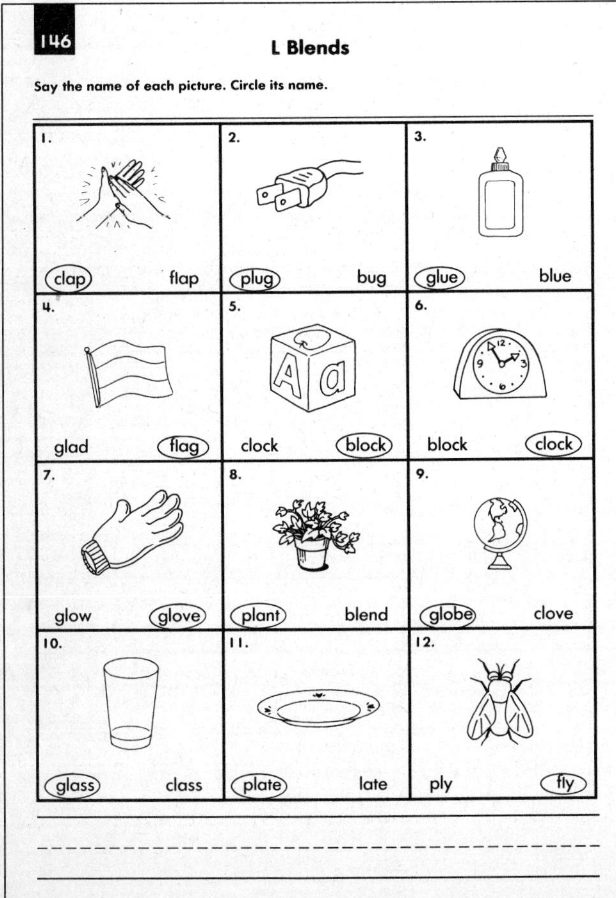

146

L Blends

Say the name of each picture. Circle its name.

1. (clap) flap	2. (plug) bug	3. (glue) blue
4. glad (flag)	5. clock (block)	6. block (clock)
7. glow (glove)	8. (plant) blend	9. (globe) clove
10. (glass) class	11. (plate) late	12. ply (fly)

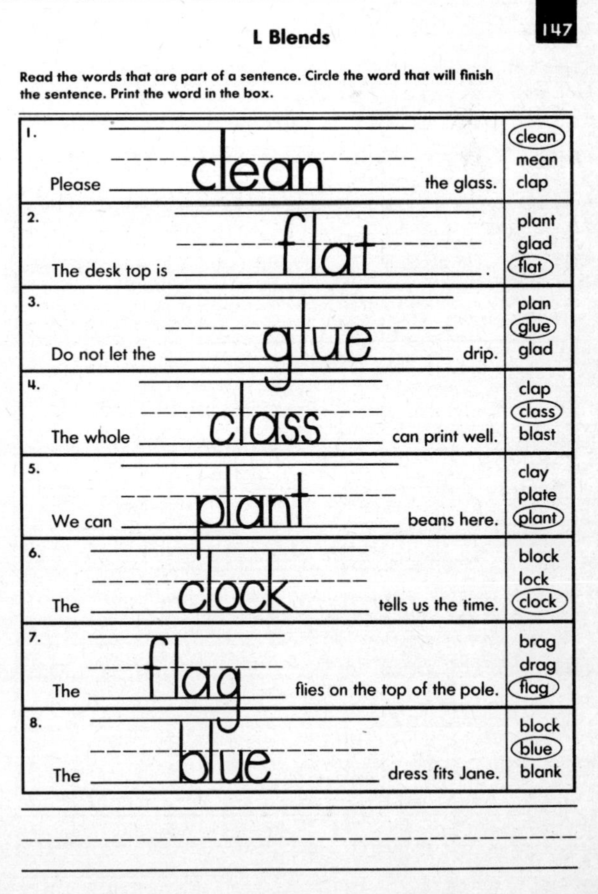

L Blends

147

Read the words that are part of a sentence. Circle the word that will finish the sentence. Print the word in the box.

1. Please clean the glass.	(clean) mean clap
2. The desk top is flat.	plant glad (flat)
3. Do not let the glue drip.	plan (glue) glad
4. The whole class can print well.	clap (class) blast
5. We can plant beans here.	clay plate (plant)
6. The clock tells us the time.	block lock (clock)
7. The flag flies on the top of the pole.	brag drag (flag)
8. The blue dress fits Jane.	block (blue) blank

Lesson 64

S Blends (pages 148–151)

Objective The child will identify *s* blends and read words that contain *s* blends.

Teaching Ideas

Listening Write the following words on the chalkboard: *stand, steam, store, stop, step*. Ask the children to listen for and identify the beginning blend in each word as you read the words aloud. Explain to the children that the sound heard at the beginning of each word is the sound of the *st* blend. Invite volunteers to trace the *st* blend in each word.

Write the following words on the chalkboard: *small, sky, sprint, stood, sweep, strap, spill, snow, slow, scrub, spray, splash.* Ask the children to listen for and identify the blend at the beginning of each word. Explain to the children that the sound heard at the beginning of each word is an *s* blend. Point out to the children that some of the words contain blends having more than two consonants. Remind the children that a blend is two or three consonants sounded together in which the sound of each letter can be heard. Ask the children to identify those words containing an *s* blend that is made up of two consonants. Then, have the children identify those words containing an *s* blend that is made up of three consonants. Ask volunteers to trace with chalk the *s* blend in each word. You may then wish to have the children name the sound of each *s* blend.

Writing Write the following words on the chalkboard: *swim, sweep, steam, state, speed, street, sneak, sneeze, sweet, sled, spring, squeak.* Ask the children to read the words aloud and underline the *s* blend in each word. Invite volunteers to write sentences using the *s* blend words. Challenge the children to use more than one of the words in each sentence. Encourage the children to share the sentences with the rest of the class.

Write the following sentences on the chalkboard.

1. Please sit still and smile.
2. Glenn tried to swim across the lake.
3. Please sweep the steps.
4. Would you please buy grapes at the store?
5. I am certain I can smell smoke.
6. His skates squeak.

Encourage the children to read each sentence aloud. Ask volunteers to circle words with the *s* blend and underline the letters that form the *s* blend.

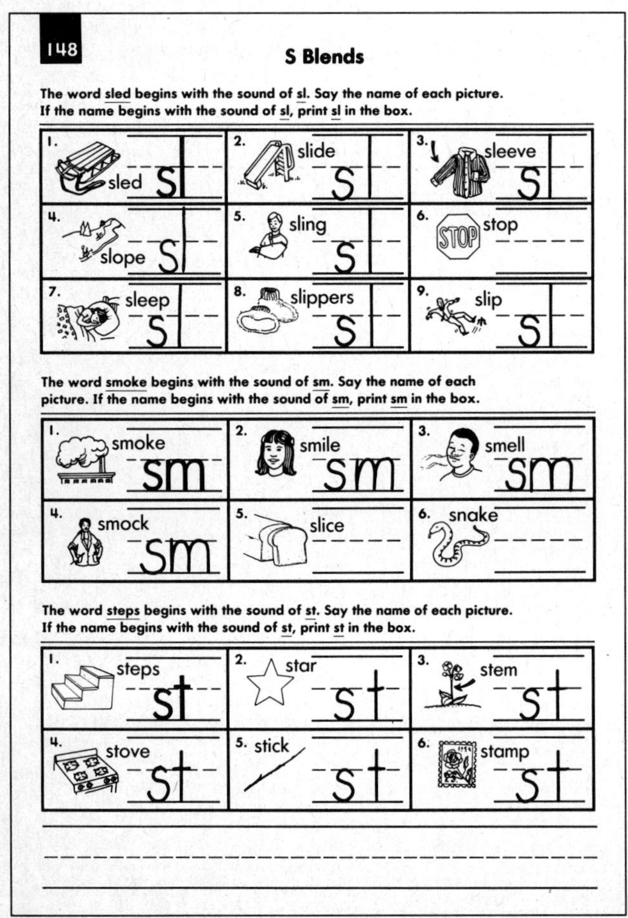

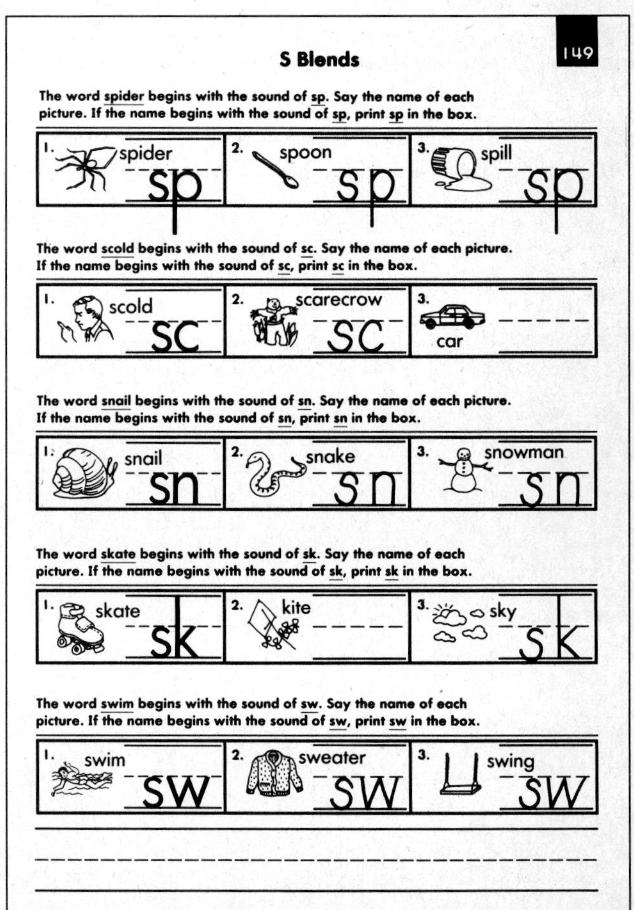

Extension

Listening Write the following words on the chalkboard: *sweet, must, rooster, just, small, straight, basket, square*. Explain to the child that each word has an *s* blend. Point to the words, one at a time, and say them aloud. Challenge the child to tell whether the *s* blend is found at the beginning, middle, or end of each word. Encourage the child to underline each *s* blend.

Reteaching

Writing Write the following *s* blends in a column on the left side of a sheet of paper: *sc, sw, sk, sl, sm, st, sn, scr, spl, str, squ*. (You may wish to use red, black, or blue marker to assist visual discrimination.) Challenge the child to suggest words for each *s* blend, providing help with spelling as needed. Encourage the child to write each of the *s* blend words.

Family Involvement Activity Duplicate the Family Letter on page 107 of this Teacher's Edition. Send it home with the children.

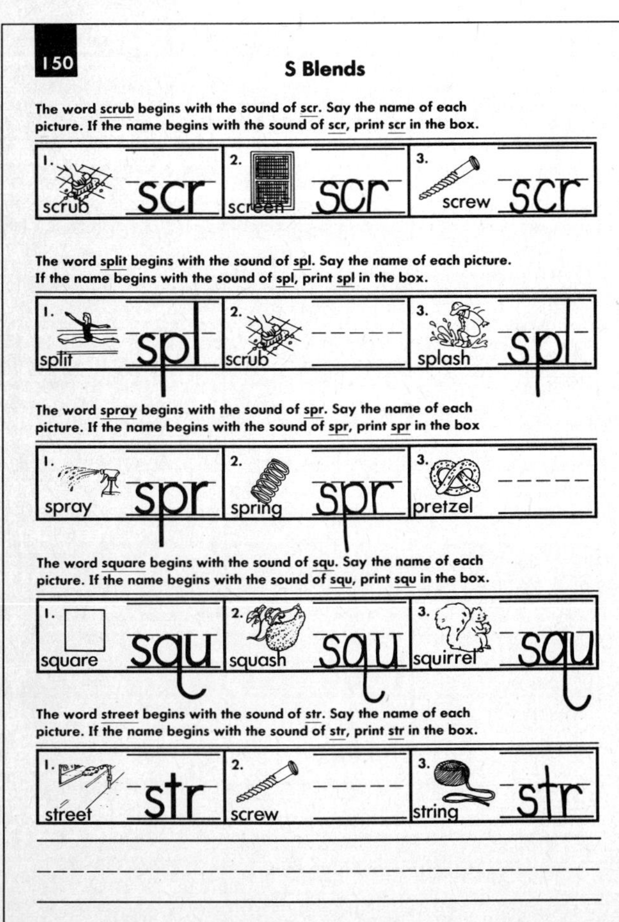

150

S Blends

The word scrub begins with the sound of scr. Say the name of each picture. If the name begins with the sound of scr, print scr in the box.

1. scrub	scr	2. screen	scr	3. screw	scr

The word split begins with the sound of spl. Say the name of each picture. If the name begins with the sound of spl, print spl in the box.

1. split	spl	2. scrub		3. splash	spl

The word spray begins with the sound of spr. Say the name of each picture. If the name begins with the sound of spr, print spr in the box

1. spray	spr	2. spring	spr	3. pretzel	

The word square begins with the sound of squ. Say the name of each picture. If the name begins with the sound of squ, print squ in the box.

1. square	squ	2. squash	squ	3. squirrel	squ

The word street begins with the sound of str. Say the name of each picture. If the name begins with the sound of str, print str in the box.

1. street	str	2. screw		3. string	str

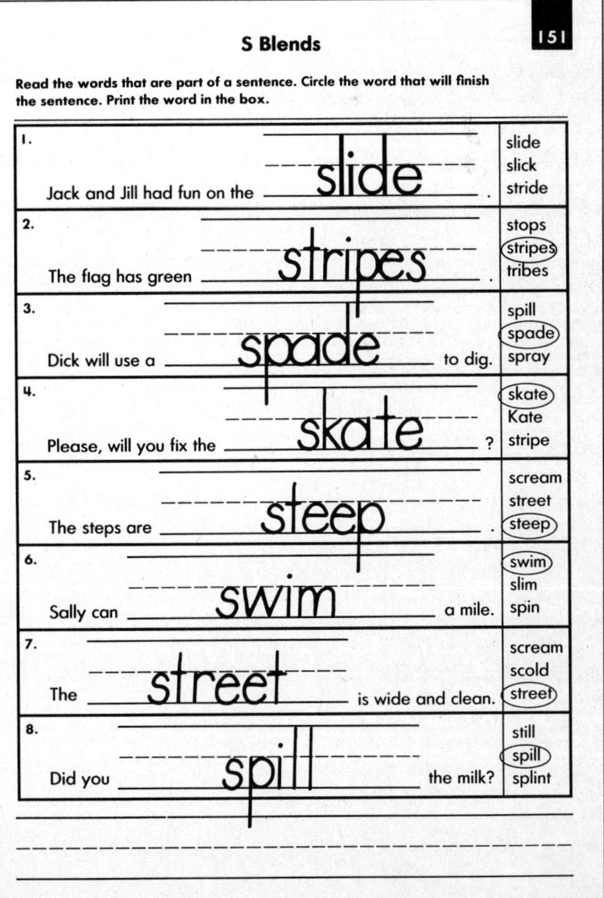

151

S Blends

Read the words that are part of a sentence. Circle the word that will finish the sentence. Print the word in the box.

1.	Jack and Jill had fun on the slide.	slide, slick, stride
2.	The flag has green stripes.	stops, (stripes), tribes
3.	Dick will use a spade to dig.	spill, (spade), spray
4.	Please, will you fix the skate?	(skate), Kate, stripe
5.	The steps are steep.	scream, street, (steep)
6.	Sally can swim a mile.	(swim), slim, spin
7.	The street is wide and clean.	scream, scold, (street)
8.	Did you spill the milk?	still, (spill), splint

Lesson 65

Vowel Y (pages 152–154)

Objective The child will read words containing the vowel *Y* and the consonant *Y*.

If *Y* comes at the beginning of a word, it is a consonant.

If *Y* is the only vowel at the end of a one-syllable word, it has the sound of long *I*.

IF *Y* is the only vowel at the end of a word of more than one syllable, it has the sound of long *E*.

Review

Speaking You may wish to review the letter *Y* as a consonant by writing the following words on the chalkboard and asking the children to read each word: *yes, yo-yo, yellow, yell, yarn.* Encourage the children to identify the sound of *Y* when it is the first consonant in a word. Invite the children to name other words that begin with the sound of consonant *Y*.

Teaching Ideas

Listening Write the following words in two columns on the chalkboard: *my, fry, by, sky; pony, funny, candy.* Point out that when *Y* appears at the end of a word, it is a vowel. (You may wish to review with the children the names of the vowel letters.) Read aloud the words in the first column and encourage the children to listen for and identify the vowel sound of *Y*. Then read aloud the words in the second column and encourage the children to listen for and identify the vowel sound of *Y*. Point out to the children that the words in the second column have two syllables. Review the concept of syllables by having the children tap each syllable of the words *funny, pony,* and *candy.* Explain to the children that the vowel *Y* has the long *E* sound when it is the only vowel at the end of a two-syllable word. Point out that the words in the first column have only one syllable. Encourage the children to tap once as you repeat each word in the first column. Explain that the vowel *Y* has the long *I* sound when it is the only vowel at the end of a one-syllable word.

Speaking Write the following words on small squares of tagboard or construction paper: *by, dry, my, bunny, puppy, dolly, jelly, baby, pony, fly.* Present the word cards to the

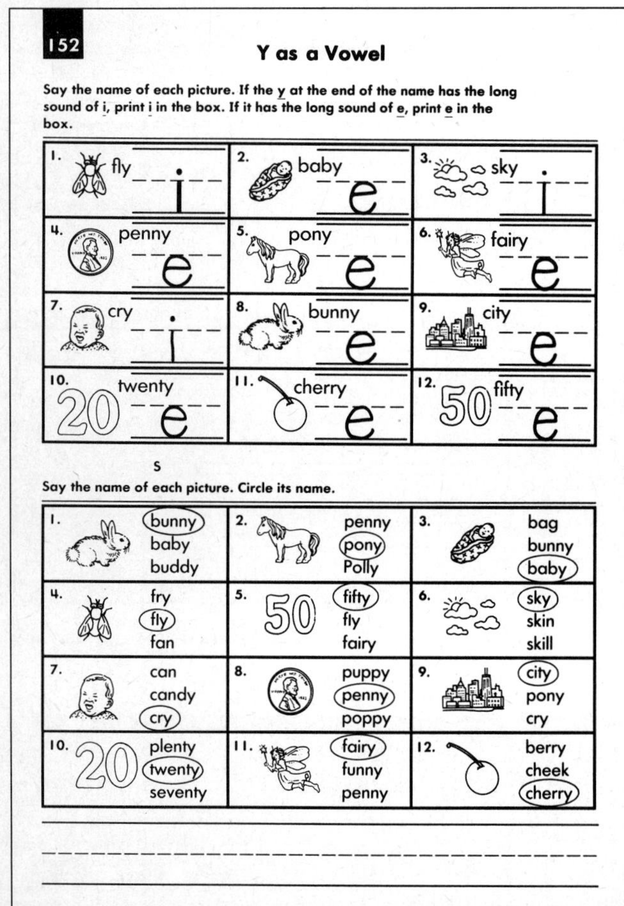

152

Y as a Vowel

Say the name of each picture. If the y at the end of the name has the long sound of i, print i in the box. If it has the long sound of e, print e in the box.

1. fly i	2. baby e	3. sky i
4. penny e	5. pony e	6. fairy e
7. cry i	8. bunny e	9. city e
10. twenty e	11. cherry e	12. fifty e

s

Say the name of each picture. Circle its name.

1. (bunny) baby buddy	2. penny (pony) Polly	3. bag bunny (baby)
4. fry (fly) fan	5. (fifty) fly fairy	6. (sky) skin skill
7. can candy (cry)	8. puppy (penny) poppy	9. (city) pony cry
10. plenty (twenty) seventy	11. (fairy) funny penny	12. berry cheek (cherry)

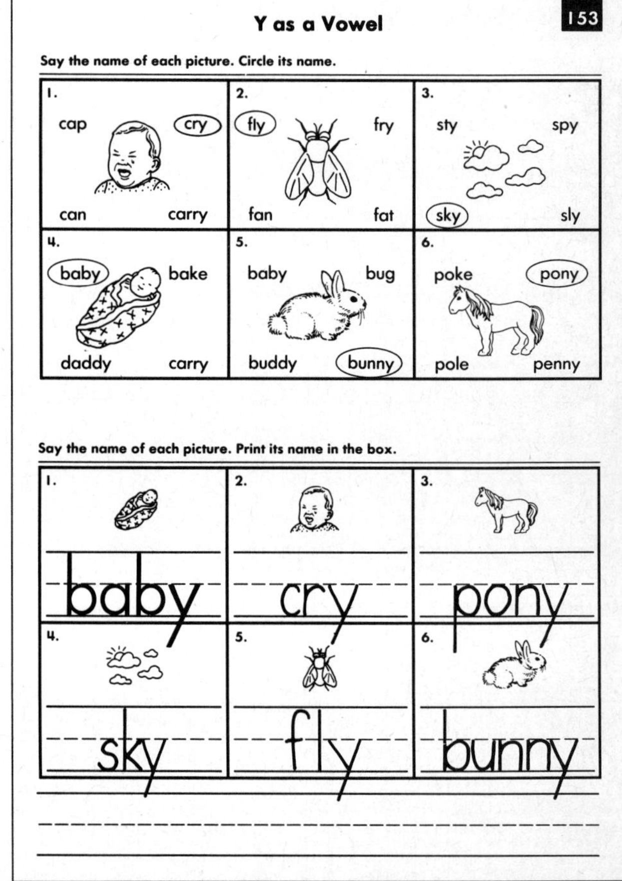

Y as a Vowel

153

Say the name of each picture. Circle its name.

1. cap (cry) can carry	2. (fly) fry fan fat	3. sty spy (sky) sly
4. (baby) bake daddy carry	5. baby bug buddy (bunny)	6. poke (pony) pole penny

Say the name of each picture. Print its name in the box.

1. baby	2. cry	3. pony
4. sky	5. fly	6. bunny

children, encouraging them to read each word aloud. Challenge volunteers to choose a word card and tell whether the word has one or two syllables. Ask the children to identify the sound of *Y* in each word and to explain the reason it is sounded as a vowel.

Write the following sentences on the chalkboard.

1. My pet dog is funny.
2. Polly will try to win.
3. Billy likes grape jelly.
4. Will you try to ride the pony?
5. The bunny is furry.
6. Sally has a baby brother.

Invite the children to read the sentence aloud and to circle the words that have *Y* as a vowel. Encourage the children to identify the sound of the vowel *Y* in each word and tell why it has that sound.

Extension

Writing Write the following words on the chalkboard: *berry, pony, sky, jelly, baby, funny, fly, cry, spy, fifty, penny, sandy, fairy, poppy*. Direct the child to fold a piece of paper lengthwise in half, forming two columns. At the top of one half, have the child write Y *AS LONG E*, and at the top of the second column have the child write Y *AS LONG* I. Challenge the child to read each word on the chalkboard, listen for the sound of the vowel *Y*, and write the word under the appropriate heading on the paper.

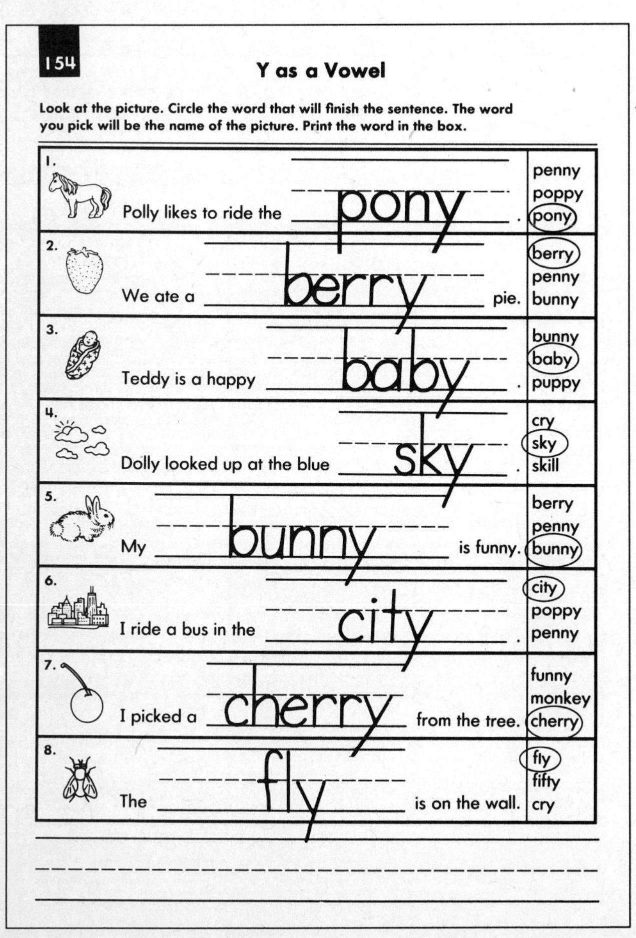
154

Y as a Vowel

Look at the picture. Circle the word that will finish the sentence. The word you pick will be the name of the picture. Print the word in the box.

1.	Polly likes to ride the pony.	penny poppy (pony)
2.	We ate a berry pie.	(berry) penny bunny
3.	Teddy is a happy baby.	bunny (baby) puppy
4.	Dolly looked up at the blue sky.	cry (sky) skill
5.	My bunny is funny.	berry penny (bunny)
6.	I ride a bus in the city.	(city) poppy penny
7.	I picked a cherry from the tree.	funny monkey (cherry)
8.	The fly is on the wall.	(fly) fifty cry

Lesson 66

Digraphs *TH* and *WH* (pages 155–156)

Objective The child will identify the consonant digraphs *th* and *wh*.

Teaching Ideas

Listening Write the following words in two columns on the chalkboard: *thumb, thirteen, thank, thin; why, when, whip, whine, whale.* Ask the children to listen for and identify the beginning sound as you pronounce each word in the first column. Point out that the beginning sound is the sound of the letters *th*. Explain to the children that when letters *T* and *H* are joined, they form a consonant digraph, with one new sound. Encourage the children to repeat the words after you. Emphasize the *th* sound in each word.

Encourage the children to listen for and identify the beginning sound as you pronounce the words in the second column. Point out that the beginning sound is the sound of the consonant digraph *wh* . Ask the children to circle the consonant digraph in each word. Encourage the children to repeat each of the *wh* words after you.

Speaking Write on the chalkboard the following words: *white, why, cloth, think, with, when, wheel, teeth, bath.* Invite the children to read the word aloud and circle the consonant digraph in each word. Encourage the children to use each word in a sentence.

Reteaching

Tactile Provide the child with a tray filled with a small amount of sand. (Small plastic meat trays could be used for this purpose.) Have the child listen for the *th* or *wh* digraphs as you pronounce each of the following words: *thumb, whip, whale, throne, whistle, teeth, white, three, thread, whine, bath.* Encourage the child to trace *th* or *wh* in the sand according to which consonant digraph is heard in the word. (You may wish to explain to the child that each response can be erased by passing a hand gently across the sand.) Reinforce correct responses by writing the word on the chalkboard.

Family Involvement Activity Duplicate the Family Letter on page 108 of this Teacher's Edition. Send it home with the children.

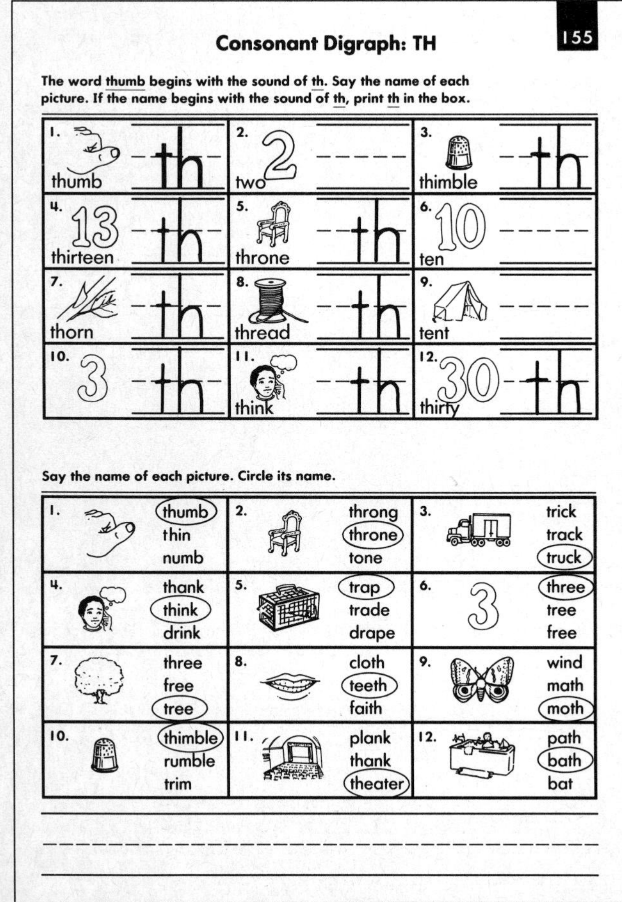

Lesson 67

Diagraphs *SH* and *CH* (pages 157–158)

Objective The child will identify the consonant digraphs *sh* and *ch*.

Review

Writing You may wish to practice recognition of the *th* and *wh* digraphs by arranging pictures of the following objects on the chalkboard ledge, asking the children to say the name of each picture and to listen for the beginning sound in each. Encourage the children to write on the chalkboard the letters that represent the beginning sound of each word: *thimble, whip, wheat, thermometer, whale, wheel, thumb.* (These pictures may be found prior to the lesson, or by the children as part of the lesson. Simple sketches on the chalkboard might also be used.)

Teaching Ideas

Listening Write the following words on the chalkboard: *ship, shot, she, shine*. Have the children listen to and identify the beginning sound in each word as you say it aloud. Point out that the sound heard in each word is the sound made by the letters *S* and *H*. Explain that *S* and *H* sounds are joined together to form the *sh* digraph. Have the children repeat the sound of the *sh* digraph after you.

Writing Write the following words on the chalkboard and invite the children to say each word aloud: *shelf, chat, much, sheep, ship, chin, wish, cheer, chop, shop, shut, chain, fresh, shake, check, shell, cash.* Ask the children to trace the *sh* digraph in each word. Encourage the children to use each of the words in a sentence.

Write the following words on the chalkboard: *chain, chop, chase, choke*. Ask the children to listen to and identify the beginning sound as you pronounce each of the words. Point out that the sound the children hear is the new sound of *C* and *H* when they are joined to form the *ch* digraph. Encourage the children to repeat the words after you, pronouncing the sound of *ch* with emphasis.

Extension

Art Write the following words on the chalkboard: *cheese, beach, shell, dish, chick, chair, fish, ship, cherry, watch.* Then provide the child with crayons, markers, paints, and squares of newsprint or white construction paper. Direct the child to choose a word and write it at the top of a square of paper. Ask the child to illustrate the word using the markers, crayons, or paints. Encourage the child to be imaginative with the drawings, making them as bright and colorful as possible. Continue the activity until pictures have been drawn for several of the words. You may wish to display the resulting picture cards in the classroom.

157

Consonant Digraph: SH

The word ship begins with the sound of sh. Say the name of each picture. If the name begins with the sound of sh, print sh in the box.

1. ship sh	2. shelf sh	3. shell sh
4. shoe sh	5. shower sh	6. skate
7. shovel sh	8. smoke	9. sheep sh
10. snail	11. shirt sh	12. shawl sh

Say the name of each picture. Circle its name.

1. **shoe** blue shop	2. smile soak **smoke**	3. sleep **sheep** sheet
4. fresh flash **fish**	5. **shade** shape shake	6. **spade** spin spine
7. self **shelf** shell	8. shy sip **ship**	9. sell shall **shell**
10. **brush** crush rush	11. fish **dish** wish	12. shoe wish **shirt**

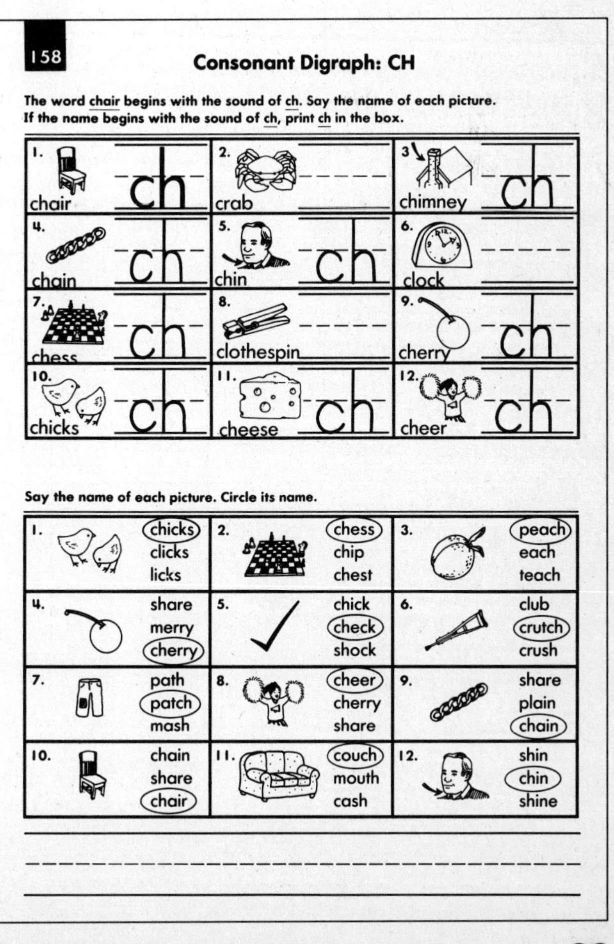
158

Consonant Digraph: CH

The word chair begins with the sound of ch. Say the name of each picture. If the name begins with the sound of ch, print ch in the box.

1. chair ch	2. crab	3. chimney ch
4. chain ch	5. chin ch	6. clock
7. chess ch	8. clothespin	9. cherry ch
10. chicks ch	11. cheese ch	12. cheer ch

Say the name of each picture. Circle its name.

1. **chicks** clicks licks	2. **chess** chip chest	3. **peach** each teach
4. share merry **cherry**	5. chick **check** shock	6. club **crutch** crush
7. path **patch** mash	8. **cheer** cherry share	9. share plain **chain**
10. chain share **chair**	11. **couch** mouth cash	12. shin **chin** shine

Lesson 68

Consonant Digraph Review (pages 159–160)

Objective The child will read words containing the consonant digraphs *th, wh, sh,* and *ch.*

Teaching Ideas

Writing Display pictures of the following objects on the chalkboard ledge: *chain, match, watch, brush, sheep, mouth, thermometer, wheel, wheat.* Have the children name each picture and identify the consonant digraph in each word. Encourage the children to write the consonant digraph on the chalkboard above the appropriate picture.

Speaking Pronounce the following words one at a time, encouraging volunteers to point to the digraph heard in the word: *church, kitchen, brushes, without, ashore, eggshell.* Challenge the children to tell whether the digraph is heard at the beginning, middle, or end of each word. You may write the words on the chalkboard to provide extra help for the children.

Write the following sentences on the chalkboard.

1. Which whistle is mine?
2. Did you hear the pony whinny?
3. Pass the dish of vegetables, please.
4. She needs a thick chain for her dog.
5. Can Chuck catch the sheep?
6. The ships came too close to the whales.

Ask the children to read each sentence aloud and to name the words with a consonant digraph. Invite volunteers to circle each consonant digraph.

Giant-Step Game Invite the children to participate in the Giant-Step Game. Tape parallel lines on the floor, two feet apart, for a total distance of twelve feet. Designate the first line as the starting line and the last line as the goal line. While you stand at the goal line, invite the children to stand behind the starting line. Ask the children to identify the consonant digraph in each word card you display, such as the following: *three, with, path, wheat, shape, fish, cheese, branch, each.* Permit the children who identify the digraph in the first word to step on the first line. Continue the game by reinforcing each correct response with advancement toward the goal. Play the game until each child has reached the goal.

Extension

Art Prepare a copy of the following sentences.

1. A thick chain was around the monster's neck.
2. The dog will watch the cat climb the tree.
3. Her face turned red when she blew the whistle.
4. The children tried to catch the sheep.

Ask the child to choose one sentence and to write it at the top of a sheet of paper. Encourage the child to illustrate the sentence by using the crayons or markers. Invite the child to illustrate each sentence, using the same procedure.

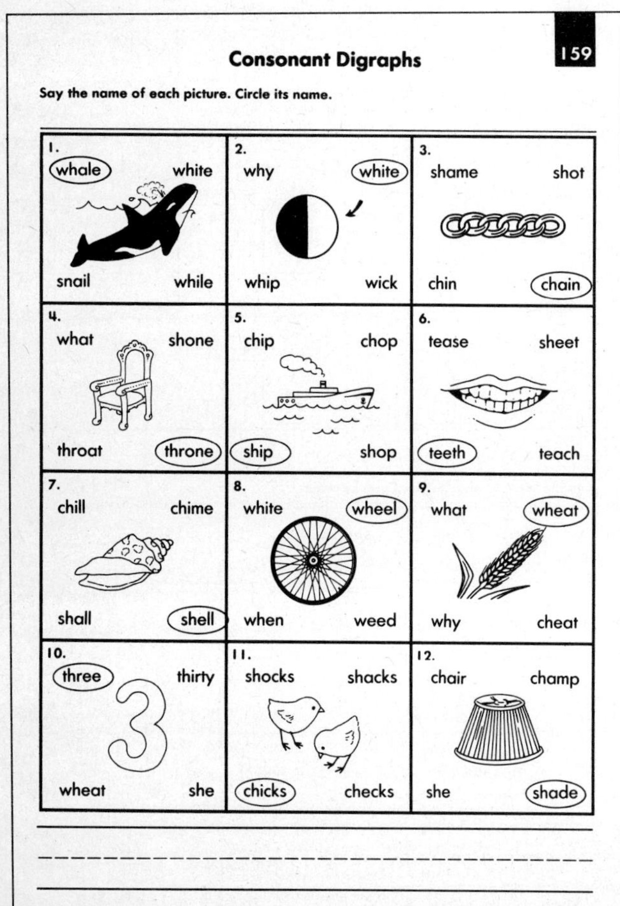

Consonant Digraphs 159

Say the name of each picture. Circle its name.

1. whale white snail while	2. why white whip wick	3. shame shot chin chain
4. what shone throat throne	5. chip chop ship shop	6. tease sheet teeth teach
7. chill chime shall shell	8. white wheel when weed	9. what wheat why cheat
10. three thirty wheat she	11. shocks shacks chicks checks	12. chair champ she shade

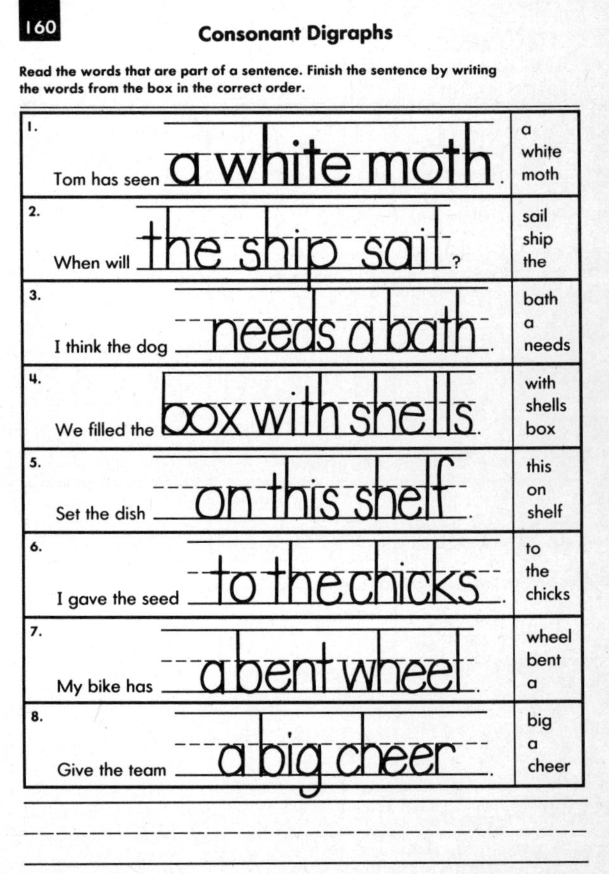

160 **Consonant Digraphs**

Read the words that are part of a sentence. Finish the sentence by writing the words from the box in the correct order.

1. Tom has seen a white moth.		a white moth
2. When will the ship sail?		sail ship the
3. I think the dog needs a bath.		bath a needs
4. We filled the box with shells.		with shells box
5. Set the dish on this shelf.		this on shelf
6. I gave the seed to the chicks.		to the chicks
7. My bike has a bent wheel.		wheel bent a
8. Give the team a big cheer.		big a cheer

Date: ______________

A Note to the Family—

We are using PHONICS IS FUN in your child's class. The skills taught in the program will help your child become a better reader. I will send a Family Involvement Activity home with your child for each phonics unit in the book. These activities are similar to those your child ______________________ does in school. Your participation in these activities will help your child develop and review the skills learned in the classroom.

The following Family Involvement Activity reviews the skills covered in Unit One. This activity involves little preparation, and the materials are common household items. For the Unit One activity, your child will write the letters of the alphabet in the correct order, write each capital letter with its small letter (we call these *partner letters*), and review the sound of each letter.

Help your child prepare an alphabet booklet by taking seven sheets of blank paper, folding them in half, and fastening them with a binding of staples or tape. Invite your child to write two pairs of partner letters on each page. Page 1, for example, would have *Aa* written in the upper outside corner of the page and *Bb* in the lower outside corner. Beside each pair of partner letters, have your child paste a picture of an object that has a name beginning with that letter. (You may prefer to have your child sketch an object for each pair of partner letters.) Additionally, you might help your child write each picture name. A completed booklet should have partner letters and a picture for each letter of the alphabet.

Please encourage your child to complete the booklet at home with the family's assistance. Completed projects may be returned to the classroom by (date)___________ and will become part of our classroom display.

Thank you for your cooperation. Your comments are always welcome.

Sincerely,

Comments: ____

____

____

____

____

____

____

Date: ______________

A Note to the Family—

We are using PHONICS IS FUN in your child's class. The skills taught in the program will help your child become a better reader. I will send a Family Involvement Activity home with your child for each phonics unit in the book. These activities are similar to those your child ______________________ does in school. Your participation in these activities will help your child develop and review the skills learned in the classroom.

The following Family Involvement Activity reviews the skills covered in Unit Two. This activity involves little preparation, and the materials are common household items. For the Unit Two activity, your child will list names of objects that begin with the consonant letters *b, c, d, f, g, h, j, k, l, m, n, p, q(u), r, s, t, v, w, x, y,* and *z*.

Help your child prepare a booklet by taking six sheets of blank paper, folding them in half, and fastening them with a binding of staples or tape. Invite your child to write two consonants on each page. Page 1, for example, would have *b* written on the upper outside corner of the page, and *c* written on the lower outside corner. Encourage your child to look through your home to find at least one object with a name that begins with the sound of each consonant letter. (You might even suggest a supervised search through the attic, the basement, or the garage.) Help your child write the name of an object that begins with each consonant beside that consonant. (For the letter *x*, you may wish to have your child list the name of an object that ends with that consonant. Additionally, the letter *z* may present a special challenge. For the similar sounds of the letters *c* and *k*, be sure your child lists words for these letters on the correct page.) A completed booklet should have two consonants and at least two words listed on each page. Challenge your child to create an attractive cover for the booklet on the top sheet of paper.

Please encourage your child to complete the booklet at home with the family's assistance. Completed projects may be returned to the classroom by (date)___________ and will become part of our classroom display.

Thank you for your cooperation. Your comments are always welcome.

Sincerely,

Comments: ____

____

____

____

____

Date: _______________

A Note to the Family—

We are using PHONICS IS FUN in your child's class. The skills taught in the program will help your child become a better reader. I will send a Family Involvement Activity home with your child for each phonics unit in the book. These activities are similar to those your child ________________________ does in school. Your participation in these activities will help your child develop and review the skills learned in the classroom.

The following Family Involvement Activity reviews the skills covered in Unit Three. This activity involves little preparation, and the materials are common household items. For the Unit Three activity, your child will write words that have the short sounds of the vowels *a, e, o, u,* and *i.*

Help your child prepare a short vowel booklet by taking six sheets of lined writing paper and stapling the sheets together on one side. Suggest the title, *SHORT VOWEL BOOK*, helping your child to spell and write these words on the cover page. Invite your child to copy one of the following headings on each page of the booklet.

Short a —hat
Short e —bed
Short i —lid
Short o —mop
Short u —pup

Encourage your child to read each heading and then to name other words that have the same short vowel sound. It might be helpful to start with rhyming words, such as *hat* and *bat.* Help your child write these short vowel words on the appropriate pages. Your child might enjoy drawing a picture for each heading.

Please encourage your child to complete the booklet at home with the family's assistance. Completed projects may be returned to the classroom by (date)____________ and will become part of our classroom display.

Thank you for your cooperation. Your comments are always welcome.

Sincerely,

Comments: ____

____

____

____

____

Date: ______________

A Note to the Family—

We are using PHONICS IS FUN in your child's class. The skills taught in the program will help your child become a better reader. I will send a Family Involvement Activity home with your child for each phonics unit in the book. These activities are similar to those your child ______________________ does in school. Your participation in these activities will help your child develop and review the skills learned in the classroom.

The following Family Involvement Activity reviews the skills covered in Unit Four. This activity involves little preparation, and the materials are common household items. For the Unit Four activity, your child will write words that have the long sounds of the vowels *a, e, o, u,* and *i.*

Help your child prepare a long vowel booklet by taking six sheets of lined writing paper and stapling the sheets together on one side. Suggest the title, *LONG VOWEL BOOK*, helping your child to write these words on the cover page. Invite your child to copy one of the following headings on each page of the booklet.

Long a —cape, mail
Long e —seat, feet
Long i —dime, pie
Long o —coat, bone, hoe
Long u —tube

Encourage your child to read each heading and then to name other words that have the same long vowel sound spelled the same way. Help your child write these long vowel words on the appropriate pages. If you wish, encourage your child to write a sentence on each page that has one or two of the long vowel words appearing on that page.

Please encourage your child to complete the booklet at home with the family's assistance. Completed projects may be returned to the classroom by (date)___________ and will become part of our classroom display.

Thank you for your cooperation. Your comments are always welcome.

Sincerely,

Comments: ____

____

____

____

____

Date: ______________

A Note to the Family—

We are using PHONICS IS FUN in your child's class. The skills taught in the program will help your child become a better reader. I will send a Family Involvement Activity home with your child for each phonics unit in the book. These activities are similar to those your child ______________________ does in school. Your participation in these activities will help your child develop and review the skills learned in the classroom.

The following Family Involvement Activity reviews the skills covered in Unit Five. This activity involves little preparation, and the materials are common household items. For the Unit Five activity, your child will write words containing various consonant blends and then create a riddle for each blend. (Your child will know that a *consonant blend* is two or three consonants sounded together so the sound of each letter can be heard, such as *pl* in *plate*.)

Help your child prepare a booklet by taking four sheets of lined writing paper and stapling the sheets together on one side. Suggest the title, *CONSONANT BLEND BOOK*, helping your child to write these words on the cover page. Then help your child list the following *r* blends on the first page after the cover page, *s* blends on the second page, and *l* blends on the third page.

r blends:	*tr*	*gr*	*br*	*pr*	*cr*	*dr*		
s blends:	*sc*	*sk*	*sn*	*sw*	*sl*	*sm*	*sp*	*st*
l blends:	*cl*	*bl*	*pl*	*fl*	*gl*			

Encourage your child to name and write two words that begin with each consonant blend. Help your child write these words on the page next to the blend. Then challenge your child to create a riddle like the following for one word in the booklet: *What word has a* cr *blend and is a name for a baby's bed?* (crib) You might help your child write the riddle on the cover page under the title, and the answer on the back cover of the booklet.

Please encourage your child to complete the booklet at home with the family's assistance. Completed projects may be returned to the classroom by (date)___________ and will become part of our classroom display.

Thank you for your cooperation. Your comments are always welcome.

Sincerely,

Comments: ____

____

____

____

____

Date: ______________

A Note to the Family—

We are using PHONICS IS FUN in your child's class. The skills taught in the program will help your child become a better reader. I will send a Family Involvement Activity home with your child for each phonics unit in the book. These activities are similar to those your child ______________________ does in school. Your participation in these activities will help your child develop and review the skills learned in the classroom.

The following Family Involvement Activity reviews the skills covered in Unit Six. This activity involves little preparation, and the materials are common household items. For the Unit Six activity, your child will write sentences containing various digraphs. (Your child will know that a *consonant digraph* is two consonants sounded together so one new sound can be heard, such as *sh* in *ship*.)

Help your child prepare a booklet by taking five sheets of lined writing paper and stapling the sheets together on one side. Suggest the title, *CONSONANT DIGRAPH BOOK*, and help your child to write these words on the cover page. Have your child write one of the following headings on each of the remaining four pages: *sh, ch, th, wh.* Encourage your child to write at least two words that have each digraph. Then, invite your child to write a sentence that includes one word for each digraph. A completed booklet should have two words and one sentence on each page. Challenge your child to illustrate each sentence.

Please encourage your child to complete the booklet at home with the family's assistance. Completed projects may be returned to the classroom by (date)___________ and will become part of our classroom display.

Thank you for your cooperation. Your comments are always welcome.

Sincerely,

Comments: ____

____

____

____

____

____

____